■   ■   ■   ■   ■   ■

To help you in your strategic and technology planning,
all worksheets in this book are available FREE on-line.

If you would like to download electronic versions
of the worksheets, please visit

www.josseybass.com/go/wiredforgood

Thank you,
Center for Excellence in Nonprofits
and
Joni Podolsky

■   ■   ■   ■   ■   ■

Wired for Good

Center for Excellence in Nonprofits (CEN™) is a 501(c)(3) nonprofit, based in San Jose, California. The center was established in December 1994 to assist nonprofit organizations in their efforts to improve quality—to strive towards excellence in all areas of operation. CEN's mission is to promote excellence in nonprofit leadership and organizational performance. CEN has established a learning community of over one hundred locally based organizations in Silicon Valley. CEN's members represent the broad array of human services and arts that makes up the nonprofit community.

Wired for Good™ (WFG), a program of the Center for Excellence in Nonprofits from 1998 through 2002, was developed to engage nonprofits in a unique technology planning process that would enable them to use technology strategically to improve their effectiveness. Taking advantage of the resources inherent to a technology-based community like Silicon Valley, WFG was a collaborative effort, drawing on the talents and expertise of corporations, foundations, volunteers, and nonprofits. The program focused on the implementation of appropriate technology as a tool for assisting nonprofits to achieve their missions. Through a series of workshops led by technology professionals and a robust review and certification process, WFG helped nonprofits align their technology use with their mission, determine what technology would be implemented and how it would be implemented, and define how the technology would be supported over time.

More information about the Center for Excellence in Nonprofits is available at www.cen.org.

3Com Corporation

3Com Corporation is one of the pioneering companies in computer networking—an industry that connects people and organizations around the world. 3Com designs and builds the networking products that help its customers communicate more effectively and operate their organizations more efficiently. As a logical extension of its business mission, 3Com also seeks to reinforce connections where communications and community intersect. Through product donations and volunteerism, 3Com encourages community investment, especially wherever 3Com employees live and work.

As a corporation, 3Com realizes that the proper use of computer networking technology requires more than the products themselves. It requires a full understanding of business processes and of the ways technology can be used as a tool to improve those processes. 3Com supports the Center for Excellence in Nonprofits (CEN) in its work with nonprofits around strategically implementing technology. Through its Wired for Good program, CEN has been successful in helping nonprofits develop technology plans with an eye to how technology can help them become more effective and efficient—enabling them to better achieve their missions and thus benefiting the communities in which we live.

3Com is proud to partner with CEN in producing *Wired for Good: Strategic Technology Planning for Nonprofits.* This is a book that will benefit nonprofits everywhere by guiding them in the development of their own strategic technology plans.

More information about 3Com products and its community investment programs is available at www.3com.com.

Wired for Good

Strategic Technology Planning for Nonprofits

Joni Podolsky

Published by Jossey-Bass
A Wiley Imprint
989 Market Street, San Francisco, CA 94103-1741   www.josseybass.com

Jossey-Bass books and products are available through most bookstores. To contact Jossey-Bass directly call our Customer Care Department within the U.S. at 800-956-7739, outside the U.S. at 317-572-3986, or fax 317-572-4002.

Jossey-Bass also publishes its books in a variety of electronic formats. Some content that appears in print may not be available in electronic books.

Wired for Good™ and CEN™ are registered trademarks of the Center for Excellence in Nonprofits.

Credits are on pages 291–293.

Library of Congress Cataloging-in-Publication Data

Podolsky, Joni, date.
   Wired for good : strategic technology planning for nonprofits / Joni
Podolsky.
      p. cm.
Includes index.
   ISBN 0-7879-6279-1
   1. Nonprofit organizations—Information technology—Planning.
I. Title.
   HD62.6.P65 2003
   658.5'14—dc21

                                                        2003001777

FIRST EDITION

PB Printing   10 9 8 7 6 5 4 3 2 1

Contents

Preface   xv

The Author   xxiii

PART 1   GETTING STARTED

  1   Understanding Technology Planning   3

      Figure 1.1 Technology Plan Pyramid   4

  2   Planning and the Technology Implementation Cycle   8

      Figure 2.1 Technology Implementation Cycle   9

      Table 2.1 Total Cost of Ownership in
           Relationship to Actions Chosen   12

  3   Assessing Organizational Readiness   14

      Figure 3.1 Triangle of Constraints   17

  4   Addressing Resistance   18

PART 2   PLANNING THE PLAN

  5   Managing the Process   27

      Worksheet 5.1 Decision Log   31

      Worksheet 5.2 Actions Required (AR) Log   33

  6   Building the Planning Team   38

      Worksheet 6.1 Process-Responsibility Matrix   44

  7   Leadership Roles and Responsibilities   46

  8   Working with Consultants and Volunteers   51

PART 3   DEVELOPING YOUR TECHNOLOGY PLAN

  9   Front Matter   59

      Example 9.1 Cupertino Community Services:
           Front Matter   61

10   Background Information   62

     Example 10.1   Services for Brain Injury:
                       Background Information   64

     Example 10.2   San Jose Repertory Theatre:
                       Background Information   65

     Example 10.3   Diabetes Society of Santa Clara Valley:
                       Background Information   66

11   Business Analysis   67

     Worksheet 11.1   Budget Reminder   70

     Worksheet 11.2   Timeline Reminder   71

     Example 11.1   Cupertino Community Services:
                       Business Analysis   83

     Example 11.2   Diabetes Society of Santa Clara Valley:
                       Business Analysis   84

     Example 11.3   San Jose Repertory Theatre:
                       Business Analysis   85

     Example 11.4   Girl Scouts of Santa Clara County:
                       Business Analysis   87

     Example 11.5   Diabetes Society of Santa Clara Valley:
                       Business Analysis   88

12   Network Services   90

     Example 12.1   Parents Helping Parents, Inc.:
                       Network Services   100

     Example 12.2   Child Care Coordinating Council of
                       San Mateo County, Inc.: Network Services   103

     Example 12.3   Hope Rehabilitation Services:
                       Network Services   104

     Example 12.4   Girl Scouts of Santa Clara County:
                       Network Services   105

     Example 12.5   Services for Brain Injury: Network Services   106

     Example 12.6   Girl Scouts of Santa Clara County:
                       Network Services   106

13   Equipment Narrative and Table   107

     Example 13.1   Youth Science Institute: Equipment Table   113

     Example 13.2   San Jose Repertory Theatre: Equipment Table   114

     Example 13.3   Junior Achievement of the Bay Area, Inc.:
                       Equipment Narrative   116

     Example 13.4   Clara Mateo Alliance, Inc.:
                       Equipment Narrative   116

     Worksheet 13.1   Hardware Inventory: Computers   117

     Worksheet 13.2   Hardware Inventory: Peripherals   118

     Worksheet 13.3   Hardware Inventory: Servers   119

14 Software Narrative and Table   120

     Example 14.1 Youth Science Institute: Software Table   128

     Example 14.2 Cupertino Community Services:
                    Software Table   129

     Example 14.3 Cupertino Community Services:
                    Software Narrative   130

     Example 14.4 Junior Achievement of the Bay Area, Inc.:
                    Software Narrative   131

     Example 14.5 Cupertino Community Services:
                    Software Narrative   131

     Worksheet 14.1 Software Inventory   132

15 Network: LAN/WAN Narrative, Inventories, and Diagrams   133

     Example 15.1 Presentation Center: LAN/WAN
                    Narrative and Inventory   142

     Example 15.2 Hope Rehabilitation Services: LAN/WAN
                    Narrative and Diagram   143

     Example 15.3 Hope Rehabilitation Services:
                    LAN/WAN Diagram   145

     Example 15.4 Child Care Coordinating Council of San Mateo
                    County, Inc.: LAN/WAN Diagram   146

     Example 15.5 Unnamed Nonprofit: Site Plan Diagram   147

     Example 15.6 EMQ Children and Family Services:
                    Site Plan Diagram   148

     Worksheet 15.1 LAN/WAN Equipment Inventory   149

16 Other Technologies   150

     Example 16.1 Parents Helping Parents, Inc.:
                    Other Technologies   154

     Example 16.2 American Red Cross, Santa Clara
                    Valley Chapter: Other Technologies   154

     Example 16.3 Cupertino Community Services:
                    Other Technologies   155

     Worksheet 16.1 Other Technologies Inventory   156

17 Facilities Plan   157

     Example 17.1 Hope Rehabilitation Services: Facilities Plan   160

     Example 17.2 Clara Mateo Alliance, Inc.: Facilities Plan   161

18 Security Plan   162

     Example 18.1 Junior Achievement of the Bay Area, Inc.:
                    Security Plan   167

     Example 18.2 Parents Helping Parents, Inc.: Security Plan   168

19 Technology Support Plan   169

     Example 19.1 San Jose Repertory Theatre:
                    Technology Support Plan   174

Example 19.2 Cupertino Community Services:
Technology Support Plan   176

Example 19.3 San Jose Repertory Theatre:
Technology Support Plan   177

20 Training Plan   178

Example 20.1 Presentation Center: Training Plan   182

Worksheet 20.1 Training Plan Matrix   185

21 Evaluation and Continuous Improvement Strategy   186

Example 21.1 Mission Hospice, Inc.: Evaluation and
Continuous Improvement Strategy   189

Example 21.2 Services for Brain Injury: Evaluation and
Continuous Improvement Strategy   190

22 Acceptable Use Policy   191

Example 22.1 Junior Achievement of the Bay Area, Inc.:
Acceptable Use Policy   193

Example 22.2 San Jose Repertory Theatre:
Acceptable Use Policy   194

23 Budget   197

Example 23.1 San Jose Repertory Theatre: Budget   201

Example 23.2 Presentation Center: Budget   204

Worksheet 23.1 Technology Budget   205

24 Implementation Timeline   210

Example 24.1 Services for Brain Injury:
Implementation Timeline   213

Example 24.2 Child Care Coordinating Council of
San Mateo County, Inc.:
Implementation Timeline   215

Example 24.3 Hope Rehabilitation Services:
Implementation Timeline   216

25 Appendixes   217

Example 25.1 Girl Scouts of Santa Clara County: Appendix   219

Example 25.2 Parents Helping Parents, Inc.: Appendix 221

26 Preparing the Document   222

PART 4 WHAT'S NEXT?

27 Managing Organizational Change   227

28 Funding and In-Kind Donations   232

29 Revisiting the Technology Plan   237

PART 5   RESOURCES

A   Comprehensive Technology Plan Outline   243

B   Flowchart Symbols   259

C   Technology Plan Checklist   261

D   Glossary of Terms   263

E   Where to Go for More Information   281

    Index   283

Preface

THE INTEGRATION of information technology (IT) into many of our daily activities has dramatically changed the way we live. It has altered the way we communicate, conduct business, and access resources. The computer has made it possible for us to increase our efficiencies and productivity, and the Internet has collapsed time and distance on a global scale. Information technology has done for the economy and the world's social infrastructure what no other new technology has done since the industrial revolution. Knowledge and information have arguably become the most valuable commodities in this new information-based economy.

For nonprofits, having access to appropriate IT tools is critical to their success in this new environment. Faced with a volatile economy, changing demographics, shifts in governmental and private funding priorities, swings in the political climate, and influential—sometimes explosive—world events, nonprofits are being called upon more and more to adapt to change—and to do so quickly. The community services that nonprofits offer are as critical as ever, but limited resources are available to deliver them. Thus, although other sectors have been relatively quick to incorporate tools that enable them to adapt to the shifting landscapes, the nonprofit sector has not had the resources to adapt as quickly.

Clearly, one of the most important tools in this necessary adaptation is technology. The purpose of this book is to provide nonprofits with a framework for planning the strategic use of technology to support the organization's mission. The following chapters are intended to supply enough information so that a nonprofit can embark on a process that will

- Align its technology use with its mission, goals, and strategies.
- Determine what technology will be implemented and how it will be implemented.

- Define how the technology will be supported over time.

At the same time, this book is not meant to be all inclusive. You will likely also need to consult with technology experts who can guide your nonprofit in its technology decisions and assist with portions of the design work, but this book will prepare you to work effectively and efficiently with these experts.

Intended Audience

Wired for Good: Strategic Technology Planning for Nonprofits has been written to assist any nonprofit interested in strategically implementing technology in order to substantially improve the way it provides services to its community. The contents of this book will be of use to executive directors, operations managers, IT managers, board members, technology committee members, and any other key individuals looking to better implement and manage technology in their organization. (I would note, however, that even though individuals from educational institutions—K–12 or universities—and governmental agencies may well find the material in this book useful, they will also find they have specific technology planning issues that are not addressed here and that will have to be researched separately.)

This book will help organizations that intend to implement new technology to do so in a way that supports their mission and carefully targets their resources. Organizations that already have technology in place but are facing challenges managing it and finding it too costly to support will also find this book useful. This guide will help them take a step back from their technology woes and focus on what they want to accomplish. With this understanding, they can select the appropriate technological tools and infrastructure to accomplish their goals.

In addition, this guide is ideal for organizations that have an excellent and well-running technological infrastructure but want to document it so that internal and external stakeholders can gain both a current and a historical understanding of it. These organizations will find that going through the technology planning process documented here will help them communicate about technology issues with current and new staff, consultants, vendors, board members, funders, and others.

Finally, the strategic technology planning process outlined in this book is designed for organizations that are seeking to engage in in-depth organizational improvement. It is not intended for nonprofits that want a quick and easy technological solution. The concepts discussed here apply to nonprofits of any size. However, small nonprofits may find their needs less complicated than those of medium-sized and large nonprofits. (For the purposes of this book, a small nonprofit is defined as having a fiscal year [FY] budget of $500 thousand or less and fewer than ten full-time equivalent [FTE] staff. A medium-sized nonprofit has a FY budget of $500 thousand to $3 million and ten to thirty FTE employees. A large nonprofit has a FY budget of more than $3 million and more than thirty FTE staff.)

Let me explain. Organizations may choose to use technology in one or both of two ways. First, organizations may use technology to make their existing operational processes more efficient. For example, paper files may be replaced with electronic data that are more easily stored and updated, or accounting processes may be streamlined. Many nonprofits may feel comfortable implementing this aspect of technology by going directly to an operational plan, such as a needs assessment or technology audit, because their basic organizational strategy is not being changed. Often small nonprofits will opt to create this kind of a plan rather than a strategic technology plan because refining existing processes is all they need at the time, and the effort can more easily be led by an IT consultant, thereby putting less strain on staff time and resources.

Many organizations, however, may decide to use technology as a tool to change their processes, fundamentally altering the way their organizations operate and meet their missions, and thus changing the way they provide services to clients. In this case, a strategic technology plan is essential, no matter what the size of the organization.

Although nonprofits of any size will need to consider all the issues covered in this book when developing a strategic technology plan, size does make a difference in how some of these issues are addressed. For example, because a small nonprofit has fewer staff, the processes it examines may have fewer steps—one person hands something to another person and the other person does something with it and the process is complete—whereas a large nonprofit may pass something through many hands before the process is finished. Therefore a small nonprofit may be able to chart a process on only one page, whereas a medium-sized or large nonprofit may need several pages. Likewise, when developing the computer network's logical diagrams, a small nonprofit may be able to combine diagrams (putting the LAN and WAN diagrams on the same page), whereas a larger nonprofit will need to keep each diagram separate. Thus a smaller nonprofit's strategic technology plan may be less complex and have fewer pages than a larger nonprofit's plan. Throughout this book there are indications where these differences between small and large nonprofits may occur. Further, the technology plan examples presented here are representative of nonprofits of all sizes.

Overview of the Contents

The materials and approach in this book are based on the content of the successful Wired for Good™ program (www.wiredforgood.org) conducted for Silicon Valley nonprofits by the Center for Excellence in Nonprofits (CEN™) (www.cen.org) from 1998 through 2002. They draw on the knowledge and experience provided by volunteer experts participating in the Wired for Good program's workshops and technology planning process. They incorporate the best practices and lessons learned from the corporate, educational, and governmental sectors, and most important, from nonprofits who have been through the technology planning process themselves. Sprinkled throughout the book are mini-case studies called Planning in Practice, and examples from technology plans drawn up by real nonprofits that have gone through the strategic planning process.

The book is divided into five parts. Part One sets the stage for understanding strategic technology planning and for determining whether or not your organization is ready for such a process. Chapter One defines what technology planning is and discusses the benefits that creating a technology plan will have for your organization. It also dispels many of the myths surrounding technology planning. Chapter Two describes in greater detail how technology planning fits with technology implementation. It explains the continuous improvement cycle and introduces the concept of total cost of ownership. Chapter Three provides guidance in determining whether your organization is ready to embark on the technology planning process. Chapter Four outlines some of the reasons people resist adapting technology, and therefore technology planning, and presents some useful advice on ways to address this resistance.

Part Two focuses on managing the technology planning process. Chapter Five discusses the costs, amount of time, and tools and resources associated with creating the plan. Chapter Six describes the technology planning team, who should be on it, and what roles and responsibilities team members must undertake. Chapter Seven takes a closer look at the roles of the executive director and the board. Chapter Eight discusses how to make the best use of consultants and volunteers, what their roles can be, and what to look for when hiring them.

Part Three (Chapters Nine through Twenty-Six) zeros in on writing the technology plan. The chapters here follow closely the Comprehensive Technology Plan Outline presented in Resource A, providing detailed guidance

---

Wired for Good™ and CEN™ are registered trademarks of the Center for Excellence in Nonprofits.

about each section of that outline. These chapters are rich with tips and with examples from actual technology plans created by nonprofits that have been through the process themselves. Worksheets are provided to assist you in preparing some of the more detailed elements of your own plan. Certain chapters in this section are fairly technology specific. Explanations are provided for many of the technology concepts addressed; however, this book is not intended to provide in-depth discussions of the technology itself. Other resources are readily available for that information. Additionally, technology is continually changing and to address specific applications in detail would have made this book only a snapshot in time. Instead, this book provides an infrastructure for planning that can be applied anytime, even as hardware and software change. Part Three, in short, presents a framework for asking the right questions, the answers to which will be your technology plan.

Part Four discusses the steps to take after the technology plan is written. Chapter Twenty-Eight addresses the change management associated with implementing new technology, providing tips to ease the organization's transition. Chapter Twenty-Nine considers finding funding and in-kind support for technology implementation and the ways that the technology plan can help you get this support. Chapter Thirty discusses revisiting the technology plan in order to maintain it as a living, useful document.

Part Five contains five resources. Resource A is a comprehensive and consolidated technology plan outline that is described in great detail in Part Three. Resource B illustrates flowchart symbols, and Resource C offers a technology plan checklist. A robust glossary is to be found in Resource D, and Resource E lists Web sites and publications that offer further information.

Acknowledgments

The following people directly contributed to the writing of this book:

Sharon Meyers, NPC Consulting, major contributor

Janette L. Rudkin, technical writer

Liz Schuler, Wired for Good program manager

Rachael M. Stark, case study researcher, interviewer, and writer

Wired for Good: Strategic Technology Planning for Nonprofits is the culmination of three years of work with the nonprofit sector on technology planning and implementation. Neither the Wired for Good program, the content of which is documented in this book, nor the book itself would have been successful without the help of many people and organizations.

First and foremost, I must thank the nonprofits that my colleagues and I worked with throughout the years. Working with them was an honor, and it was their openness to learning and to teaching others that made it possible to document the best practices and lessons that appear in this book. In particular I wish to thank those nonprofits that were willing to have their staff interviewed and that provided examples of their technology plans so that others could learn from them.

I wish to thank the advisers, volunteers, consultants, and sponsors involved in the Wired for Good program. The success of the program, the participating nonprofits, and the writing of this book could not have been accomplished without all of them. In particular, I am grateful to 3Com Corporation, which, in addition to consistently providing in-kind equipment contributions to the Wired for Good program participants as well as volunteer support, provided sponsorship of this book.

I must offer my thanks to both the board and the staff of CEN for providing a supportive and creative environment in which to work. My special appreciation goes to Bob Kardon, CEN's executive director from 1997 to 2002, for his wisdom, vision, and leadership. I am also thankful to Molly Polidoroff, CEN's current executive director, for her enthusiasm and commitment to carrying this book project forward.

I am grateful to Sharon Meyers and Harris Meyers, of NPC Consulting, who were consummate partners in the development of the content of the Wired for Good program. Sharon's significant contribution to this book can be found especially in Part Three and the Glossary. Her gift of being able to translate the often complex concepts of technology planning into a clear and easy-to-follow process added tremendously to this book. Harris's encyclopedic knowledge of technology and his thorough work in leading the process of reviewing technology plans for the Wired for Good program enabled him to provide great guidance in determining which technology plan examples to use in this book.

I have learned much from Liz Schuler, Wired for Good's program manager, through her refinement of the program's workshops and content, not to mention her sense of humor and personal support. Along with Harris, Liz chose the outstanding technology plan examples exhibited in this book. Liz did an impressive job of incorporating the examples so they would provide clear and understandable illustrations for the reader.

I am indebted to Rachael Stark, an excellent interviewer and writer of the Planning in Practice case studies included in the book. Her enthusiasm for the project and her willingness to help under a short deadline are much appreciated. Janette Rudkin did herculean work in pulling together three years of program notes and workshop materials into a comprehensive and useful manuscript.

Madeleine Fackler not only reviewed book chapters and provided valuable volunteer contributions to the Wired for Good program but is also a wonderful friend and mentor. Thank you to Tom Battin, a good friend and colleague, for reading the manuscript and providing constructive suggestions based on his many years of experience providing IT consulting to nonprofits.

I wish to express special appreciation to Johanna Vondeling, associate editor at Jossey-Bass, for her enthusiasm for and advocacy of this book and for her encouragement and helpfulness.

Finally, enough cannot be said to thank my family, friends, and colleagues for their love, patience, guidance, and support.

Belmont, California   Joni Podolsky
January 2003

The Author

JONI PODOLSKY is founding program director of Wired for Good, a program of the Center for Excellence in Nonprofits in San Jose, California. In that position she was responsible for helping Silicon Valley nonprofits use technology strategically to improve their effectiveness, a goal accomplished by taking them through a unique technology planning process.

Podolsky has a decade of experience working with nonprofits. Prior to joining the Center for Excellence in Nonprofits, she was a project director of Smart Valley, Inc., helping Silicon Valley school districts plan for and implement technology in the classroom and in district offices. In addition to authoring *Wired for Good: Strategic Technology Planning for Nonprofits*, Joni is author of the Smart Valley guidebook *District Administrator's Guide to Planning for Technology*. She has spoken about technology planning for nonprofits at conferences and workshops nationwide and in various industry and nonprofit publications. She welcomes correspondence regarding this book; please write to her at jonip@cen.org.

Wired for Good

Part One
Getting Started

THE FIRST STEP in the strategic technology planning process is understanding what this process is and how it benefits your organization. More important, this first step involves determining whether your organization is ready for such a process. The four chapters in Part One address this first step. Chapter One defines what strategic technology planning is and presents the reasons why this process is critical to long-term success in the use of technology. Besides outlining the benefits of technology planning, this chapter dispels some of the myths surrounding such planning. Chapter Two describes in greater detail how technology planning fits with technology implementation. It explains the continuous improvement cycle and briefly discusses total cost of ownership. Chapter Three offers guidance on determining whether or not an organization is ready to embark on the strategic technology planning process. Chapter Four summarizes some of the reasons why people resist technology, and therefore technology planning, and provides some useful advice on how to address this resistance.

Chapter 1

Understanding Technology Planning

AT ITS BROADEST level, a technology plan is a communications tool. Its purpose is to provide a framework for improving an organization's effectiveness through the implementation of appropriate tools. The plan is a document that aligns an agency's technology use with its strategic goals, defines what technology will be implemented and how it will be implemented, and determines how the technology will be supported over time.

As Figure 1.1 illustrates, a technology plan can be envisioned as a three-tiered pyramid. At the top of the pyramid are the *mission, goals,* and *strategies.* Supporting the mission are the technology *applications,* or *tools,* that enable an organization to achieve its mission, such as e-mail, the Web, office software, and databases. Finally, supporting the applications, or tools, is the *infrastructure.* This includes both the physical infrastructure, such as the organization's desktop computers and network, and such things as training, budget, and support and maintenance. All tiers are required to complete the pyramid. Without a clear articulation of the organization's mission, goals, and strategies, people will find it impossible to know the right tools and to establish the infrastructure needed to achieve the mission. Therefore the strategic technology plan is centered around the organization's mission, the foundation upon which all decisions in the plan are made.

There are many benefits to developing a technology plan. Although today most nonprofits recognize information technology as a mission-critical tool, putting IT in place and trying to use it well is often an exercise in frustration. Those nonprofits that have implemented technology without a plan will often admit later that their piecemeal approach has increased stress on staff, cost more than expected, and in many cases made the issues they were trying to improve, such as financial, organizational, and client or member management, worse, not better. These organizations now realize

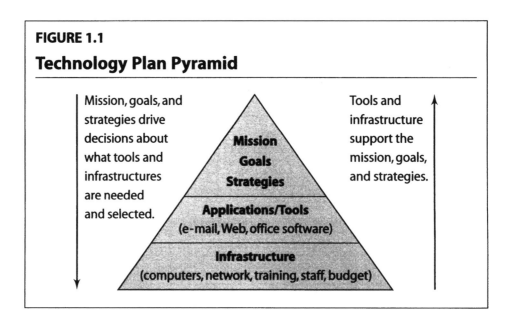

FIGURE 1.1

Technology Plan Pyramid

Mission, goals, and strategies drive decisions about what tools and infrastructures are needed and selected.

Tools and infrastructure support the mission, goals, and strategies.

Mission
Goals
Strategies

Applications/Tools
(e-mail, Web, office software)

Infrastructure
(computers, network, training, staff, budget)

that the *total cost of ownership* (TCO) of technology goes beyond any initial investment in hardware and software. The TCO also includes such factors as user training, ongoing support, maintenance costs, and costs of consumables. Even donated technology has costs associated with it. For example, a donated used computer may need to be stripped of all its previous owner's software and data. New software will need to be installed, the memory may need to be increased, and the computer may need to be made network-ready. It will also need periodic maintenance and regular software upgrades, and most important, the user will need to be trained in operating it.

Although developing a technology plan is not a guarantee that all the frustrations and extra costs associated with implementing technology will disappear, the process does help staff better understand and then mitigate these issues as much as possible. The planning process removes the guesswork and allows staff the opportunity to thoughtfully integrate technology that furthers the agency's mission.

Do all nonprofits need a technology plan? Conventional wisdom says yes, though the plan need not necessarily be worked out all at once. Developing a technology plan is not a linear process. An organization may need to develop its plan in stages and at different levels, going deeper as time goes on. For example, an agency that is having ongoing technology crises may need to start at the operational rather than strategic level, addressing such issues as getting a printer to work. Many organizations will tackle these operational issues at the same time as they work on their strategic technology plan. Organizational culture, priorities, and available resources will all be factors in determining the approach to planning that works for you.

Here are some key reasons why technology planning is essential. (The accompanying sidebar reveals five myths about technology planning.)

Planning can ensure technology that supports the mission and strategic goals. Creating a technology plan is an opportunity for an organization to focus on its mission, goals, and strategies. It is a good opportunity for revisiting your strategic plan and making sure the staff and board are aligned with it. Technology planning is an opportunity to rearticulate strategic goals and quantify how technology will be used as a tool to achieve them. A technology plan focused on mission is most likely to outline technology that facilitates improvements in the organization. This decreases the danger of implementing technology for technology's sake. Additionally, once you are focused on organizational goals, you can identify clear measures that indicate when and how the organization is being successful in achieving those goals.

Planning is an opportunity to improve existing processes. In order to determine how technology can best serve the mission, an agency must first evaluate its existing processes *without regard for technology.* A *process* is a sequence of repeatable steps that lead to some desired end or output. Focusing on process improvements reveals inefficiencies of all kinds, not just those related to technology. Among the nontechnological inefficiencies may be redundancies, overlaps, or steps that should be eliminated altogether. Technology is a wonderful tool, but it can be a hindrance when the process it is meant to improve is inherently flawed. Only after the processes are examined and documented should staff have creative discussions about how technology can increase capacity and improve effectiveness.

Planning creates organizational learning. For any kind of planning it is often said that the process is more important than the product. Although the technology planning document is an important result of the technology planning process, it is that act of developing the plan that provides the most benefit. Staff engaged in the planning process are likely to make unexpected discoveries along the way, and it is sometimes these unanticipated "aha" moments that provide the most important results. For example, focusing on process improvements reveals ongoing inefficiencies. Researching technology solutions often inspires creativity in new ways of doing things. By working together to create the technology plan, staff become more closely aligned and will ultimately learn new and better ways of working together.

Planning focuses on the now as well as the future. A technology plan helps an organization think through technology that is appropriate now as well as technology possibilities for the future. A rule of thumb is to tie the technology plan closely to the organization's strategic plan so that the agency is thinking through the appropriate tools needed to accomplish the specific goals and strategies that it is striving to achieve in both the future and the present. Therefore, if the agency has a three-year strategic plan, then the technology plan should also be a three-year plan. If the strategic plan is for five years, then so should be the technology plan. Like the strategic plan, the technology plan is a living document. It should be revisited at least yearly, or more frequently if needed. This practice enables the nonprofit not only to adjust for organizational changes but also to keep up with the rapidity of technological changes.

Planning enables the organization to effectively target resources. Without planning it is easy to purchase equipment that is not needed, that is inappropriate, or that is not robust enough. Developing a technology plan encourages an organization to think about what it already has and whether it is maximizing the use of what it has. The process of technology planning not only reduces the potential for wasteful purchases but also enables you to identify the new equipment, support, and training that are needed. By taking the time to budget for your agency's present needs and think through future needs, you may spend more effectively now and also save money later on. The process also helps you think through total cost of ownership, making sure that you budget for both the obvious and not-so-obvious costs of technology.

Planning establishes a framework and process for making decisions. Because it focuses on mission, the technology plan provides a context for making decisions about incorporating or changing technology. Without planning you risk making wrong decisions and ending up with something that is too complicated or does not serve the agency's needs. Planning is an opportunity to think through organizational goals and to research possible solutions. In this way developing the technology plan can help you avoid potential difficulties that come from having made poor choices.

Planning creates a historical record. The technology plan is a critical tool for communicating historical information to current staff, new employees, the board, consultants, volunteers, and vendors. It provides a record that documents past, current, and future thinking, such as the criteria used in making key decisions. More tangibly, it incorporates such things as inventories, diagrams, maintenance records, and service contracts, which are essential information for those who need to know where the organization stands. This significantly cuts down the time you need to orient new staff or others who are providing technology services to your organization, and guides them to provide an appropriate level of support.

Planning provides a basis for fundraising. These days, it is difficult to find funders for technology who do not ask the question, Does your agency have a technology plan? They have a vested interest in making sure that the technology they fund will help the agency achieve its mission, and that the agency has realistically planned for the resources and training to support the technology. Additionally, sections of the technology plan can be used in proposals. Clearly articulating your technology needs will make it easier for you to obtain what you need. An agency "wish list" might even be posted to the agency's Web site or inserted in its newsletter.

Five Myths of Technology Planning

1. *It is only about technology.* This is not true. A technology plan is really an adjunct to your strategic plan, focusing on organizational mission, goals, and strategies. It is a guide for making appropriate decisions about the tools and related elements needed for your organization to fulfill its mission.

2. *It outlines technology goals.* People often refer to technology goals when they really mean organizational goals. There are no such things as technology goals, because technology is simply a means for achieving organizational goals. Therefore a technology plan outlines technology *strategies* (not goals) that facilitate the achievement of organizational goals.

3. *A technology plan will enable your agency to save money, or conversely, a technology plan will result in more expenditures.* Each of these statements may be true or false. Writing a plan will enable you to target resources more effectively, providing a framework you can use to evaluate true cost of ownership and budget accordingly. However, technology can be expensive, and writing a plan does not change that reality. Planning does encourage you to justify all expenses, making certain they support the agency's mission. Direct costs associated with writing the plan itself are often minimal. The major cost is the staff time needed to develop the plan.

4. *A technology plan can be developed in just a couple of weeks.* The actual amount of time it takes to develop a strategic technology plan will vary depending on the scope of the plan and the resources and time the agency can allot to its creation. However, a typical nonprofit should expect to spend approximately six months to a year developing the plan.

5. *You need to be an expert in technology to write a technology plan.* In fact, although you will need to draw on someone with technological expertise at various points in the planning process, technology plans written solely by IT staff are usually not as effective as those written by a team that is representative of the agency as a whole or that is led by an individual with a big-picture view of the organization.

Chapter 2

Planning and the Technology Implementation Cycle

TECHNOLOGY PLANNING is the most critical step in establishing technology change in an organization. But how does it fit in with the overall technology implementation? Because technology implementation is not usually a linear process, it is best to think of it as a cycle rather than as a straight line. Figure 2.2 illustrates the *technology implementation cycle*. It is based on a standard project management tool, the PDSA (plan, do, study, act) cycle.

The *plan* stage is the one addressed in this book. It is the stage where discoveries are made. It consists of identifying issues and opportunities and researching solutions and further actions. In this stage you are

- Selecting the issues and processes that will be addressed

- Describing the improvement opportunities

- Documenting the current processes surrounding the improvement opportunities

- Determining possible causes of problems in the current processes

- Developing solutions and creating effective and workable action plans

- Determining targets for improvement and measures for success

Remember that the term *improvements* does not describe only problems that need to be fixed but also new opportunities. For example, an organization may not have considered expanding its services beyond a certain geographical reach. Once the Internet becomes available to that organization, however, a geographical expansion may become a realistic possibility—one that may *improve* the organization's ability to achieve its mission.

After planning comes the *do* stage—the implementation of the technology plan. It is in this stage that the solution or process change described in the technology plan is instituted. It is also during this stage that the milestones and measures for success are monitored.

FIGURE 2.1

Technology Implementation Cycle

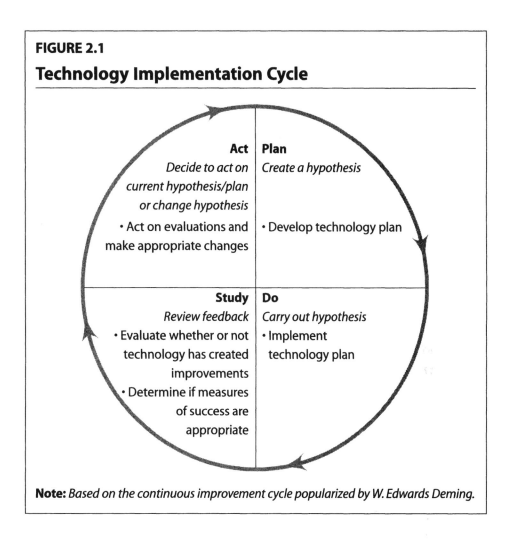

Act
Decide to act on current hypothesis/plan or change hypothesis
• Act on evaluations and make appropriate changes

Plan
Create a hypothesis
• Develop technology plan

Study
Review feedback
• Evaluate whether or not technology has created improvements
• Determine if measures of success are appropriate

Do
Carry out hypothesis
• Implement technology plan

Note: *Based on the continuous improvement cycle popularized by W. Edwards Deming.*

It is important to remember that you may decide not to implement the entire technology plan all at once. In fact it is often recommended that you take a phased approach, integrating solutions in small increments. The advantage to this is that you have the opportunity to test the improvements with a minimum of cost and staff stress. Gradual implementation also gives staff time to acclimatize to the change that instituting new technologies creates.

The next stage is the *study* stage. During this time the results of the technology changes are reviewed and evaluated. Is the solution having the intended effect, both internally and externally, for clients and other key stakeholders? If not, why not? Do additional changes need to be made? Are there any unintended consequences to the changes? Additionally, it is during this stage that you confirm or establish the means of monitoring the solutions—are the measures identified in the plan valid or do they need to be adjusted to be more realistic?

Finally, in the *act* stage, you reflect and act on your learnings. You assess the results and the problem-solving process and recommend changes. For example, are the measurement tools you are using effective? Is the process for rolling out the technology improvements working? Do you have the right people involved in the processes? If further changes are needed to make the technology change more effective, this is the time to enact those changes. If no further changes are needed, then standardize the new processes. Most important, in the act stage you actively communicate your achievements to key stakeholders and celebrate your successes. This enables everyone to feel a sense of accomplishment along with the sense of having been an active part of the change process.

Notice that the technology implementation cycle is cyclical and continuous. At any given time you may find that you are in the plan stage for some issues and already implementing changes in the act stage for others. This occurs because some changes are easy to implement, whereas others may take more time and careful deliberation. For example, standardizing operating systems on all an agency's computers may be a relatively easy change to make, but developing a centralized database will probably take many months of planning and implementing before that database can be fully used in the organization. Agencies may also veer off the linear course when emergent issues—such as computers crashing or printers malfunctioning—cannot wait for the completion of the technology plan. These issues need to be resolved when they arise, even if the planning stage is not yet complete. You may also consider a phased approach to expend your resources on technology gradually, spreading out the costs and staff time rather than using them all at once.

What happens if you skip the plan stage and move right on to the act stage? This often happens and may be a normal part of the process. However, you will still need to come back to the plan stage at some point. The trade-off for acting first is that without proper planning it is likely that the agency's total cost of ownership (TCO) will increase, resulting in unnecessary expenditures and increased stress on staff.

As noted in Chapter One, TCO refers to all the costs associated with owning and using technology—both obvious costs, such as the purchase price of a computer, and not-so-obvious costs, such as user training, hardware and software support and maintenance, and the like. Evaluating total cost of ownership not only helps an agency budget for all costs associated with owning technology but also enables it to evaluate the trade-offs that will occur for every decision made. For example, in many organizations, when a computer crashes an employee cannot do his work, which makes that employee all but useless. What is the cost associated with the lost productivity? Is it better to spend the money up front for reliable equipment and staff who can provide maintenance and support, or is it better to take the risk of using an older, perhaps donated piece of equipment and relying on volunteers to resolve computer problems in their spare time? What are the costs associated with each decision? What are the trade-offs? These are the types of questions that are addressed in a technology plan, as the accompanying example illustrates.

PLANNING IN PRACTICE
Total Cost of Ownership of Donations

Michael Edell, former executive director of the AIDS Community Research Consortium, said that "a lot of corporations that get rid of computers are getting rid of computers for very good reasons, because they're not up to date." He described this phenomenon with a telling image: "It's almost like someone donating clothes to a person for a job interview and the shirt or blouse that was donated has a hole in it."

Edell described the technology planning process as a wake-up call, highlighting things like unsatisfactory hardware and incompatible software. When his agency did an inventory of all its software, agency staff noticed how old and incompatible much of it was. This encouraged the agency to work toward better compatibility.

When staff looked into it, they discovered that buying the licenses for up-to-date and compatible software, using nonprofit discounts, would be relatively cheap. Before that, they had just kept whatever software was on donated machines when they received them and upgraded it if they could. This cost them a lot in time and aggravation.

Once the technology plan outlined the agency's needs, Edell knew what technology donations to ask for from corporations and foundations. The plan also gave him the courage to politely but firmly refuse any offers he might receive of "a blouse with a hole in it."

Table 2.1 presents examples that reveal how costs can increase depending on the decisions an organization makes about how to act on key issues. This table is a great tool to use with board or staff members to illustrate the trade-offs that result from various decisions.

TABLE 2.1

Total Cost of Ownership in Relationship to Actions Chosen

	The "TCO-Savvy" Nonprofit		The "Doing the Best We Can" Nonprofit		The "Worry About It Tomorrow" Nonprofit	
	Actions	**Costs**	**Actions**	**Costs**	**Actions**	**Costs**
Professional development	Devotes an appropriate amount of technology budget to staff development.	Because it's planned for, is a predictable cost. May be more up-front money, but will ultimately reduce costs later on.	Provides some staff training, but usually during a crisis when the agency or staff member can no longer get by without it.	Loss of productivity, which could be the cause of the crisis in the first place.	Assumes that staff "will learn on the job."	Higher and longer learning curve. Staff may or may not learn all that is needed to make maximum use of the technology. Increased stress and loss of productivity.
Support	Provides regular computer support, either part-time or full-time, depending on number of computers.	Increased head count and overhead, but significantly reduced computer downtime.	Relies on a patchwork of overworked staff to maintain network and fix problems. Does not track the amount of time its network is down or computers are not in use.	Staff burnout, loss of productivity, and unreliable technology.	Relies on the "Hey Joe" sort of informal support.	Staff burnout, loss of productivity, and unreliable technology.
Software	Recognizes that the greater the diversity of software packages and operating systems, the more support that will be required. Makes provisions for regular upgrading of software packages.	Consistent, yearly budget item. Reduced support costs by standardizing all desktops.	Utilizes centralized software purchasing, but choice of application and respective support left to individuals, departments, and staff members.	Increased staff time spent on supporting computers, rather than their own jobs.	Expects support personnel to manage whatever software happens to be installed on a computer.	Increased software costs and support and training costs. Possible file incompatibilities, making it difficult for staff to collaborate on documents.

Replacement costs	Budgets to replace computers on a regular schedule, usually every three years, whether leased or purchased.	Consistent, predictable costs budgeted for on an annual basis. Reduced support costs on aging machines. Reduced staff frustration and loss of productivity.	Plans to replace computers when they no longer can be used.	Perceived savings on annual capital expenses. However, unpredictable costs not always planned for in budget set up potential for crises, increasing staff stress, and loss of productivity.	Assumes that when computers are purchased they will last forever.	Increased support costs on aging machines. Inability to upgrade software, and unable to take advantage of all available resources to improve effectiveness and efficiencies.
Donations	Has a published list of hardware and software donations it will accept, based on the programmatic use of the equipment, ability to support and maintain it, and the budget to upgrade it when necessary.	Line item for hardware and software needed is still in budget, but when savings occur through donations, funds are allocated to other items, providing overall savings.	Doesn't have a published list of acceptable donations, and makes decisions on what is accepted on a case-by-case basis.	No direct costs, but decreased opportunity for appropriate donations. Sometimes results in a disappointed well-meaning patron when donation is not accepted.	Accepts everything and anything it can get.	Nonprofit becomes a dumping site for people to discard their equipment. Nonprofit pays high costs in adapting the equipment for its needs (for example, adding memory or network interface cards), or finds no use for the equipment at all and uses it as a big doorstop.
Connectivity	Plans its network with connections that provide enough bandwidth to manage current and future needs.	Potential higher immediate expenditures, but lower costs for the future.	Has the bandwidth it needs today, but has no plan for scaling upward as demand grows.	Future upgrade costs may be high.	Has a phone and a modem; what more do you need?	Increased staff frustration, inefficient communication with internal and external stakeholders, loss of productivity, and lack of potential to use IT tools that will increase effectiveness and efficiencies.
Policy development	Involves stakeholders in analysis of the best approach to acceptable use policies for technology. Forms policies that are appropriate for the organization's needs and working culture.	Reduced confusion on technology acceptable use, security procedures, and so forth.	Copies policies from other organizations or corporations without adequate revision.	Practices are potentially inappropriate for organization's environment. Increased staff dissatisfaction. Potential for security breaches and unnecessary work.	Assumes it will all work out!	Potential for costly lawsuits and staff turnover. Unsecured information environment.

Source: *Adapted, with permission, from Consortium for School Networking (CoSN, www.cosn.org), "Taking TCO to the Classroom" (www.classroomtco.org).*

Chapter 3

Assessing Organizational Readiness

BEFORE EMBARKING on the development of your technology plan, it is important that your agency be ready. In order to achieve the maximum benefits such a planning process creates, the agency must be prepared to make technology planning a priority and to involve key stakeholders. The following questions will help you determine if your organization is ready or if your agency still has preliminary work to do.

Do you have a well-defined mission statement and strategic goals for your entire organization? Because the technology plan is about implementing the appropriate tools to support the agency's mission and strategies, it is important that a clear mission statement and strategic goals already exist and that all stakeholders understand and agree upon the mission and goals. These materials do not necessarily need to be in the form of a strategic plan, although a strategic plan does provide the best foundation from which to start.

Do you have support and commitment from the board? The board plays a critical role in approving expenditures and securing the resources necessary to implement an agency's technology plan. The board's understanding of and buy-in to the reasons for embarking on this process are necessary if you are to be successful in your efforts.

Do you have the active support and involvement of the executive director? As leader of the organization and carrier of its vision, the executive director establishes a vision for the technology plan. She must incorporate the planning efforts into the organization's culture and make the planning a priority for the agency. The executive director must also directly participate in the planning efforts by attending necessary meetings and applying necessary resources. (The roles of the board and executive director are discussed further in Chapter Seven.)

Are you able to make technology planning an organizational priority? Determine what other major agency projects during the next six to twelve months are going to dominate staff time, efforts, and resources. For example, if the agency is about to embark on a capital campaign, is experiencing critical staff turnover, or is embarking on any other significant changes or transitions, this is not necessarily the best time to also embark on a strategic technology planning process. This said, however, some transitions—such as moving to a new site or building a new facility—can go hand-in-hand with technology planning. During these kinds of transitions, a good technology plan is critical to determining the technology infrastructure needed. (It can be far more expensive to make building alterations to accommodate a computer network after the fact than to do it when other construction work is being accomplished. For example, wire can be pulled for computer data lines at the same as telephone lines are installed, and determining in advance the location of the server room will enable you to make sure that appropriate air conditioning, electrical connections, and security are built in.)

Can you allocate sufficient staff resources for both the planning and implementation? A common assumption is that planning can be added to the staff's regular, full-time work. It is important to recognize that the technology planning effort is a key part of that work. Trade-offs and allowances need to be made in order for staff to manage the process *within* their full-time jobs, not on top of them. Also take into consideration holidays and staff vacations. You need to be ready to bring on additional resources, such as a consultant, if necessary, to make the plan happen.

Do you have enough money in your budget, or a commitment to raise the funds, to implement the technology plan? Determine whether the organization has the financial resources to embark on this process. Although creating the plan will help you target your budget more strategically and may ultimately improve your financial situation, it is important that the agency have enough resources so that you can make technology planning a priority and that you are able to implement the plan once it is written.

Do you have a skilled project manager who can be the team leader, coordinating the planning and implementation activities? Ideally, this manager is someone on staff who has a history with the organization, is familiar with policies and procedures, and knows the organization's culture. The project manager needs to be someone who has good project management skills and the ability to convene and rally a team.

Do you have access to knowledgeable, objective resources on technology? These resources might be available in the form of a volunteer, board member, nonprofit technology assistance provider, nonprofit management support organization, or other entity that can help you make clear, unbiased decisions about your technology choices.

Planning in Practice
Using Times of Transition to Your Advantage

Times of transition are sometimes the worst times to do technology planning and implementation, but then again, sometimes they are the best times. Jaclyn Phuong Fabre, executive director of Cupertino Community Services, was able to use the planned transition of building and moving to a new facility at a new site to make positive changes in her agency's technology. When she had become executive director, two years before, a task as simple as creating computer-printed labels for a mailing was a major event. Since then, she had been able to increase the use and knowledge of technology from that basic level but wanted to do even more.

Phuong Fabre did not want searching for records and information to get in the way of providing service. She felt this particular transitional period was the optimum moment to make some critical changes in how the agency operated and was "the perfect place for bringing new stuff and technology."

"Transition can be hard, but it can encourage expansive thinking," Phuong Fabre said. "Why would we want to bring old technology into a brand-new building? We're raising all this money. We're going to have a fantastic new office. We have the opportunities to put in all these new technologies like DSL. Why should we hang onto the old stuff?" Over the past year, through the technology planning efforts, the agency has prepared staff who were less technology minded to embrace it. Summing up, Phuong Fabre said, "This transitional time offered a lot of great opportunities for us."

A tool for assessing whether your organization is ready to embark on technology planning is the Triangle of Constraints (Figure 3.1). Any project comprises three elements—*scope, time,* and *resources.* A project can be successfully completed when one or even two of these elements are constrained, but when all three are constrained, the project will not be successful.

For example, if an agency has fifty processes to examine (scope), and the deadline for the technology plan to be finished is only six months away (constrained time), then the amount of staff time and money (resources) applied to completing the plan must be unconstrained. Alternatively, if

FIGURE 3.1

Triangle of Constraints

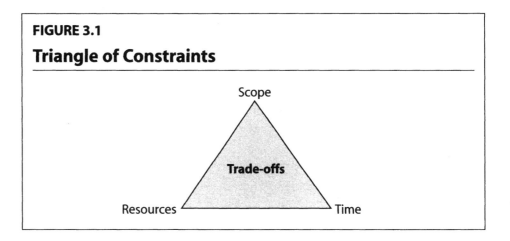

there is limited staff time and money and the plan needs to be completed in six months, then the scope of this plan would need to be far smaller, perhaps focusing on only one or two critical processes rather than all fifty. If the agency finds that all three elements are constrained, then it is not yet ready to embark on the technology planning process. The agency will need to spend more time examining what trade-offs it is willing to make before beginning a project like this.

Chapter 4

Addressing Resistance

FOR BOTH LEADERSHIP and staff, initiating technology planning and achieving agreement to make that planning a priority for the agency may be a daunting task. The person who spearheads the effort may be one of any number of people. Often the directive to develop a technology plan comes from leadership—the executive director, the board, or another member of the executive team. Often the idea comes from another staff member. No matter who brings the idea forward, it is important for all staff and leadership to buy into the process if the plan is to be effective. However, implementing new technology represents change, and change can bring out fears about and resistance to technology, and therefore to the technology planning effort. (More on change management can be found in Chapter Twenty-Seven.) This resistance is normal and must be addressed head on. Resistance is not necessarily a bad thing; it can help you develop a better plan. Resisters often identify issues that should be articulated, and they often need help in doing so.

One way to address resistance is to remove the word *technology* from the discussion. After all, what is really being talked about is identifying the tools the agency needs in order to be successful. Focus at first on your organization's mission and processes, without regard for how technology will be used. Only after that is done should discussions on the tools needed to improve the processes take place. This helps everyone to understand *why* technology is needed and ensures that the only technology installed is that which will improve something in the organization. When resistance comes up, try to find out what the person is reacting to, then steer the discussion back to *why*, not *how*, the agency is implementing technology. Most people get nervous when they bog down in the details of how technology will be implemented. They need constant reminders of the returns—the *why*.

PLANNING IN PRACTICE
Getting Everyone on Board

How do you get everyone on board with technology planning? For Christine Camara, executive director of Services for Brain Injury, the key was making sure everyone understood why the agency was embarking on this effort. "I think it is important to make sure the staff are very well aware of why you are going to do this technology plan," she said. "It becomes part of how they see technology aiding them in their jobs. Talk to them about [this question]: 'What are the things that you'd like to have happen that would make your job easier?'"

In the field of human services, writing and record keeping often take away from staff's direct service and treatment time with their clients. Camara showed staff members how technology could help them with this common and frustrating situation. The organization found training in technology use that matched each staff member's level of skill and experience. This kept those staff less familiar with technology interested and positive while more expert staff created the technology plan. This was a formula that motivated both groups, Camara said. "As we worked on the technology plan, they were keeping time by being in the loop with some technology."

Training was a strategy that worked equally well for the Community Association for Rehabilitation. As associate director Peter Beckh said, "The fear and most resistance [took the form of] 'I can't possibly learn that; it's way too complicated.'" As a remedy for lack of knowledge, the organization offered education. It sent people to relatively inexpensive training for specific software they would use in their day-to-day work, "things they were already doing and could do better by using the computer," said Beckh.

Jaclyn Phuong Fabre, executive director of Cupertino Community Services, found that acclimating staff to change by adapting something familiar helped convince staff that technology would help them. One strategy the agency employed was computerizing forms that had previously existed only on paper. Making computerized versions as familiar and usable as possible sped up the process of acceptance. More technologically savvy people in this organization made the new applications very easy to use. They created on-screen versions that looked as much as possible like the original paper ones, so the change was not as great for less technologically experienced staff.

Phuong Fabre joked, "Most people just thought it was a phase that we were going through. They could not really see what the point was unless it directly affected their lives." By immediately creating something useful for them, such as the computerized forms, the agency made it easier for them to understand the applicability of technology and how it could improve their lives. Then when the technology planning team described what people would be able to do with technology once the agency moved to its highly anticipated new site, staff started to see what technology could do for them individually.

Another way to help those resisting technology planning is to get them involved in the planning process itself. For example, you might have them help with researching the technology possibilities. This will begin to help them envision how technology can be used as an effective tool and generate excitement. You might also go to see demonstrations, particularly in nonprofits providing similar services, or bring in vendors. Participate in relevant e-mailing list discussions to find out the best practices and lessons learned by others. Talk to friends and colleagues, getting their ideas. Get practical examples and focus on successes and challenges. Bring in case studies, and articles from magazines and newspapers that talk about the technology being examined. Do whatever is necessary to help generate vision and excitement.

Here are some common reasons people present for not buying into technology and the writing of a technology plan. Each reason is followed by responses you might use to soften this resistance.

"It costs too much." Not only will developing the plan cost money, but technology in general is too expensive to implement, so why waste the time writing a plan? Try to get to the root of what is meant by "costs too much." If the issue is that the agency does not have the money to implement the plan, consider changing the scope of the plan to implement the technology in smaller phases, then seek the necessary resources through fundraising or in-kind donations. If the concern is that technology in general is too expensive, conduct some benchmarking research to determine what similar agencies usually spend on technology. Finally, always go back to the return on investment. If the return (for example, increased productivity or better access to services by your clients) is small, then it is a reasonable decision not to do the project.

"It's too much work and time." And it is hard, thoughtful work because it addresses issues at the core of the organization. Most agencies are at staff capacity as it is; adding technology planning on top of staff's more than full-time jobs seems like a luxury the organization cannot afford. Examining the organization's busi-

ness strategies is part of the job. Even without technology as the impetus, it is critical to examine strategies on an ongoing basis. Although it is true that trade-offs will need to be made so that staff can make technology planning a priority, make sure the planning team is adequately staffed so that the burden of the work does not fall on only one or a few individuals. Consider getting some skilled consultants or volunteers involved. (There is more on working with consultants and volunteers in Chapter Eight.)

"We tried it before and got nothing out of it." This attitude might be taken toward technology planning or toward implementing the technology. Examine what went wrong before. Perhaps the solution did not solve the problem and instead compounded it. Determine what it will take to make sure that the same problems do not happen again. Return to the vision of the technology possibilities and how they will improve the organization's ability to provide services.

"Technology is constantly changing and it's too hard to keep up." It seems as though once the plan is written, it will already be obsolete. Determine the appropriate technology that will meet the agency's needs at the time the plan is written. Account for the need to upgrade technology in the plan's budget and timeline so that changes happen in a methodical way that addresses the organization's ongoing needs. Remember, the technology plan is a living document. It is designed to help your organization manage change more effectively. Having to update your technology plan is a sign that your agency is accomplishing this.

"We lack talented staff in this area." There is no one engaged in the agency who knows anything about technology. Find other agencies who have developed a technology plan or implemented technology similar to the technology you are thinking about for your agency. Learn from their strategies, best practices, and lessons gained from experience. It is true that hiring appropriate IT staff can be costly, so think creatively about ways and means of providing guidance to existing staff—for example, collaborating with other agencies or finding college students or volunteers who can help mentor staff. In today's technology-rich society, it is easier than you might think to find someone with the appropriate technological expertise to help.

"It will distract us from the agency's mission." Technology is not what the agency is about, providing direct services to the community is. Refer back to the return on investment—what needs to be improved in order to provide services better? How can technology help? Remember, the agency is not going to implement anything that does not improve something. Determine whether it might actually be a disservice to the agency's constituency if the agency did *not* examine the most appropriate tools to provide services effectively and efficiently.

"I'm uncomfortable with technology." Technology is too difficult to understand; people fear appearing "dumb." The more someone is exposed to technology and how it supports the organization's mission, the less mysterious technology will seem. Provide as much training as is needed. People need time to experiment with the technology and learn how it works. Reward those who take the risk and try new tools, even if they initially make mistakes. Include them in decision-making processes and in evaluation of these new tools. Remind them that they do not need to be experts in technology, that in fact the tools are in place to support their efforts in their own area of expertise.

"Technology will replace humans in their jobs." The agency is implementing technology so that it can reduce the need for staff and volunteers. It is true that technology may replace humans in doing some rote tasks, such as providing information on programs or applications for services on the agency's Web site. This makes it possible for the client to access certain information or services without interacting with agency staff. Nonprofits are a relationship-oriented business, however. Technology cannot replace the important client and staff interaction needed to deliver the agency's mission. Before deciding which tasks can be replaced by technology, determine whether or not it is important for each task to involve human interaction to maintain the relationship-oriented value of your agency. If, for example, you are trying to help funders feel a personal connection with the agency and one of the strategies you employ is to handwrite thank-you notes, then it is reasonable to choose not to have your donor database automatically generate thank-you notes, even though this may be a more efficient way to get the job done.

Because providing community services well requires relationship building, it is important to remember the role of IT. It is a tool for facilitating relationships or creating efficiencies so that staff have more time to spend providing important services. If implementing a specific tool detracts from either of those purposes, then do not put it in place. Again, focus on the benefits that using technology will have for fulfilling the agency's mission.

It is important to validate and address these concerns. A first step is to encourage staff to identify their personal worries and resistance. Although some of the resistance will take the form of practical concerns (about money, time, resources, and the like), some of it will be emotional (for example, being afraid of appearing "dumb"). To learn people's feelings and impressions, take an informal survey. Then, in addressing the resistance, keep coming back to the purpose of the technology plan—to apply the appropriate tools that will make the organization more effective.

PLANNING IN PRACTICE
The Role of a Supportive Organizational
Culture in Acceptance of Technology

Sister Patricia Marie Mulpeters, executive director of the Presentation Center, felt that hospitality was a characteristic sign of the mission of this retreat center. This was as true of how the staff treated each other as it was of how they treated their guests. A supportive environment, a strong sense of community, and a strong belief in trust and cooperation characterized the agency's organizational culture even before it began working on its technology plan. This supportive organizational culture carried staff through the planning process gracefully.

The Presentation Center had a mostly Spanish-speaking maintenance and kitchen staff and a number of older, active volunteer Sisters who had been born well before the time of computers. This could have been a recipe for substantial resistance to technology. But with an eye to the good of their mission and the good of their people, they supported each other while creating an excellent plan.

The technology plan of the AIDS Community Research Consortium also benefited from a supportive organizational culture. Executive director Michael Edell described how the organization had a strong spirit. It helps HIV-positive people live longer and healthier lives. In addition to life-threatening illness, clients often have other serious troubles, such as no job, no home, and low literacy. The supportive atmosphere the organization created toward clients is shared with the staff. As Edell said, "It's our nature to be a safety net for those folks. So, having said that, it's our nature to be a safety net for each other."

This supportive atmosphere served the agency well during the technology planning process. Among the multiracial, multigender staff, the most skittish people were those who knew the least about technology going in. They were worried that if they failed to do well with technology, they would look like poor performers.

To avoid a scenario of searching for "poor performers" to blame for any problems that might occur, leadership decided to frame technology planning as an ethical debate, with no one cast in the role of the villain. If the organization had been a past poor performer in preparing staff for technology, the leaders reasoned, why should it blame this on the staff now? With this sort of supportive organizational culture and safe environment, fear and resistance to technology did not last long.

Part Two

Planning the Plan

THIS SECTION is about managing the planning process and the roles and responsibilities of the individuals who are a part of it. Chapter Five discusses the costs, time, tools, and resources associated with creating the plan. It gives guidance and tips on project management techniques that are useful not only for the planning process but for technology implementation as well. Chapter Six offers greater detail on organizing the technology planning team, selecting who should be on it, and determining roles and responsibilities. Chapter Seven discusses the importance of leadership in the planning process and, in particular, takes a closer look at the roles and responsibilities of the executive director and the board. Chapter Eight outlines how to make the best use of consultants and volunteers, how to define their roles, and what to look for when hiring them.

Chapter 5

Managing the Process

AFTER YOU have decided that your agency needs a technology plan, you have achieved key stakeholders' buy-in and involvement, and you have determined that you can make technology planning a priority for the next six months to a year, you are ready to start developing the plan. Managing the technology planning process is like managing organizational change. The technology plan is documentation for that change. Therefore, managing the technology planning process is analogous to managing any new project within your organization. It consists of

- Developing a team
- Conducting necessary meetings
- Listing the planning tasks
- Developing a timeline for completing the plan
- Setting priorities
- Determining roles and responsibilities
- Budgeting for the creation of the plan
- Tracking and charting progress
- Communicating frequently and effectively

Developing a Team

The process of developing a team is fleshed out more fully in Chapters Six, Seven, and Eight. Briefly, however, the technology planning team consists of the individuals responsible for providing key input into the plan and for writing the plan. Their job is to conduct research, chart processes, compile data, propose solutions, and document and communicate their findings and plans. The team must ensure that the change the technology plan represents is conducted with as much thoughtfulness as possible and must communicate frequently and effectively with the rest of the organization during the planning process.

Conducting Necessary Meetings

Although there is nothing unique about having regular meetings, some issues related to technology planning may change the way these particular meetings need to be conducted. One issue to be aware of is that because the team represents multiple levels of stakeholders, including some external resources, you may find that you have convened a group of people who have never worked together on a project before. For example, you might have a board member working with the agency's receptionist. They may have never met, much less worked together on a team. It is important to acknowledge the group's diversity and take steps to establish appropriate group norms.

Two other issues that often arise in technology planning meetings are the "Gee whiz!" and the "I know the best solution" factors. The "Gee whiz!" factor is the excitement that is generated by technology gizmos and gadgets. Like children finding out about a new toy, team members may find technology fun to talk about and play with and may easily lose sight of the team's ultimate goal—to plan the *appropriate* application of technology for the agency (not necessarily the technology that is the most fun or the coolest available). This goal is not always as alluring to talk about as the latest and greatest technological toy, so make sure the team develops a clear agenda for each meeting and sticks to it.

The "I know the best solution" factor pops up when a team member has expertise in a particular type of technology or vendor and insists that it is the best solution for the agency. This too can distract the team from the real goal, because it makes it difficult for the team to be open to examining all the possible solutions.

If possible, it is often helpful to bring in someone from outside to facilitate the sessions, especially when the team first begins to meet. Facilitators can make sure the team stays on track. They can also bring in new perspectives and objectivity. Facilitators will provide a framework for the meetings and make sure that everyone has an opportunity to provide input. The facilitator you choose should have knowledge of process improvement strategies, excellent facilitation skills, and at least a user-level knowledge of IT.

Planning in Practice

Don't Let the "Cool" Factor Get You Off-Track

Jim Gomes, president of the Environmental League of Massachusetts, described how he needed to tell tech-craving staff that technology implementation is about getting work done effectively and not necessarily about the most elegant solution or neatest hardware. He said that some may feel they need certain technology, but "that's not what we are doing here." Gomes reported that he saw some nonprofits create Web sites not because they really needed one, but because they felt pressured to have one—to gain admission to what he humorously described as the "cool, cutting-edge nonprofit organization club." A Web site seemed to be part of the entrance fee.

Gomes ran into the problem of board members' making unhelpful suggestions about technology, sometimes recommending tools that were too fancy. He said, "We have board members who know a fair amount about computer technology, but that can be a negative if the board members are not also very well versed in what we do day-to-day.... It can be a distraction, having to talk through with them why we don't really want to do it that way. 'Yes, you know more about computers than we do. But that's not the point. We know more about what we do day-to-day than you do.'"

Patricia Suhrcke, executive director of the Cambridge Forum, said, "most important is how does [the technology] relate to your mission." If nonprofits cannot clearly relate mission components to anything they do with technology, she said, it's easy to get pulled off course by the latest bells and whistles and staff who have various interests and expertise. In her experience, the director is the main person who can keep the mission central to technology planning: "nobody is as solid on the mission and putting the pieces, the activities, of the organization together to further that mission as the director."

The agenda for the first meeting should be to establish how the group members want to work together. Articulate your decision-making processes by determining who drives the decisions, including approval on individual decisions included in the plan and on the plan in total. Get clear on everyone's roles and responsibilities. Brainstorm agenda topics for subsequent meetings. Determine how work on the technology plan will be accomplished between meetings. Figure out who else needs to be involved in the process and when.

TIPS

- Set long- and short-term objectives for the team and communicate them throughout the organization before the first meeting.

- Make as many basic decisions about roles and responsibilities as possible before the first meeting occurs, and document them.

- Always have a clear agenda for each meeting and stick to it. (Have a strategy in place for keeping the team on track; for example, create a "parking lot" where issues that are important can be noted and revisited at a more appropriate date.)

- At the end of each meeting, determine tangible action items (note who is assigned to completing the task and a deadline for when the task will be complete) and determine the next meeting date.

- Keep a *decision log* to track the dates decisions are made, participants in making the decisions, and the reasons for the decisions.

  Use Worksheet 5.1 to begin your team's decision log.

Listing Tasks

Listing tasks consists of itemizing everything that needs to be done to develop the plan. Resource A, Comprehensive Technology Plan Outline, will guide you to many of the necessary tasks. What tasks does your organization need to accomplish in order to complete its technology plan sections? Ask the team to brainstorm and make a list. Some of these tasks will be unique to your organization; however, tasks that most agencies are likely to face are conducting staff surveys, researching technology possibilities, hiring consultants or arranging for volunteers, selecting meeting dates, and so forth.

TIPS

- Make sure that as you create your task list you match it with the sections that need to be completed in the technology plan.

- Note task interdependencies: What tasks need to be completed before others can be completed?

- Use project management tools such as Gantt charts, flowcharts, tree diagrams, affinity diagrams, and the like. These well-known project management tools can be easily found in project management software, books, and Web sites. (Although you can use special software to help with project management, it is not essential. You can often use basic office software such as spreadsheets to achieve the same results. Even pen and paper will work.)

WORKSHEET 5.1

Decision Log

Decision No.	Date Made	Decision Description	Participants	Reason for Decision

- Keep an *actions required log* to track who is assigned to each task, the date the task was assigned, and when the task is due.

  Use Worksheet 5.2 to begin keeping your team's actions required log.

Developing a Timeline

A timeline not only helps you see how to get from the here and now to your final goal but also acts as a tracking device, outlining the tasks that need to happen, how long they last, and when they need to be completed. The first step in developing a timeline for the creation of a technology plan is setting a deadline.

Clear deadlines are helpful in keeping everyone on task and moving forward. Depending on many factors, including the scope of its plan and the resources available to it for this process, a typical nonprofit can expect to spend six months to a year developing the plan. To some, this may seem like a long time, but to others this may seem very aggressive. Referring back to the Triangle of Constraints model discussed in Chapter Three, the fewer the resources available and the bigger the scope you anticipate for the technology plan, the more time you will need to develop the plan. The time it takes to create the plan can be reduced by applying more resources, such as delegating more staff time to the project, or by narrowing the scope of the plan to address only a few technology strategies.

The next step in developing the timeline is identifying key milestones. A milestone has no duration. It might be a completed event or occurrence, or it might be a deadline by which something must happen. Working toward milestones keeps the team progressing. Achieving a milestone is an opportunity to celebrate the team's accomplishment. Brainstorm with the team the milestones it needs to meet on the path to creating a technology plan. Refer back to the task list and to the technology plan outline in Resource A to determine what to put on your timeline.

TIPS

- Do not hesitate to add tasks and milestones as needed.

- Recognize that you will change task start dates, end dates, and durations as needed, but be aware of the impact these changes will have on subsequent tasks and milestones.

- Delete tasks and milestones that become obsolete or irrelevant as you progress.

- Always keep your final end date in mind.

- Allow time for overall proofreading and edit passes.

WORKSHEET 5.2

Actions Required (AR) Log

Action No.	Date Assigned	Assigned To	Action Description	Deliverable	Date Due	Date Done

- Allow time to get approval on sections of the technology plan and the plan as a whole. Remember that approval may not come from just one individual; it may need to come from an entire department (or at the very least a department head).

- When using project management tools, such as a Gantt chart, see whether you find it easier to develop the task list and timeline in the same format. Start by listing the tasks, then add milestones, durations, and start and end dates.

Setting Priorities

Once tasks and milestones are identified, you can begin to prioritize. Ask yourself such questions as

- What has to happen first, second, third?
- Are there some tasks that only one person (or certain people) can do?
- When is that person available?
- What else is that person doing that may conflict with the technology planning tasks?

Examining priorities can also result in identifying *critical path* items—things that have to happen before another thing can happen. Note that this critical path may affect your budget. For example, does something need to be purchased, or must a consultant be hired before other things can happen?

Determining Roles and Responsibilities

Now that you have identified tasks, created a timeline, and set priorities, you need to match people with the tasks that need to be accomplished. This process is described in Chapter Six.

Budgeting for the Creation of the Plan

In addition to developing a budget for the implementation of the selected technology and outlining that budget in the technology plan, you must budget for the costs associated with creating the plan itself. In terms of direct expenses, these costs are few. Direct costs may include such items as hiring people with the necessary expertise to assist in the technical areas of the plan, hiring facilitators to help with the planning meetings, and purchasing supplies (such as binders to hold the plan and butcher paper for creating flowcharts during meetings). These costs will vary depending on your organization's available resources. However, the highest cost associated with the development of the technology plan is staff time.

The amount of staff time needed will fluctuate depending on the number of people on the team, the scope of the plan, and the culture of the organization. You may also find, depending on the overall timeline for the plan, that staff time devoted to planning will vary from week to week. A good rule of thumb is that the plan's project manager should budget at least approximately sixteen hours (two days) of the workweek to work on the technology plan. Other team members should expect to spend approximately eight hours (one day) per week. This ratio changes, of course, if you have someone who is dedicated full-time to working on the plan.

Tracking and Charting Progress

As the team progresses in the development of the technology plan, it is important to track its progress along the way to see clearly not only what has been accomplished but also what work still needs to get done. This tracking also provides the team with a sense of accomplishment as they see each item getting checked off.

TIPS

- Enlarge the technology plan outline and task list to poster size and post them on the wall so that everyone can easily see the progress being made.

- Use butcher paper and Post-It notes to document flowcharts and provide the flexibility to move items around. Post flowcharts on the wall as well. Not only does charting the organization's progress on the wall keep the planning team moving forward, it gives staff not directly involved in the planning effort a sense of what is being accomplished.

Communicating Frequently and Effectively

Ongoing communication is critical, not only for the technology planning team but also for other staff and key stakeholders. Keeping everyone engaged in the process as you progress will make technology implementation easier and help everyone adjust to the changes required by incorporating new processes and tools. Many things need to be communicated; some examples are tasks, milestones, project priorities, decisions, and of course any actions that those with whom you are communicating are assigned to complete.

One of the first decisions the planning team will need to make is what else, besides the items just listed, needs to be communicated, to whom, when, and how frequently. And the team must consider communication not only between team members but with other key stakeholders as well. Additionally, the team members will need to determine how they would like to receive communication. To move forward, they will need information from others, such as clarification about the way certain individuals accomplish tasks in their jobs and about individuals' opinions and preferences.

TIPS

- Remember that communication may be either formal or informal. No matter how well crafted a team's communication strategy, it is normal for people to talk on the side. The team must be clear about its key messages to provide consistent information and avoid any confusion among the team members and other key stakeholders.

- Use multiple methods of communication, such as memos, e-mail, minutes distributed in writing, staff meetings, one-on-one meetings, and so on.

- When in doubt, overcommunicate. Some people say there is no such thing as too much communication. This is almost true. You know you have communicated enough when people beg you to stop.

PLANNING IN PRACTICE
Keeping Technology Planning a Priority

Pam Brandin, executive director of the Peninsula Center for the Blind and Visually Impaired, kept her technology planning team progressing by means of a big chart on the wall. Tacked to the wall of the conference room where the agency held staff meetings and board meetings, the chart showed both needs and progress in a graphic way. With verbal descriptions provided for blind staff, the chart kept the planning process in the forefront of everyone's minds.

In addition to seeing a sort of picture of what was going on or having that visual described, people also heard a lot. Staff meetings and board meetings included progress reports on the planning process. Team members offered their updates and impressions. Cross-functional teams had spokespeople in each department who informally reported back to their departments and answered questions from departmental staff.

Keeping people well informed had a good effect. Staff members gained greater understanding of how the whole agency worked, not just their part or their department or their job. Brandin said, "They see things in context and not just . . . advocating for something very specific without understanding how it's going to fit into whole scheme of things." People became more attentive during staff meetings when people in other departments described what they were doing. Staff had lots of job satisfaction, at least in part because of seeing the organization as a whole and seeing their individual value in that whole.

Chapter 6

Building the Planning Team

AS DESCRIBED in Chapter Five, one of the critical first steps in developing the technology plan is establishing a planning team. This team could have as few as three people or as many as ten (for ease of working together, it is unadvisable to have more than twelve members). Even in a small organization, a technology plan should be developed by multiple people. The scope of the work is too much for just one individual, and most important, it is easier to get the widespread support needed for implementation when multiple stakeholders are involved.

Although the mission of the team is to develop the technology plan, there are many additional benefits to the organization when people work together in this process. This practice ensures that the effort is collaborative and that no single person must shoulder the full responsibility of writing the plan. Multiple points of view are represented so that better decisions are made. A core group of people is established to be cheerleaders to other key stakeholders for both the planning effort and its implementation. Shared language is developed so that misunderstandings are at a minimum. Finally, this work provides people with the opportunity to develop and communicate a shared vision.

Understanding Necessary Team Skills

Together, the team members should be representative of the entire organization, and they may include key board members or other volunteers. The following list consists of skills the team needs. Note that you may find that a single person on the team embodies many of these skills and also that some skills may require separate individuals.

- Team skills (such as communication, facilitation, and decision making)

- Project planning skills (ability to develop timelines, budgets, evaluation, and the like)

- Process planning skills (information mapping, process management)

In addition, the following people will be needed for their roles as well as their knowledge. The roles and knowledge these people bring may not be needed at the same time nor to the same degree throughout the planning process.

- People with decision-making and budgetary authority. (Determine early on who drives the decisions, including approving individual sections of the plan and the plan in total.)

- Individuals directly affected by the plan, such as program managers, administrative staff, volunteers, and board members.

- The facilities or operations manager.

- Experts in network architecture, network installation, and network support.

PLANNING IN PRACTICE
Get the Big-Picture People on the Planning Team

Pam Brandin, executive director of the Peninsula Center for the Blind and Visually Impaired, knew what she needed in her technology planning team. The team included a blind employee and representatives from each department. Having a cross-functional team that knew all the elements and issues involved was important.

With the advice of department supervisors, Brandin recruited one person from each department. She asked for people who would be good at thinking about the agency as a whole. More than anything, she looked for systemic thinking and big-picture skills. Out of a team of eight, two had specific technology expertise. The rest did not but were willing and eager to learn. Technology skills, Brandin knew, can be learned. But without the ability to see the big picture, people may find it impossible to create a mission-based technology plan.

Scott Render, CEO of the American Red Cross, Santa Clara Valley Chapter, discovered that skills in communication and persuasion can be more important than specific technical skills in technology planning. He thought the agency's information systems (IS) person would lead the technology planning process, but it did not turn out that way. Instead, the communications person ended up taking the lead. With stronger coordination and communication skills, the communications person became the bridge between technology and department management. The IT person did the strictly technical work and the communications person got managers to write their parts of the plan. People skills ended up being more central to technology planning than purely technical ones.

Understanding Key Roles and Responsibilities

Key roles and responsibilities for the team include

- Team sponsor (for example, the executive director or the board)
  - Makes the team's mission a priority
  - Allocates appropriate staff time
  - Is both an internal and external advocate for the process
  - Commits to allocating or securing the appropriate funding and in-kind resources
- Project manager or team leader (may be the executive director or someone to whom the executive director delegates; note, however, that experience shows that the IT director is not necessarily the best person to lead this effort, as it is important that the plan's project manager have a big-picture view of the organization)
  - Makes sure the plan is written in a clear, consistent manner
  - Maintains business linkages to the project (that is, makes sure the team stays within organizational priorities, such as mission, vision, and budget)
  - Determines team membership
  - Owns the vision, mission, and expectations of team
  - Respects bottom-line constraints and project boundaries
  - Chooses an appropriate decision-making style
  - Does "real" work herself
  - Makes sure the entire team is aware of logistics of all pertinent activities
- Key contributor(s) (program managers, administrative staff, IT director or consultant, bookkeeper, and so forth)
  - Provides direct inputs, including information and work, that affect the results and success of the technology planning

- Helps establish vision and strategies to be included in the plan
- Polls other key stakeholders and communicates their feedback to the rest of the team
- Conducts appropriate research
- Writes or causes to be written specific elements of the plan

- Administrator (usually an administrative assistant)
  - Coordinates team meeting schedules
  - Takes notes or minutes and distributes them to the team
  - Orders appropriate supplies, such as binders to hold the plans
  - Performs other administrative tasks as needed by the team

- Supporter(s) (stakeholders who are not on the planning team, such as departmental staff, board members, volunteers, clients, or anyone else affected by the organization's technology)
  - Responds to team requests for information
  - Participates in group or individual meetings, when asked
  - Fills out appropriate surveys

Planning in Practice
Ask for Help When You Need It

Christine Camara, executive director of Services for Brain Injury, knew that her development director, the organization's accidental techie (who was neither trained nor hired to be the technology staff person but who, because of his interest and skills, has become the person that everyone goes to), would be perfect as the project manager of the technology planning process. But this organization provides essential services that are unavailable anywhere else, and the development director is an integral part of making those services happen. Camara knew they would need about 25 percent of the development director's time to be devoted to the planning effort. She said, "We were committed to the technology plan, but not at the exclusion of our other activities." So they "pulled out the old job description and asked, 'how do we make this happen?'" Not, it turned out, without some help from others in the organization. For the duration of the planning process, the agency worked around the development director's job description and shifted some of his responsibilities to other staff to let him have time to do the planning work.

Jaclyn Phuong Fabre, executive director of Cupertino Community Services, had a small staff and said, "I can't afford to take that many staff out of other work for the [planning] process." However, the agency had a volunteer who had been helping staff with technology. In order to allow him to attend daytime meetings and be available on short notice, they hired him as consultant. That way, Phuong Fabre said, "he's there not just as a volunteer . . . he's there not at his whim, but at ours."

Anne Dunham, executive director of Youth Science Institute, got the idea to hire a consultant from the representatives of larger agencies whom she met at Wired for Good program meetings. She noticed some of them were hiring outside help to assist in the technology planning process. Youth Science Institute was undertaking a capital campaign at the same time as the technology plan and found its staff overwhelmed.

Dunham's education director knew a woman just starting a consulting practice who had previously directed an organization similar to Youth Science Institute. She was skilled and respected and turned out to be the perfect solution to their problem. The extra help allowed the planning team to not only attend Wired for Good meetings but also take a little time away from the office afterwards to focus exclusively on their planning efforts.

Mapping Roles and Responsibilities

An excellent tool for determining and clarifying roles and responsibilities is the *process-responsibility matrix.* Use Worksheet 6.1 to begin your own process-responsibility matrix. This worksheet helps you identify who is the owner, key contributor, or supporter of each process that needs to be accomplished in order to develop the technology plan.

An *owner* is an individual who has responsibility for the effective operation of a specified piece of the technology planning process. One way to identify the owner is to think about who would get praise if the results were good and who would take the heat if they were not. For example, an owner could be the person in charge of researching appropriate technology solutions. Although the owner does not necessarily need to be the one actually conducting the research, he is responsible for making sure the research gets accomplished. There should be only one owner of any given process.

A *key contributor* is an individual who provides direct inputs (including information or work) that affect the results and success of completing a piece of the technology plan. This is an individual who must contribute to the process in order for the owner to achieve results. For example, a key contributor could be the one conducting the research on technological solutions. This person is not the owner of the process because she could be one of many investigating the technological possibilities. There can be multiple key contributors.

A *supporter* is an individual whose contributed input to a piece of the technology planning process adds value. The results of that process could be produced without this individual's input, but the input makes the results of the process better. For example, a supporter could provide an opinion on the different technologies being considered. As with the key contributor role, there can be multiple supporters.

The value of filling out a process-responsibility matrix is that it provides a visual picture of who is doing what and the degree to which each person bears responsibility for each process. Holes and overlaps are then easily identified, so the team can determine how to make sure everything gets accomplished, perhaps by hiring a consultant or adding more members to the team. As the team fills out the matrix, opportunities arise for making sure everyone has a shared understanding of each process. A collective language begins to emerge. Additionally, the team members develop a deeper understanding of each other's roles. They also gain a greater appreciation for the work ahead of them and can plan their jobs accordingly.

Process-Responsibility Matrix

Instructions

1. Fill in the names and contact information of your planning team in the first table below.

2. Down the left side of the second table list the tasks that must be accomplished to complete the technology plan. These tasks may include completing the main sections and subsections of the technology plan itself as well as other tasks such as research. Add rows and columns as necessary.

3. Complete the top row of the second table with the names or titles of the members of the technology planning team. Then in the cells under the names, insert the letter "O," "K," or "S" to indicate whether each person is the "Owner," "Key Contributor," or "Supporter" for completing each particular section or subsection of the technology plan or some other task.

Owner. The individual who has ultimate responsibility for effective development and completion of a particular piece of the technology planning process. (One way to identify the owner of a task is to think about who would get praise if the results were good and who would take the heat if they were not.) There should be only one owner for each section, subsection, or other task.

Key contributor. An individual who provides direct inputs (including information or work) that affect the results and success of completing a piece of the technology planning process. This is an individual who must contribute to the process in order for the owner to achieve results.

Supporter. An individual whose contributed input to a piece of the technology planning process adds value. The results for the section could be produced without this individual's input, but the input makes the results better. There may be multiple supporters.

Technology Planning Team

Name	Contact Information

Process-Responsibility Matrix

Main Section	Subsection	Name	Name	Name	Name	Name	Comments

Chapter 7

Leadership Roles and Responsibilities

LEADERSHIP PLAYS a critical role in the technology planning process. Although the roles of the executive staff as leaders are paramount, all levels of staff will manifest leadership qualities during this process. For example, an administrative assistant who is on the planning team will need to be an advocate for the work the team is doing. He will have to understand both the organization's vision and the vision of the technology plan and be an articulate spokesperson, coach, and change agent to the staff who are not as integrally involved in the process.

The roles that individual staff take on will vary—sometimes they will be leaders, sometimes followers, and sometimes neutral parties. However, it is important to recognize that almost everyone must take on some leadership responsibilities throughout the planning process if that process is to be successful.

This said, what are the specific roles of the executive director and the board during the technology planning process?

Role of the Executive Director

Because technology planning is most often seen as an operational issue, it is easy for many executive directors to delegate this process to other staff members and not be very involved in it at all. However, technology, and technology planning, is much more than an operational issue, it is a strategic issue as well. Technology is a tool that can change the services a nonprofit provides, not just how the nonprofit provides them. It has systemic implications for the entire organization, affecting every aspect of it, at every level. Because of this, the role the executive director plays in the technology planning process is crucial.

The executive director need not take a hands-on role in developing the technology plan, managing the logistics, or getting the plan written. However, the executive director does need to make sure that the technology plan supports the organization's mission and vision. More than that, the executive director must overtly support the vision of strategically integrating technology into the organization and be an advocate for it to both internal and external stakeholders. It is the executive director who has the ultimate say on whether or not technology planning can be made a priority for the agency over the next six months to a year, and it is the executive director who makes sure that both internal and external resources are appropriately applied to this endeavor. Not only should the executive director be personally invested and involved in the technology planning effort, but she must get others invested and excited about the effort as well. In this way the role of the executive director in relation to technology and technology planning is no different then her role around other organizational initiatives—she is a visionary, strategist, change agent, coach, politician, and fundraiser.[1]

PLANNING IN PRACTICE

The Role of the Executive Director in Technology Planning

Patricia Suhrcke, executive director of the Cambridge Forum, summed up the dual roles of an executive director in nonprofit technology planning when she remarked, "Sometimes I feel like I'm the cheerleader; sometimes I feel like I'm the brake." She felt her role was to serve as an educator during the technology planning and implementation process, getting everyone in the organization on the same page by focusing on the agency's mission and on the use of technology to further that mission.

But although she wanted to generate the vision and excitement for what the agency could do with technology, she also wanted to keep everyone grounded in reality. The Cambridge Forum already used technology for standard office functions such as databases, word processing, desktop publishing, and providing outreach and content through its Web site. Suhrcke wanted to see the agency use more sophisticated databases and a wider range of content on its Web site, but at the same time, she wanted to make sure leadership and staff made responsible decisions so the agency wouldn't be left with debt or equipment that it couldn't handle in the future.

---

1. See B. Nanus and D. Dobbs, *Leaders Who Make a Difference* (San Francisco: Jossey-Bass, 1999).

During the technology planning process, the executive director carries out these key roles and responsibilities:

- Articulates vision, both for the organization and the technology planning process

- Gains support and commitment from the board so it will allow financial resources to be applied to the plan and its implementation and will assist in fundraising efforts when appropriate

- Provides personal advocacy and organizational priority to the technology planning initiative

- Allocates staff resources for the planning and implementation processes (recognizing that staff planning efforts are not in addition to their jobs but a critical part of those jobs)

- Assigns a skilled project manager to lead the logistical efforts of getting the plan done

- Secures necessary funding and in-kind resources

- Develops strategic collaborations and partnerships, both internally and externally

- Participates in key decision-making processes

- Participates in or leads key meetings as necessary

The amount of hands-on work the executive director takes on in technology planning is a matter of the size of the organization, resources available, and leadership style. For example, the executive director of a small nonprofit with few resources may take on the role of project manager for the technology planning process, whereas the executive director of a large nonprofit with a large staff may delegate most of the work and not participate in the logistics at all. Executive directors of medium-sized nonprofits may both delegate and participate in the hands-on work. These executive directors carefully balance their involvement in the planning process with the needs of the agency, organizational culture, and personal leadership style.

Regardless of the degree to which executive directors are involved in the logistics of developing the plan, their paramount role is to help sort out those issues that are most critical for the agency. With their big-picture view of the organization, they are uniquely able to keep the appropriate emphasis on such important issues as mission, vision, costs, resources, and the like.

Role of the Board

First and foremost, the role of the board is to approve the organization's financial commitment to both the completion and implementation of the technology plan and, if necessary, to assist in securing the funding. The board members must have a shared understanding of the vision that makes writing the plan necessary and must be committed to finding the resources to make the technology strategies the plan represents a reality. Through fulfilling this role, the board also supports the staff in developing the technology plan.

Beyond the role to support staff and secure resources, the role board members play in the technology planning process varies from organization to organization. The following are typical ways that individual board members can be helpful during the planning process.

Participate as technology planning team members. Whether or not the board has individuals with technological expertise, having one or a few board members participate on the team is valuable for a couple of reasons. First, they are often able to provide a more objective point of view than are staff who are mired in the day-to-day work of the organization. Those board members who work in the private sector are likely using technology tools in their organizations and can give good examples of the ways technology can be used to improve efficiency and effectiveness. Second, they can serve as an effective communication link between board and staff. They can back up staff in recommendations for technology implementation because they were part of the process of developing those recommendations. Because they are communicating with their fellow board members, they have more license than staff to communicate with, if necessary, undiplomatic honesty.

Serve as mentors to staff. This is a good role for someone on the board who does have technological expertise. Not only can this board member be a good sounding board, she may be able to offer ideas and suggestions based on experience. This individual can also help the team research technological possibilities.

Assist with hiring consultants or volunteers. Hiring technology consultants and volunteers can be a daunting task (see Chapter Eight for more information). Board members can be excellent resources here, able to help the team in developing the hiring criteria, interviewing candidates, and providing feedback on the candidates' qualifications. This gives staff more confidence in the selection process. Once someone is hired, board members can also help oversee that consultant's or volunteer's work.

Locate resources. In addition to helping with fundraising campaigns, board members often have connections to the community that will help the agency secure other resources. Be it within their own company or another organization, they may be able to locate in-kind donations of equipment, software, peripherals, furniture, and the like. They can also be helpful in finding potential consultants and volunteers—for example, colleagues who are interested in helping with a specific technological project, such as building a Web site.

Both as individuals and as a unit, the board plays a crucial role in the technology planning process. Carefully examine the skills, talents, and experience of the individuals on your board and recruit members as appropriate to participate in the process. Having a board that is invested in the planning will make implementation much easier in the long run.

Chapter 8

Working with Consultants and Volunteers

UNLESS YOUR AGENCY has IT expertise in house, you will inevitably need to hire a consultant or knowledgeable volunteer to assist you in both the technology planning and implementation efforts. This chapter discusses tips and best practices for hiring such consultants and volunteers.

Consultants

Hiring IT consultants is very similar to hiring other consultants to work with your organization. The area in which you may find some difference is that it may be more difficult to determine the credibility of IT consultants' knowledge, because their expertise is highly specialized. A common pitfall is relying too heavily on consultants' expertise without questioning whether that expertise fits the needs of your organization. Just as people often do when discussing their health with a doctor, it is easy to trust that consultants know what they are doing and to fail to make sure you understand the reasoning behind their diagnosis and treatment plan. When you place this kind of blind trust in IT consultants, you may end up implementing technology that does not fit your organization's needs, and that can be expensive. For example, they may implement a solution that is more complicated than is needed, creating unnecessarily high costs in maintenance, support, and training; or they may implement a solution that is not robust enough and does not solve the issue the technology was meant to improve.

Good IT consultants try to understand the individual agency's problem, not just offer standard solutions. Further, they do not assume that technology is necessarily the answer to all problems, and they provide multiple options, not single solutions. Good IT consultants talk to you in a language you understand, translating difficult jargon and acronyms and using metaphors and analogies you can relate to. In fact they are conscientious teachers while conducting the work, so that staff have an understanding of what they are doing and, if appropriate, can do the work themselves next time. Good IT consultants know their own strengths and weaknesses and are not afraid to articulate them to you. Finally, good IT consultants either develop a succession plan so that you are not permanently dependent on them or develop a maintenance plan that includes agency staff, so that their permanent services are at a minimum.

When hiring a consultant, go through a process similar to the one for hiring staff. Develop a job description and determine the criteria on which you are basing your hiring decisions. Interview multiple consultants so that you can make some comparisons and have a variety from which to choose. The IT consultant you hire to help the agency with aspects of the technology plan will most likely be the same consultant with whom you will work when implementing the plan. For this reason, keep your long-term technology implementation, support, and maintenance needs in mind when you are interviewing consultants to assist with the technology plan. Here are some sample interview questions:

- Whom have you worked for in the past, and what did you accomplish with those clients or employers?

- Have you worked with nonprofits before? If so, describe your experience with them.

- Have you ever consulted with someone on an issue similar to ours? What were the results of your work with that client?

- How would you collaborate with (or distance yourself from) staff, the executive director, and the board?

- Describe a situation when you had to work with a difficult person and explain how you resolved the situation.

- What led you to IT consulting as a career?

- What other projects are you currently working on?

- Give me an example of an analogy you use when explaining technical jargon.

- What is your work process, including the manner in which you set priorities for servicing your clients?

- What is your turnaround time for solving an immediate technology problem?

Make sure you check candidates' references. Here are some sample questions to ask a reference:

- Did the consultant quickly understand the needs of the organization and its technology needs?

- Was the work completed on time, on schedule, and within budget?

- How were changes in the work plan negotiated?

- Did the consultant work at an appropriate pace?

- How did the consultant communicate with (or train, or mentor) staff?

- How did the consultant handle a situation in which a member of the staff disagreed with the consultant's recommendation?

- Did the consultant develop an appropriate succession or maintenance plan?

- Would you hire this consultant again?

IT consultants can be found through multiple sources. Some consulting organizations specialize in technology consulting for nonprofits. They are often referred to as *nonprofit technology assistance providers,* and many such organizations can be found throughout the United States. Another phrase often used to describe nonprofit IT consultants is *circuit riders.* Though there are many different subdivisions among circuit riders, they are typically characterized as consultants who travel to nonprofits to assist them with technology. Additionally, many nonprofit management support organizations also provide IT consultants, technology training, and strategic technology planning assistance. Finally, check with other nonprofits and find out whom they use as their consultants and how they found these individuals. Ask board members, friends, and other colleagues for suggestions. Put an announcement on your Web site, in messages sent to e-mail lists, and in your newsletter.

The following tips will help you work successfully with the IT consultant you hire:

TIPS

- Make him aware of your situation—the services your agency provides and its unique challenges. Do not let the IT consultant forget what kind of organization he is assisting.

- Technology consultants often speak in technical terms. Always ask for jargon clarification.

- Have an agenda or list of topics to discuss for any meeting. You may need to reel in your consultant. Do not let the discussion go off on a tangent. This might mean you need to run the meeting.

- Set clear boundaries for the work to be accomplished and negotiate any changes to the consultant's responsibilities up front.

- Be judicious in asking your consultant to do pro bono or discounted work, even if she offers it. (Often boundaries begin to blur when a consultant does free or discounted work, leading to the consultant's feeling used or manipulated—even when she is the one who changed the boundaries in the first place.) If the consultant does do free or discounted work, have her invoice you anyway, indicating a zero balance. This puts the value of the work on record (and supports a nice story about how you leveraged maximum resources with lower expenditures).

- Clarify roles with the consultant. Is he there as a project manager, to provide expert advice, or both? Who does he report to within the organization?

- Be an informed consumer. Remember, you need to own this. The agency will have to live with any choices made, long after the consultant is gone. You need to make the decisions. When you accept a suggestion made by the consultant, know why it is appropriate to accept it.

Volunteers

Volunteers can be great assets to an agency's technology planning and implementation efforts. However, the same rules should apply to hiring volunteers as apply to hiring consultants. Because technology affects your entire organization and mistakes can be costly, you want to make sure the volunteers hired are highly knowledgeable and reliable. Indeed, some organizations decide they would prefer to pay the fee for a consultant rather than rely on the free resource of a volunteer because payment produces a fiduciary accountability that is sometimes difficult to achieve with volunteers. Additionally, volunteers are usually helping in their spare time. It is normal for their other responsibilities or activities to take priority over the work they are doing for you, decreasing their ability to be a reliable resource.

For these reasons, it is advisable to hire volunteers to help with short-term projects or tasks rather than with regular, long-term support. Here are some examples of tasks volunteers might appropriately take on during the technology planning process:

- Conducting research on possible technology solutions

- Mentoring or advising staff

- Documenting selected sections of the technology plan

- Facilitating meetings, thus allowing all agency staff to be participants

- Proofreading the finished technology plan
- Reviewing the plan for general understandability and completeness

---

PLANNING IN PRACTICE
Blessed with Volunteers

Cathy Ferrari was an experienced volunteer, already working in the development office of the Presentation Center when that agency began its technology planning process. Ferrari was strongly committed to the mission of the Sisters at the Presentation Center. Sister Patricia Marie Mulpeters, the executive director, became aware that Ferrari also had computer skills. As a longtime stay-at-home mother and active volunteer with technology expertise, Ferrari had the perfect combination of skills, commitment, and time.

Ferrari was able to put a lot of time into the technology plan so that the process did not use up paid staff time needed for the business of running a retreat center. Her contribution made possible the creation of a very high level plan. She was able to offer twenty to twenty-five hours a week of volunteer time, preparing flowcharts, reading, and going to meetings. She was a core member of the technology planning team.

When it came time to implement the plan, Sister Patricia Marie realized that she needed Ferrari's help even more. So she hired her as a part-time staff person whose primary responsibility was technology. Her formal title was assistant director of marketing and development, but everyone called her "the technology guru."

Michael Edell, former executive director of the AIDS Community Research Consortium, also credited the success of his agency's technology plan to a skilled volunteer. A tech-minded volunteer took the lead in attending classes with Edell. The volunteer served as keeper of the plan, compiled the plan sections, and interviewed staff to answer questions outlined in a technology planning rubric. The volunteer had been a client of the organization. Living on disability support, he had lots of time to devote to technology planning. He and Edell made up a small but dedicated technology planning team of two.

For the implementation phase of the agency's plan, Edell once again turned to skilled volunteers. He asked local computer companies to donate staff time on weekends to run wire. With a volunteer crew from a local computer company, the agency did it in one weekend. "It was," said Edell, "the only way we could do it."

Part Three

Developing Your Technology Plan

THE PURPOSE of the chapters in this part of the book is to offer guidance on assembling and writing the actual elements of the technology plan. The chapter headings follow the section headings of the comprehensive technology plan outline provided in Resource A. Likewise, the subheadings coincide with the subsections of the comprehensive technology plan outline. In addition to describing each section of the technology plan, these chapters provide two important resources:

- Examples from actual technology plans developed by real nonprofits

- Worksheets to assist your agency in information gathering for the technology plan and in organizing and presenting the plan

Recalling the pyramid model (Figure 1.1), Chapters Nine through Eleven focus on the first tier by looking at your organization from a business perspective so you can transfer this information to the plan. You will articulate your organization's mission, goals, and strategies. You will describe how your agency does business, then look at how your agency can improve upon what it does. And finally you will explore how technology might help your agency improve the way it does business and better achieve its goals. Note that even though only a few sections are devoted to this part of the technology plan, it is often the most time intensive and difficult part to write. Documenting business processes and improvements involves the participation of representative stakeholders from all the organization's functional areas. Further, it is often during this stage that many important discoveries are made within the organization. You may decide to move forward and develop the rest of your technology plan while you are still working on these sections. However, many of these discoveries will need to be addressed before you can move forward.

Chapters Twelve through Sixteen address the second tier of the pyramid model—applications, or tools. They delve into the specifics of the technology your organization currently has and how it needs to be enhanced to implement the technology strategies identified in Chapter Ten. Note that the information required for the plan sections described in Chapters Twelve through Eighteen is highly technical in places. If your agency does not have technical expertise on its staff, consider hiring someone with that expertise to work with you on the plan.

The remainder of the chapters in Part Three relate to the third tier of the pyramid model, the infrastructure needed to support the applications that support the mission, goals, and strategies. Chapters Eighteen and Nineteen discuss issues important to supporting technology strategies once they are implemented. Support takes the form of both taking care of the equipment itself and taking care of end-users so that they can do their work.

Chapters Twenty through Twenty-Two discuss business issues surrounding the ownership and use of technology, including guidelines for its use, and describe how the agency can maintain its technology plan as a viable guiding document.

Chapters Twenty-Three and Twenty-Four will help you devise the budgetary and project timeline information necessary to a successful deployment of your agency's technology strategies.

Chapter Twenty-Five describes the technology plan appendixes that should be provided, containing supplemental information about the organization, its current technology, its staffing, and any additional information that will help readers understand the technology plan as a whole. Finally, Chapter Twenty-Six discusses how to prepare a technology plan with maximum flexibility and readability.

Although the discussion in this section is directed to the person leading the planning team or responsible overall for the planning process, the team members are of course participating in all the tasks described.

Chapter 9

Front Matter

THE FRONT MATTER of the technology plan (Section I in the outline shown in Resource A) should quickly orient readers to what will follow in the detailed sections of the technology plan. The front matter should include these subsections:

A. Cover page

B. Table of contents

C. Executive summary

A. Cover Page

The content of this subsection is self-evident.

B. Table of Contents

Although a table of contents may seem like an obvious item to include, its importance cannot be understated. It allows readers to understand quickly both the breadth and depth of your plan.

TIPS

- List every section of your plan, along with at least its major subsections (the first-level heads in each section), so readers can find specific topics easily.

- List figures and diagrams to facilitate "quick looks."

- List appendixes by number (or letter) and name rather than only number or letter, for clarity.

C. Executive Summary

The executive summary provides a thumbnail sketch of the plan's highlights. Consider including a brief statement of what your organization is about, its staffing level, and its annual budget; the major changes the organization is planning (and not only those related to technology); the timeframe covered by the technology plan (in fiscal years); major business areas the organization is striving to improve with technology; major technology strategies the organization is planning; and an overview of the technology plan budget.

TIPS

- Make sure the executive summary occupies no more than one page.

- Use a bulleted list to present key points concisely.

- Align the list of business areas targeted for improvement and the list of technology strategies with actual sections and subsections of your plan, by either name or number. Readers can then easily locate the details on any key point by looking for the same phraseology or item number in the table of contents.

Example

Example 9.1: Cupertino Community Services, a small, community-based organization (www.CupertinoCommunityServices.org). In this executive summary example, note the succinct statement of the organization's background, of the key points of the organization's technology plan, and of the major impacts of technology. By simply skimming the bullet points, a reader can pick up the gist of the agency's plan and then refer to the table of contents to find details about any key point.

EXAMPLE 9.1

Cupertino Community Services: Front Matter

CUPERTINO COMMUNITY SERVICES

TECHNOLOGY PLAN

EXECUTIVE SUMMARY

- Cupertino Community Services, Inc. (CCS), is a private nonprofit, community-based agency that provides direct assistance, referrals, and housing services to the West Valley Community. We have 10 staff (8 FTE) and an annual budget of approximately $800,000.

- In 2002, CCS will experience a major transition as we move into a newly constructed office site, approximately 4 times the size of the current site. The new office is a part of our Heart of Cupertino Project, a development of 24 affordable housing units and social service facility, to be completed in December 2002.

- Our Technology Plan is based on this transition and covers 3 periods—pre-transition, transition, and post-transition. The 3 periods somewhat parallel 3 fiscal years (July–June) starting with FY 2001–2002 and ending with FY 2003–2004.

- Within these 3 years, our technology goals are:

  - Streamline intake processes among all departments

  - Streamline service delivery and case management tracking among all departments

  - Improve information and referrals process

  - Improve telephone communication

  - Improve checks processing

  - Improve communications with clients, volunteers, and donors

- We will be focusing on the following technology areas:

  - Centralized databases

  - Acquire up-to-date hardware and software

  - Acquire up-to-date office equipment that meets our operational needs

  - Up-to-date networking with secure shared broadband access to Internet and e-mail

  - Improve Web site and Web communications

  - Staff training

- The total budget for the implementation of this Technology Plan is estimated to be $98,924.

Chapter 10

Background Information

BACKGROUND INFORMATION introduces your organization and the members of your technology planning team to external readers: consultants, funders, volunteers, vendors, and so on. It also provides a history of how the technology plan was developed; this will be of interest to internal readers—members of the board of directors, for example, or new employees. This section of your agency's technology plan (Section II in Resource A) should include these subsections:

A. Mission statement

B. Brief description of your organization

C. Technology planning team members

A. Mission Statement

State your organization's mission as simply as possible. If the agency has a formal, written mission statement, include it as is. Ideally, the statement should be a one- or two-sentence explanation of the organization's purpose for being.

B. Brief Description of Organization

The better you and your team understand your organization and can convey that understanding to readers, the more appropriate your technology choices will be. Expand on the brief statement made in the executive summary, but still keep it brief. Include pertinent facts that will help others understand the organization. Consider including items like these:

- Primary purpose of the organization (health and human services, arts and culture, or youth development, and so forth)

- When founded

- Number and type of clients served

- Number of full-time equivalent (FTE) employees

- Number of volunteers

- Number of office locations

- Geographical service area

- Current fiscal year budget

- Structure (departments and reporting relationships)

TIPS

- Keep this section brief—no more than three pages. You might even be able to combine the mission statement and brief description effectively.

- Use this part of your technology plan to lay the groundwork for the business analysis section to follow.

- Consider using an organizational chart showing both the departments the agency has and their reporting relationships. This uses much less space than narrative text. If a department's function is not obvious from its title, *do* include narrative to describe its function.

C. Technology Planning Team Members

For each team member, provide his or her name and position or affiliation with the organization. Indicate which member(s) of the committee is (are) the principal author(s) of the technology plan. Additionally, describe each member's role on the team. For example, does the person bring knowledge of technology, finances, or organizational processes? Also describe the role each member played in the writing of the plan. For example, which sections did each help write? Although you can provide this information in narrative format, it is helpful to use a table or bullet points for clarity.

Provide each team member's contact information, such as title, telephone number(s), and e-mail address(es). Be sure to indicate which member of the team is the project manager. Also indicate who is responsible for keeping the team list and contact information up-to-date. You may find it easier to provide contact information separately from role descriptions, for example in the format of a phone list.

Examples

Example 10.1: Services for Brain Injury, a small health and human services organization that assists brain-injured people to reach their highest level of independent living (www.SBIcares.org). This mission statement not only states the organization's mission but also provides indications of the organization's culture and values.

EXAMPLE 10.1

Services for Brain Injury: Background Information

1. Introduction

1.1. Mission Statement

Service for Brain Injury's mission is to assist brain injured individuals reach their optimum level of independent activity through accessible, affordable services; support their caregivers; and provide community prevention programs targeting children.

SBI's Value Statement

Services at SBI are driven by the needs of brain injured individuals and their caregivers, delivered in a collaborative continuum with measurable outcomes, available to a diverse and underserved population, and provided by dedicated staff and volunteers at an affordable cost.

SBI's Vision Statement

SBI will grow in depth and breadth, thereby expanding its core capacity to become a recognized leader in brain injury services, methodology, and outcomes.

Example 10.2: San Jose Repertory Theatre, a large arts organization (www.sjrep.org). This organizational chart lists positions, rather than individuals. This makes the organizational structure clearer to external readers.

Example 10.3: Diabetes Society of Santa Clara Valley, a medium-sized health care organization that provides education and information on diabetes (www.diabetesscv.org). This technology committee table is clear as well as informative, including each member's role on the committee, role in writing the technology plan, and technology background. (Members' names on this table are pseudonyms.)

EXAMPLE 10.2

San Jose Repertory Theatre: Background Information

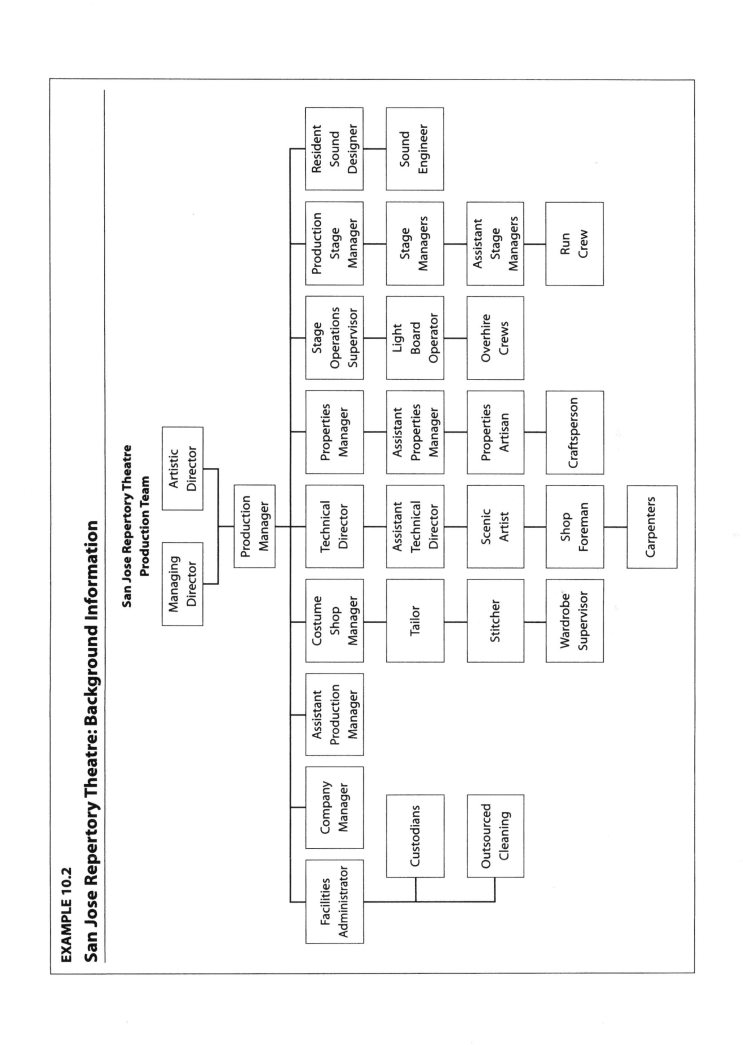

San Jose Repertory Theatre
Production Team

EXAMPLE 10.3

Diabetes Society of Santa Clara Valley: Background Information

Table 1: TECH COMMITTEE AND PROJECT TEAM MEMBERS (1.3 AND 1.4)

Name	Company	Position	Role on Tech Committee	Role in Tech Plan	Technology Background	Phone Number	E-Mail
John Doe	Telecom. Company	Web Programmer	Web site and donor software lead	Contributing author	5 years programming/ Web site authoring experience	(650) 555-5555	john@email.com
Bob Jones	Cable & Wireless Services Company	Sr. Staff Internet Systems Expert	E-mail and ISP lead	Consultation in security	20+ years in advanced systems and high-speed networking	(408) 555-5555	bob@email.org
Jane Doe	University	Student	Web site design	Proposed Web site design	Web site design	(408) 555-5555	jane@email.com
Barbara Smith	DSSCV	Director of Development and Public Relations	N/A	Attended workshop; assisted with funding plan	None	(408) 555-5555	barbara@email.org
Sarah Johnson	DSSCV	Executive Director	Client representative	WFG project lead	Little (married to a network engineer)	(408) 555-5555	sarah@email.org

Chapter 11

Business Analysis

THE PURPOSE of the business analysis section of the technology plan (Section III in Resource A) is to help align your organization's technology strategies with its mission and strategic goals. This section also clarifies how the organization does business in order to achieve its goals and thus achieve its mission. Articulating the business analysis section is a five-step process.

1. Review your organization's strategic goals. Keep them in mind as you proceed with Steps 2 through 5.

2. Articulate how the organization currently does business internally. Do this by identifying major business processes and writing them down. This is a *discovery activity*. Ask people what they do and how they do it. At first, you will hear about discrete tasks. As you learn more, tasks will take shape as larger processes.

   Ask for each process that you identify: How does this process help the organization achieve its strategic goals and mission?

   Why do this? If you do not understand how a process contributes to the organization's mission and goals, any changes you make may end up worsening a situation rather than improving it.

3. Identify ways to improve the business processes. This is a *brainstorming activity*. At this point, whether an improvement lends itself to a technology solution is not important. You are just evaluating what improvements can be made. You may find, for example, that the same data are entered more than once or that clients have to fill out several forms that

This chapter is adapted with permission from a workshop titled "Business Strategies," developed and led by Sharon Meyers of NPC Consulting (www.npcconsult.com).

have a lot of common data. These are not problems that necessarily lend themselves to technological solutions.

Ask for each process: How might we do this job better? Faster? Easier?

Why do this? To best determine appropriate technology strategies for your organization, you need, first, to understand where it can benefit from general improvements in organizational life.

4. Identify which improvements can best be accomplished by using technology. This is a *sorting activity.* Put improvements that lend themselves to technology in one group and those that do not in another group. For example, what if people in your organization cannot get proper training on how to use the spreadsheet templates for departmental budget planning? Clearly, an improvement in employee training is needed. It may simply be that no one has been given the responsibility for teaching others how to use the templates. This example calls for a procedural solution, not a technology solution.

Ask for each improvement: Is technology the best way to make this improvement?

Why do this? Because you are developing a technology plan, from now on you will be interested only in those business process improvements that will benefit from technology solutions.

5. Identify specific technology strategies that can facilitate the process improvements you have identified in Step 3. This is a *refinement activity.* Set aside processes that you wish to improve but for which technology is not the best path to improvement. (The organization will definitely want to look at the latter at another time, but they cease to be part of technology planning at this point.) You are seeking to understand how technology or automation can help the organization do the business that it does. Only after you understand the processes, how they help the organization accomplish its goals and how to improve them, can you finally start talking about technology.

Ask these important questions: How is technology going to help us accomplish our mission and goals? How is this technology going to improve how we do business?

Why do this? This information will become the core of your technology plan. You have identified how the organization does business, how it can improve upon those processes, and how technology might help.

The outcome of this five-step process is a set of technology-based strategies for business process improvement that is directly related to your organization's mission and strategic goals. The information you identify here will supply the majority of the content for the business analysis section of your technology plan, under these subsections:

A. Strategic goals

B. Current business processes

C. Process improvement goals

D. Technology strategies

E. Measures of success

The subsections fall into two groups. In the first three subsections, you are documenting the organization with enough depth that you can make informed decisions about the technology strategies you will plan for in the rest of the plan. In the other two subsections, you are identifying specific technology strategies to plan for and the ways that implementing those strategies will affect the organization over the long term.

Building business process descriptions and filling in all the other business analysis subsections are often iterative. You and your team define a few processes, begin to think of improvements and so forth, then a few more processes come to mind. *Do not become discouraged.* Team members can build and fill in this section of the technology plan at the same time they continue gathering some of the information needed in subsequent subsections, such as current descriptions of software and hardware inventories, what the organization's network looks like, the site plan, and so forth.

Track Budget and Timeline Needs as You Go Along

As you go through the process of developing a technology plan, starting with identifying the agency's technology-based process improvement strategies, it is helpful to use *budget reminder* sheets to keep track of anything that will require money. Use the budget reminder sheet shown in Worksheet 11.1 to begin writing down items that have costs associated with them. They may become line items when you come to writing up a budget, in Section XV of the plan. This will make it easier to identify *all the costs* when you get to the budget section of the technology plan later on. Do not forget items like training and ongoing maintenance.

Use *timeline reminder* sheets to keep track of anything that has a deadline, that someone needs to do, or that requires any action from outside the organization. This will make it easier to develop a timeline for your technology plan later (Section XVI). So, fill out the reminder sheet on Worksheet 11.2 as you go along.

WORKSHEET 11.1

Budget Reminder

Process Improvement or Technology Strategy	Budget Item(s)

WORKSHEET 11.2

Timeline Reminder

Process Improvement or Technology Strategy	Timeline Item(s)

Although many pages in this chapter are devoted to discussing how to develop goals, processes, process improvements, and technology strategies, what ends up in your technology plan may occupy just a few pages. Nevertheless, it is important to go through the five-step business analysis process to ensure that your end product—technology planning, acquisition, and implementation—will in fact result in your organization's ability to accomplish its mission and goals.

A. Strategic Goals

How does your organization achieve its mission? How do its strategic goals directly relate to its mission? *Strategic goals* are what an organization wants to accomplish over a specific period of time. *Tactics* are plans of action—how the organization will go about achieving its strategic goals.

Recalling your agency's mission statement from your background information section (Chapter Ten), state your organization's strategic goals, which it must achieve to accomplish its mission. If your organization does not already have a set of written strategic goals, then take some time to develop them now. If the organization has written strategic goals, but they now seem somehow incomplete, take the time to update them. Everything you decide with regard to planning for technology should be in support of these strategic goals.

Be careful to state strategic goals in business terms (not in tactical or technology terms). This ensures that the only technology put in place is that which will serve your organization's strategic goals. It also helps to clarify what the measures for success are going to be. For example, a goal stated in technology terms, such as "develop a client service database," does not say how achieving the goal will help the organization achieve its mission. Ask yourself *why* the organization should develop the database. Your answer will most likely be a strategic goal. Some examples of strategic goals are:

"Expand educational and community service programs."

"Provide professional development and training activities to staff and board members to increase the organization's expertise in grantwriting and fundraising."

"Better monitor and understand the needs of the community to effectively respond to those needs."

"Improve communications with clients, volunteers, and donors about services, and volunteer and giving opportunities."

TIPS

- Number the goals, so they can be easily referred to later in the plan document. It is easier to refer to "Goal 1" than to restate the entire goal.

- Make sure goals are organizational, not technological. It is easy to confuse a technology strategy with a goal. But, remember, technology is not a goal. It is only a toolbox whose contents help you do a better job.

B. Current Business Processes

What happens with people and to information from start to finish? Who does what, when, and how? In simplest terms a business process is a task. It is the way that something gets done, encompassing all the steps one or more people take to accomplish a specific outcome. In this subsection of the plan, you are taking a procedural approach to looking at your organization. The information included here is from Step 2 of the business analysis process. Consider what happens to information from start to finish as your organization conducts an aspect of business: what data go in, what reports or data go out, what are people doing? To understand a business process, answer these key questions:

- How is the task accomplished? That is, what steps have to happen and in what order?

- Who is responsible for the process? Does this person know he has this responsibility?

- Who helps accomplish it, and what do they do?

- What inputs are required?

- What information is required and when?

- What decisions are required and when?

- What results are desired or required? Are reports of the results needed?

As discussed in Chapter Six, the person responsible for a process is its *owner*. This person is responsible for the result. All business processes have an owner, whether explicit or implicit.

The people who help with a process are *key contributors*. They are essential to completing a process successfully. They actively participate in some way, perhaps by providing necessary data or by accomplishing a task or by contributing to a decision.

Start by brainstorming as a team and writing down as many of the main processes that occur in your organization as you can think of (for example, processing a request for assistance, applying for a grant, publishing a newsletter). Simply make a list. Have others in the organization review the list, add to it, modify it, or subtract from it.

You may find it helpful at this time to identify the strategic goal or goals that each process supports. This ensures that the work people do is actually in support of the organization's strategic goals, and not "busy work" or "interesting but possibly unnecessary work."

Once you have identified several business processes, pick one that seems simple and straightforward. Answer the key questions outlined earlier in this section. For example, let us consider a process identified as "pay the bills." Who receives and opens the mail? If the mail is a bill, does that bill get logged in or is it handed to another person? What does that person do with it? What approvals are needed before payment can be made? How are those approvals acquired? Who authorizes a check to be written? Who stuffs the envelope and mails the check? What happens to your copies of the bill and the check? Are there any reports about bills paid within a specific time period? Who owns the "paying of bills"? Go through the key questions for each high-level business process you have identified.

How do you organize this information once you have gathered it all? It can be written in a narrative format: "First, this happens, and so-and-so is responsible for getting it done. Then that happens, and someone else is responsible." Or it can be presented as a list or a table. However, both of these approaches will likely be unsuccessful when the process to be described is a complicated one that involves several things happening at once or that requires several tasks to come together so that a decision can be made. A better approach may be to develop a flowchart.

Drawing a process as a flowchart lets you, both pictorially and concisely, capture a starting point and identify steps along the way, decision points, information inputs, and reports. Describing complex and long processes is definitely a time when "one picture is worth a thousand words." Some complicated processes may be very difficult to chart. This is an indication that they are seriously flawed. Do not focus at this point on how to improve these flawed processes. Just capture them as they are. You will have the opportunity to think about improvements as you prepare the next section of the technology plan.

You likely have noticed by now that one process may be made up of several more detailed processes, and each of those may be made up of yet more processes. You are probably telling yourself, "Wait, I could be describing processes for a very long time." Rest assured, this is not what is being suggested!

Although you must decide for yourself how much detail to include in your process description or chart, here are some tips to help you decide. Remember, you are trying to find out or help others find out how best to apply technology strategies to help your organization achieve its goals. A rule of thumb is to include enough information so that anyone can understand the process taking place and can decide if technology might help simplify work or outcomes, but not so much that the end result is a job training tool or encyclopedic description of the most intricate workings of the organization. It is perfectly all right to describe some processes in more depth than others because they are more complex or because potential technology solutions are far reaching. Simple processes call for simple charts.

In describing organizational processes, by whatever method you choose, make sure that you are describing tasks that people do, actions that they perform. For example, Accounting is not a step in a business process, it is a department. Think about what Accounting does. In the "pay the bills" example, Accounting might "pay the invoice after all approvals are submitted." Hence, "pay the invoice after all approvals are submitted" would appear as a step in the process flowchart for the "pay the bills" process.

TIPS

- Describe processes in sufficient detail to maintain both a high-level and detailed view. You want the reader to understand what it takes both to accomplish processes and improve them but not to be overwhelmed with details.

- A strategy that is often effective is to describe all processes at a high level, in simple terms and symbols. Then, *after* you look at technology strategies to improve processes, go back and add detail as necessary to more fully understand the implications of the proposed technology solutions.

- Although you may want a fairly comprehensive list of business processes for organization management purposes, in the technology plan include only the flowcharts or descriptions of those that you ultimately decide to improve by means of a technology strategy. (Descriptions of the remaining processes may be included as an appendix to the plan, to provide readers with a more thorough picture of your organization and to demonstrate that the organization has performed due diligence in analyzing the best areas to apply technology strategies.)

- Number the processes for easy reference later in the technology plan. (It is easier to refer to "Process 1" than to identify that process with a long text description.)

- Make sure all flowcharts show a clear beginning and end. Show, for example, what the triggering event or action is, and how it ends.

- Indicate where decision points are and what happens depending upon the decision made.

- Use consistent symbols throughout flowcharts and include a legend of the symbols used, telling the reader what each symbol means. (See Resource B for a set of common flowchart symbols.)

- Chart your current processes as they are. Do not decide on improvements right now. They will come later.

- It is useful to explain why people do something a particular way, especially when established procedures have some historical significance that may not be obvious to the current process participants. These notes are useful in determining process improvements. The explanations can be part of a text description, a column in a chart, or annotations to a flowchart.

- If you encounter complex processes that are difficult to chart, and hence might be seriously flawed, use a separate piece of paper to capture your ideas for improvements. This will be valuable information for writing the next subsection of the technology plan, where you outline process improvement goals.

- Complex processes, involving several departments, many decisions, and several key contributors, may require more detailed documentation than processes that are simple, short, and straightforward, involving only a single department, no or few decisions, and only one or two people.

C. Process Improvement Goals

How can your organization make its processes more efficient? How do these improvements help it achieve its strategic goals? Now that you have described how the organization does business on a day-to-day basis through the various processes people perform to accomplish their work, in this subsection of the technology plan (corresponding to Step 3 of the business analysis) you are identifying which of the processes described need improvement and the improvements identified for each.

You may think of several possible improvements for a single process. Make sure that the improvements you ultimately select help the organization achieve its strategic goals and are in line with the organization's vision and culture. Some characteristics to look for in identifying areas for improvement are these:

- Duplicated effort in different processes. For example, are three different people taking down demographic information about the same client?

- Unnecessarily complicated processes.

- Processes that are causing staff members or clients to complain.

- Information the organization wishes it had but cannot easily obtain from current processes.

- Activities or tasks that are done manually and for which automation might save people's time or free people to do more critical tasks.

As you may have found in working on the previous subsection, you are likely to gather more information than you can use in the technology plan. To begin determining what to include, select the processes and improvements that do not suggest a technology strategy as part of the improvement. Move these items to an appendix, or set them aside for later consideration. A good way to document improvement ideas is with a chart or table, as it is a clear and concise way to present information.

TIPS

- Look for general ways to improve processes before focusing on technology. You may discover ways to improve some processes without using technology.

- Include only the processes and improvements that involve technology in your technology plan. Move processes and improvement suggestions not related to technology to an appendix as supplemental information for readers.

- Be sure to relate improvement ideas to the specific processes to which they apply.

- Use a table to present processes (by name or number) in one column and then their improvements in the next column or, conversely, to list the improvements and then the processes to which they apply.

D. Technology Strategies

Can your organization use technology to better achieve its process improvements? If so, how can the selected technology help? This subsection, corresponding to Step 4 of the business analysis, describes specific technology strategies to achieve your organization's process improvements (the applications tier of the pyramid model). These specific technology strategies form the basis for the rest of the technology plan (the infrastructure tier of the pyramid model)—that is, the network design and upgrades; the software, hardware, and network purchasing plans; and staff training. These strategies inform the agency's needs for improvements in facilities, security, technology support (including network and data management), acceptable use policies, budget planning, and resource and time management to carry out the plans.

Examine which process improvement ideas identified may benefit from the use of technology as a tool. How will technology be beneficial? What will be gained? (When you document this in the technology plan, you will need to be specific about the technology being proposed as a solution in each instance. However, at this earlier point in the plan's development, you may not yet know these specifics.)

PLANNING IN PRACTICE

Process Improvements: File Sharing Then and Now

The Environmental League of Massachusetts staff lobbied for more effective file sharing when the league got a grant to build a collaborative network of environmental groups. At the time the league started the collaborative, its state of the art for file sharing consisted of passing floppy disks from hand to hand. President Jim Gomes remembered that everyone had a box of floppy disks on his or her desk. The staff advocated for a local area network (LAN). Gomes recollected, "Shortly after we got the network, we left the era of the floppy disk."

Pam Brandin, executive director of the Peninsula Center for the Blind and Visually Impaired, had an even more dramatic reason for needing a wider variety of ways to share files. Blind and low-vision staff and clients were completely unable to use files in conventional paper format.

Brandin pointed out that "computers are really the basic information and communication tool for blind and visually impaired people." Low-vision staff and clients used screen reading software to greatly enlarge print on the monitor or had voice output that read text to them aloud. Blind computer users had voice output or printed Braille output. Although expensive, refreshable Braille output was available in what looked like a long pin cushion. The pins are variously raised and depressed to form the Braille letters.

Computer file sharing in these accessible formats greatly simplified life for blind staff members. Before this, the agency used to have human readers read paper files to blind staff. With this technology, these staff could find, read, and write the information they needed independently. Electronic file formats have been useful for sighted staff as well. Remote access to client files allowed staff visiting clients in the field or working from home to get the information they needed and send reports back in a timely fashion.

Sister Patricia Marie Mulpeters, executive director of the Presentation Center, did not need to send files in Braille, but she did need to tell the kitchen how many vegetarians to expect in each retreat group. The administrative offices were a good distance from the kitchen and cabins where food was cooked and meetings held for guests to the retreat center.

The Sisters of the Presentation Center knew they needed a better system of communication between retreat center departments. They were spending a lot of time physically carrying paper from one end of their large site to the other and interrupting work in the kitchen with calls about changes in reservations. Sister Patricia Marie knew a computer network would make sharing information faster and easier. Even before implementation was complete, they were hopeful that better file sharing would allow them to spend more time creating a peaceful environment for their guests and less time running around with pieces of paper.

For each technology strategy, answer these questions:

- Which processes are affected? A given technology strategy may improve more than one business process. Whose work is affected?

- Why is this strategy a good one for improvement?

- What is the purpose of the process improvement, and who will use it? Be specific (a description such as "use a database" is incomplete).

Note that if your organization does not have an IT department, network manager, or other technology staff, you will benefit from the advice of a knowledgeable, objective technology person (most likely a consultant) during your work on this and subsequent sections (see Chapter Eight for information about the role of IT consultants or volunteers). This outside expertise can help your organization to avoid costly technology choices that do not improve the way it does business or meets its goals.

In writing down the technology strategies, be sure to indicate the business processes and process improvements to which each technology strategy applies. Once again, this can be clearly and concisely accomplished with a table, perhaps one that includes all three types of information in one place.

TIPS

- Some organizations find it helpful to prioritize their technology strategies. You need not place each one in order from first to last in importance. Sorting them into priority categories such as *high, medium,* and *low* may suffice. This will help your organization implement its plan in phases, as it has the budget and resources.

- When you do not have technology expertise within your organization, get planning help from knowledgeable and objective outsiders—consultants or reliable volunteers whom you feel you can hold accountable.

- Use a table to list technology strategies, business processes (by name or number), and their improvements.

E. Measures of Success

Once the process improvements involving technology are implemented, how will you know whether they are successful? In the previous sections you have documented how your organization does business and you have written up critical business processes; you have determined how these processes can be improved and which ones can be improved through the use of technology; and you have identified technology strategies to help with these improvements. Now determine how you will know whether the improvements you envision have been achieved. The way to learn whether the technology strategies are contributing to the kinds of improvements the organization wants is by using measures of success. *Measures of success* are quantitative statements of improvement over time—measurements of things that can be compared to previous results of measurements of the same things.

Define at least one measure of success for each technology strategy. For each measure defined, ask: How will we be able to measure this? and, In what period of time do we want to see this improvement? Avoid vague terms like "better customer service" or "satisfied clients." Instead say, for example, "The time required to return a call to a client will be reduced by 20 percent within six months." Or, "The time required to approve a request will be reduced by 10 percent within one month." Be as specific as possible. Also make sure that the measure is something that can be taken several times.

Remember these three things that measures are not:

- They are not milestones. A milestone occurs once in time. You achieve it and keep on going. "The new server is installed" is a milestone.

- They are not goals. A goal is the end result you want to achieve. For example, "Phone messages will be returned promptly" is a goal statement. A statement of measurement for this goal would be "We will return 100 percent of messages by 5 P.M. of the day they are received." This statement quantifies the improvement desired, making it possible to measure progress toward the goal.

- They are not something you measure once and never measure again. Because measures of success are intended to help you check improvement over time, you will need to take the measures more than once.

To evaluate whether or not your organization is achieving the improvements it desires, first take a *baseline measurement* to determine the starting point for improvement. An organization cannot know whether it has improved unless it knows what it started with. For example: How long does it currently take to return a call to a client? What is the shortest possible time? What is the longest time that anyone can remember (or will confess to)? Ask several people and take an average. This will become the baseline measure for "time taken to return a call to a client."

Next, decide how frequently to measure progress: weekly, monthly, quarterly, semiannually? Note that each measure of success will require resources to both take the measure and analyze it. Your organization needs to take the measure frequently enough that staff can understand what is happening, but not so frequently that it overburdens people's ability to take the measure and use it. If the improvement is to be accomplished over a very short time period, for example, one to three months, you need to take only a baseline measurement and a final one. If the improvement is to be accomplished over a longer period of time, for example six months or more, then schedule one or more interim measures to make sure that the process involved is moving along its intended path to improvement. Taking interim measures permits the appropriate person to take corrective actions if the progress hoped for is not being made. In making these corrective actions, determine the cause of the lagging progress. For example, maybe employee training is inadequate, or computers were not delivered on time and users have not had enough time to learn new procedures.

Lastly, determine when to take the final measure. If the organization wants to see improvements in six months, then schedule the final measure for six months from now.

Surveys are an excellent tool for measuring improvement, but an initial survey must be taken before changes can be measured. You can also ask people to maintain activity logs, recording, for example, the day and time a client phone message was taken and the day and time the call was returned. Then periodically collect the logs and collate the data.

TIPS

- Ask, "How will we measure this?" for each measure of success you define.

- For each measure of success, define both the quantitative measure and the time period for improvement.

- Allow yourself time to get the measurement tools ready before scheduling the baseline measurement. For example, you might need to design a user survey or an activity log and then train people how to use it.

- Identify the people who will take the measures and the people who will analyze and publish the data. Include these tasks in the Implementation Timeline section of your technology plan (Chapter Twenty-Four). Building this into your plan will help avoid job stress later on.

- Decide on an appropriate time to take a baseline measurement (and as noted above, include in the Implementation Timeline section of your technology plan).

- Decide how many interim measurements to take and when they will occur.

- Decide when you hope to take your final measurement.

- Define how to handle a performance degradation: that is, the measure does not show improvement, it shows the exact opposite.

- Describe what the organization can do if performance improvement is not achieved in the hoped-for time frame.

Examples

Example 11.1: Cupertino Community Services, a small, community-based organization (www.CupertinoCommunityServices.org). Note this organization's concise list of goals. The statement of strategic goals need not be long and complicated, whatever the size of your organization.

Example 11.2: Diabetes Society of Santa Clara Valley, a medium-sized health care organization that provides education and information on diabetes (www.diabetesscv.org). Some organizations prefer a more detailed statement of goals, with specific objectives, as exemplified in this set of goals.

Example 11.3: San Jose Repertory Theatre, a large arts organization (www.sjrep.org). The narrative descriptions in this example illustrate how to achieve clarity along with brevity. Note how the descriptions of process improvements, technology strategies, and measures of success parallel and correlate, respectively, with the descriptions of business processes, process improvements, and technology strategies. This structure maintains order and clarity among the subsections.

Example 11.4: Girl Scouts of Santa Clara County, a medium-sized, community-based organization that is a chapter of a national organization (www.girlscoutsofscc.org).

EXAMPLE 11.1

Cupertino Community Services: Business Analysis

Business Strategy

Strategic Goals

CCS developed a five-year strategic plan in 1997. At that time, CCS Board of Directors and staff set five goals, which covered the improvement or enhancement of budgeting, staff training, program services, advocacy, and communication.

CCS has experienced major transitions and changes since those goals were set. Ninety percent of the staff is new, including the Executive Director. The major concentration for the past three years has been placed on the Heart of Cupertino Project.

CCS will be going through the strategic planning process this year (2002). Below is a draft of the strategic goals that are currently being reviewed in the strategic planning process. These proposed goals are modifications of the goals set in 1997 to reflect CCS's current operations and forthcoming changes. The Board of Directors has not yet formally approved these goals.

Goal 1: To increase funding and allocate adequate resources to fulfill our mission and implement the following strategic goals:

Goal 2: To better monitor and understand the needs of the community to effectively respond to those needs.

Goal 3: To evaluate programs and adjust CCS services and processes to meet the changing needs of the community.

Goal 4: To be at the forefront of social services policy development and public awareness.

Goal 5: To improve communication with clients, volunteers and donors about services, volunteer and giving opportunities.

CCS technology plan will address all of the above goals, with emphasis on Goals 3 and 5.

This table shows not only a description of a business process but also the correlation of the business process with additional, vital information for a successful technology plan. Note that the table includes measures of success along with descriptions of the business processes, process improvements, and technology strategies.

Example 11.5: Diabetes Society of Santa Clara Valley, a medium-sized health care organization that provides education and information on diabetes (www .diabetesscv.org). This is an excellent example of an integrated approach to describing business processes. It includes a brief narrative, a flowchart, and a table that correlates the business process to additional, vital, information. Note how the integrated approach incorporates process improvements, proposed technology strategy, and measures of success for this business process. The integrated approach can work for an organization of any size.

EXAMPLE 11.2

Diabetes Society of Santa Clara Valley: Business Analysis

2.1. Strategic Goals

Although the Diabetes Society does not have a written formal strategic plan in place at this time, there are a number of goals and objectives outlined in each department head's plans for the year:

Goal 1: Assess the needs of people with diabetes in Santa Clara Valley.

> Objective 1: Conduct a comprehensive community needs assessment.
>
> Objective 2: Outreach to and partner with the County in conducting the needs assessment.

Goal 2: Increase revenue and diversify our funding base.

> Objective 1: Submit 50 proposals for at least $400,000.
>
> Objective 2: Create and submit a marketing sponsorship proposal to underwrite a camp.
>
> Objective 3: Upgrade our Web site to allow for on-line donations.
>
> Objective 4: Restructure contracts with health insurance organizations to cover actual costs of our educational program.

Goal 3: Increase the support of volunteers on all levels within the organization.

> Objective 1: Recruit a Volunteer Coordinator.
>
> Objective 2: Recruit four (4) new members to the Board of Directors.
>
> Objective 3: Expand Board committees by recruiting two (2) new members to each committee.

Goal 4: Develop a more efficient method for recording, managing, and reporting donor and client information.

> Objective 1: Select and acquire a new database software (DonorPerfect) to meet the needs of all departments.

Goal 5: Empower and educate individuals with diabetes to improve their overall health and well-being.

> Objective 1: Conduct a quality diabetes self-management education program that meets the national standards established for diabetes patient education programs.
>
> Objective 2: Continue to assess the quality of the diabetes education program through outcome measurement of HA1c and behavioral changes.
>
> Objective 3: Establish a permanent data collection process to identify and implement process improvement measures.
>
> Objective 4: Continue to assess and identify areas in the program where changes and improvements are needed.
>
> Objective 5: Conduct an Annual Program Review in January 2002 by the Program Committee to review outcomes.

EXAMPLE 11.3

San Jose Repertory Theatre: Business Analysis

2.2. Current Business Processes

E: Volunteer Management

The tasks performed in this process are as described in Appendix B Chart E. The House Manager/Volunteer Coordinator is the Owner of this process and the only person who performs record keeping for our volunteers in the Volunteer Program at the Rep. All reports and records are for the use of the Volunteer Coordinator. Upon request, copies of these may be furnished to the Foundation and Grants Manager for grant applications. The current process was established because customizing fields for specific tracking needs was not viable due to the limitations of *ACT!,* and utilizes Netscape Messenger e-mail client to support the Volunteer program.

F: Volunteer Scheduling

The tasks performed in this process are as described in Appendix B Chart F. The House Manager/Volunteer Coordinator is the Owner of this process and the key person who schedules volunteers for shifts. Assistant House Managers, when working, are able to schedule, cancel and arrange changes in shift. Currently, the only report in this process is the schedule notebook where shifts are manually written. In order to contact the Volunteers, they need to be looked up in either *ACT!* or Netscape for contact information such as phone numbers or e-mail addresses. As with the Volunteer Management process, the inability for *ACT!* to be able to customize volunteer records creates the need to use alternate methods to keep a schedule for the volunteers.

2.3. Process Improvement Goals

E: Volunteer Management

Ideally, all information kept on a volunteer would be stored in a single location, or in locations that can be utilized as resources interactively. The need to categorize a single volunteer in multiple applications takes additional time doing basic Program administrative duties that could better be spent in expanding the Volunteer Community at the Rep. By using multiple applications to track volunteers, any updates in one system must be updated in each application, and therefore exponentially increases the data management time spent coordinating volunteers.

F: Volunteer Scheduling

In conjunction with volunteer management, the scheduling of volunteers takes a great deal of the Volunteer Coordinator's time. The amount of time needed to schedule volunteers for shifts should be accomplished during the "between" show times.

Unfortunately, even during the run of a show, there are still unfilled shifts to schedule. During this time, the Volunteer Coordinator's time is mostly occupied with running Front of House for Rep productions, limiting the time available to contact volunteers. With the current volunteer tracking system, the process of contacting volunteers quickly becomes difficult. With a Volunteer Program consisting of several hundred participants, the need to simplify the process of requesting volunteers, scheduling, and confirming shifts is the main improvement needed.

EXAMPLE 11.3

San Jose Repertory Theatre: Business Analysis, Cont'd

Having a single coordinating system to schedule and track such a large staff would improve the functionality of disseminating information to volunteers. This would enable the needs and opportunities of volunteers to be catered for on an individual basis, thereby making the process more efficient.

2.4. Technology Strategies

> **E: Volunteer Management &**

> **F: Volunteer Scheduling**

Selecting a Contact Management database that specifically relates to the needs of volunteer management is the best technological application to improve both the Volunteer Management and Scheduling processes. Finding a preexisting system that allows basic contact information and categories of jobs to be recorded, events to be scheduled and the tracking of hours worked, while still allowing unique fields to be established would, in effect, eliminate all of the multiple entries needed currently. The only other factor would be a compatibility with the Rep's existing e-mail client, Netscape Messenger. Currently Red Ridge *Volunteer Works* is being researched and tested by the Volunteer Coordinator and Systems Staff. Total cost for this project is $1,500.00 based on Red Ridge product. We anticipate installing the new system in May of 2002 so details can be worked out during the final show of our 2001–02 mainstage season.

2.5. Measures of Success

> **E: Volunteer Management &**

> **F: Volunteer Scheduling**

By having all volunteer information consolidated into one system, the Coordinator will reduce the time needed to distribute requests to volunteers by eliminating the need to cross reference schedule, contact information, and contact application information. This reduction should cut the time spent on volunteer management and scheduling paperwork and data entry by twenty-five (25) percent. This measure will be taken annually before the beginning of each mainstage season.

2.6. Anticipated Challenges

> **E: Volunteer Management &**

> **F: Volunteer Scheduling**

The greatest challenge of installing a new volunteer coordination system will be data conversion and training. To address these issues, we are already working on an MS Excel worksheet table of all volunteer information. This worksheet allows all the needed information to be ready for import into the new volunteer coordination system. As for the training issue, the Financial Systems Manager will work with the Volunteer Coordinator to create an Assistants Guidebook to address the basic operations of the new system, and set training guidelines for any new House Management staff.

EXAMPLE 11.4

Girl Scouts of Santa Clara County: Business Analysis

Table 2.7

Strategic Goal—Funding: GSSCC will cultivate a strong, renewable donor base resulting in adult generated, diversified funding that supports increasing operational demands and capital development.

Business Functions—fund development.

# & Appx	Business Process	How Accomplished Currently	Process Improvements	Technology Improvements	Measurements of Success
1. 19.8.a 19.8.b	Processing & managing gifts	Entry into Blackbaud Raiser's Edge for donor letters; entry into MAS90 for accounting.	Reduce redundant data entry	Shared database (db) to integrate receipts w/ accounting; shared db w/ membership to eliminate duplicate data entry	By July 2003, an accurate, integrated shared database with fund dev., membership, and accounting will: 1. reduce data entry time by 50%, and 2. reduce cost of data entry by 30%.

Strategic Goal—Girl Development: GSSCC will provide program that responds to the current and future needs of girls from diverse communities and empowers them to reach their full potential resulting in a diverse membership that is at parity with the county population.

Business Functions—membership, program, registration.

# & Appx	Business Process	How Accomplished Currently	Process Improvements	Technology Improvements	Measurements of Success
3. 19.8.c	Registering a member/ Unplaced girls	Service Unit registrars add member into troop. When filled, completed registration forms are sent to Council for data entry. (Process takes up to 6 months.) Unplaced girls are placed in a temporary troop until contact with Service Unit registrar to determine open spaces. (May take up to 9 months.)	Get information into WinPCMS faster	Service Unit registrars enter member information directly to db using extranet OR Prospective members register themselves via on-line transaction	By July 2003: 1. decrease # girls in unplaced troops by 50%, 2. increase # troops by 5% 3. decrease registration process by 3 months, 4. increase accuracy of girls in troops to at least 90%, and 5. increase registered members by at least 5%.

EXAMPLE 11.5

Diabetes Society of Santa Clara Valley: Business Analysis

Product Inventory

The Product Inventory business process was chosen for inclusion in this technology plan because it is an area in which we are not adequately and responsibly managing well. Although our product inventory has been low over the last two years, it is because of cash flow rather than interest from our customers. This is a business strategy that has the potential to expand and become more profitable for us. Before that can happen, we must develop our inventory and sales processes for efficiency.

The process outline shows the Office Manager as the owner of this process. As part of her overall responsibilities of managing the office, office equipment, and office supplies, she also manages diabetes product supplies by doing product inventory and ordering diabetes products as needed. With a small staff, there is no one else who is in a position to perform product inventory on a regular basis. Our Office Manager has been doing it for several years now. She does it manually by "eyeballing" our supplies on a monthly basis. If she sees that supplies are low in-between inventory, she is able to order at that time as well. She does inventory this way because it is easy and effective for now. However, when we dramatically expand our supply and sales, this method will no longer be effective.

The only use of technology in this process is through our bookkeeper. She maintains a spreadsheet in Microsoft Excel to list product inventory. She then makes several entries into our accounting software, QuickBooks. She is able to calculate the value of products and provide an inventory value on our Balance Sheet—our product is listed as an asset. Also, the value of products that are sold to people on Medicare is listed on our Balance Sheet as Accounts Receivable (she receives these receipts from the Receptionist). When a Medicare payment is received that value goes down on the Balance Sheet.

EXAMPLE 11.5

Diabetes Society of Santa Clara Valley: Business Analysis, Cont'd

Product Inventory — FC.4

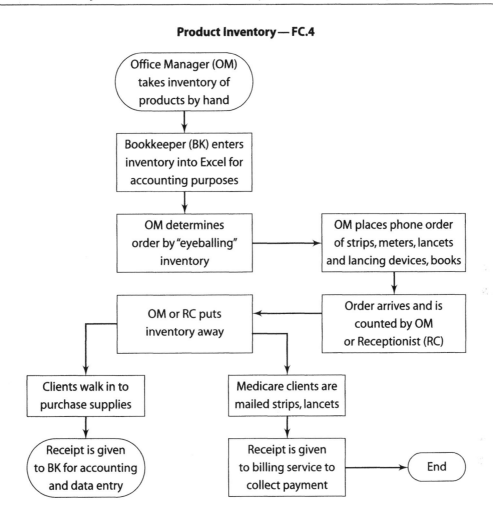

Table 5: Product Inventory

Process Improvement	Technology Strategy	Measure of Success
Create a more efficient and accurate way to track inventory and inventory value. Reduce staff time spent entering inventory and dollar values.	Acquire purchasing software and a bar code scanner.	Staff time reduced by 50 percent each month taking inventory starting 1/03 versus 12/02. Achieve exact value rather than estimate starting 1/03.

Chapter 12

Network Services

STARTING WITH the network services section of the technology plan (Section IV of Resource A), you move from an analysis of how your organization does business into a detailed look at what technology it currently uses, followed by how it plans to change or improve upon current practice to achieve its business process improvements. The importance of this and subsequent sections of the technology plan is that it is extremely difficult to know how to move forward until you understand where you are now.

For smaller organizations, the network services section may have only a few subsections, for example e-mail, printing, a server that stores files, and possibly a public Web site. Larger organizations may provide numerous services or multiple forms of the same service and may have many servers in multiple locations and therefore have many more subsections in this section of their technology plans. In fact a large organization may suffer from *too much* technology, possibly the result of uncontrolled acquisition and individual purchasing decisions throughout the organization. In this case the organization may conclude that what is needed is a consolidation of resources along with some procedural guidelines for both technology administration and end-user purchases and usage.

In any case, striving to understand what your organization currently has will lead to informed decision making about what to do next.

What are network services? *Network services* are all of the services that a technologically networked environment can provide to facilitate collaboration and information sharing. In this section of the technology plan, you describe the network services your organization currently has (even if it has none) and what needs to change in order to implement the technology strategies you described in an earlier section. Perhaps the organization needs to modify or enhance current services or needs to add new services.

Every network service that the technology plan calls for should ultimately help your organization achieve its strategic goals. Common network services to consider for implementing your technology strategies include these:

File sharing. For file sharing, you need one or more places where users can both save and retrieve files from any desktop computer connected to the network. File sharing makes it easier for staff to collaborate on documents. Additionally, it provides security for data because files can be backed up in a central location, and it makes preventing unauthorized access to files easier. It also makes virus checking easier, because that task can be performed routinely on all the centrally stored files.

Printer sharing. This service allows multiple people to send work to a single printer on the network.

Internet access. This service allows multiple people to access the Internet through a single, centrally administered connection. This is different from giving each person a modem and a phone line to dial up an Internet service provider (ISP).

Web server. This is a computer that provides access to the following Web sites:

- Public (on the Internet): the Web site that the general public sees.

- Internal (usually called an intranet): a web site that only internal users, such as employees, see. An internal web site provides important organization-wide information that employees need in order to do their work. Examples are upcoming events, calendars, policies and procedures, and links to web resources commonly used throughout the organization, such as expense report forms.

- Partners, or extranet: an extranet serves the same purpose as an intranet, except that the community of users is larger, including people who are outside the organization but with whom the organization has regular communication and business dealings.

E-mail server. This is a computer that provides e-mail access from a centrally administered location for people affiliated with the organization, including employees, volunteers, and sometimes clients.

Domain name service (DNS). The service that makes it possible for users within the organization to receive e-mail from people outside the organization and to host a public Web site. In technical jargon, it links a user name to an Internet Protocol (IP) address.

Remote access. The use of network resources by a user who is away from the workplace, working at home, for example. Providing remote access can be as simple as providing one modem and phone line to permit one user at a time to *dial in* to the server to read mail and access files. It can be as complicated as implementing virtual private networks (VPN), the electronic equivalent of a tunnel from the server to the user's remote computer, for any number of users.

Database. When information is centrally stored in an electronic database, multiple people have access to the same data from their desktop computers. Access to such databases can also be obtained through a Web site interface, a solution that requires special programming and configuration work.

CD-ROM sharing. This service allows multiple people access to a single CD-ROM or set of CD-ROMs installed at a central location. Note that CD-ROMs shared in this way must be made for networked environments and must come with a license that permits sharing on a network.

Fax. This service allows people to print from their computers directly to an outgoing fax facility. You do not have to print out a document, take it to the fax machine, and send it. A fax service may also allow incoming faxes to be delivered to people at their desktop computers as e-mail message attachments.

Many of these services are provided by using a *server.* A server is simply a computer that is configured to deliver one or more network services. It is usually kept in a secure (for example, locked) air-conditioned room with limited access. A typical server has special hardware and software that takes care of backing up all data on the server every night, when few users would be accessing the data files or services. It has significantly more storage than an average desktop computer.

The network services section of the technology plan should include a description of the network services you currently have and a description of any network services the organization wants to enhance, modify, or add. You need not write about network services that you do not have and do not plan to get. However, it might be useful for keeping track of information to simply state "do not have" for each service you do not have and "not planned" for each service you do not plan to get. This can help you avoid the situation in which you gather a substantial amount of information and then lose track of what you have already described.

It is also helpful to make the discussions about what you have now and what you plan to get adjacent subsections, as shown in the following list. Most organizations have these subsections in their technology plans:

"Current Public Web Site" and "Proposed Public Web Site"

"Current Internal Web Site" and "Proposed Internal Web Site"

"Current Shared Databases" and "Proposed Shared Databases"

"Current E-Mail Services" and "Proposed E-Mail Services"

You should feel free to add subsections if you currently have or are proposing network services that are not included in the previous list.

For every network service you currently have or propose to implement or change, several common questions will always apply. Keep these in mind while determining what services you currently have, how you want to improve them, and what new services you propose to implement.

- How does our service work now?
- Who uses it now, and how?
- Why do we want to improve it?
- What are the improvements we want to make?
- Which processes will be improved, and how?
- Which strategic goals do the improvements serve?
- What will the improvements cost?
- How long will the improvements take?

TIPS

- Confine discussion of proposed capabilities to the appropriate subsection..This will make it easier for readers to follow the plan.
- If you do not *currently have* one of the listed network services, simply state that fact in the subsection to help the readers track the status of all the services under consideration. It will also keep readers from wondering if you left something out that should have been included.
- If you do not plan to *change* a current service, simply state that fact under the *proposed* subsection for that service. This will keep the reader from wondering if you left something out.
- If you do not plan to *implement* one of the services, or have no need for it, simply state that fact under the *proposed* subsection for that service. This, again, will keep the reader from wondering if you left something out.
- There are different ways to present network services information. Find a style of presenting it that suits your organization, then use that style consistently throughout.

The remainder of this chapter fleshes out the typical network services subsections:

A. Public Web site

B. Internal web site

C. Shared databases

D. E-mail services

E. Other current and proposed network services

A. Public Web Site

1. Current Public Web Site

Web sites that are open to anyone who wants to look at them are *public Web sites*. For this part of the technology plan, describe your organization's current public Web site, using these questions as guidelines:

- How is your organization's current public Web site hosted? Is it hosted by an ISP or on the agency's own Web server?

- Who uses your current public Web site? The general public, volunteers, clients, donors, employees?

- What does each category of users access the Web site for (be specific)? For example, does the Web site provide either general or specific information, allow volunteers to access a database of your volunteer needs and sign up to help, allow site visitors to make contributions? Is it static, that is, the same for every visitor, or dynamic, with content tailored to the visitor?

- How is your current public Web site maintained and updated? By an employee, volunteer, contractor? How often is it updated? Can employees post their own content, or must they go through someone else?

2. Proposed Public Web Site

Questions to consider for a proposed public Web site section parallel the ones just supplied for a current public Web site. If you plan to *improve* the current public Web site, note what is *different* from your current offering. If you propose to *develop* a public Web site, answer the questions from the perspective of a new service and new user. Use these questions to guide you in describing the proposed public Web site:

- Why do you want to improve your organization's public Web site (or to develop one)?

- What business processes are being improved with this technology strategy?

- How will the proposed public Web site be used differently from the current one?

- Will different people use the proposed public Web site?

- From where will users access the proposed public Web site? For example, from their homes, workplaces, or organization offices; on the road?

- Where will the proposed public Web site be maintained?

- How will the proposed public Web site be maintained and updated?

- How much will the changes cost? (Add these items to your budget reminder sheet [Worksheet 11.1] and be sure to include them in Section XV, Budget.)

- By what time does the organization need these changes? (Add this item to your timeline reminder sheet [Worksheet 11.2] and be sure to include it in Section XVI, Implementation Timeline.)

You may of course decide *not* to develop or upgrade your organization's public Web site. In that case, make sure you formally state that decision in the technology plan.

TIPS

- Be aware when deciding whether to have a static or dynamic Web site that dynamic Web sites require far more maintenance.

- Maintaining a Web site is always more time consuming than people expect it to be. Be sure to revisit the maintenance plans often.

- If the organization plans to host the Web site itself, on a computer on its network, be very careful about security. Security is also vital if the Web site handles any confidential information, such as credit card information.

B. Internal Web Site

1. Current Internal Web Site

Some web sites are used only internally, within an organization. These internal-use-only web sites are called *intranets*. The questions to answer about a current internal web site are identical to the ones for a current public Web site, except that your focus will be the distribution of information that applies only to people inside your organization. Refer to the question list for a current public Web site when describing your organization's current internal web site.

2. Proposed Internal Web Site

The questions to consider for a proposed internal web site reflect the ones for a proposed public Web site, but with the change in focus described for the questions for the current internal web site. If you plan to *improve* your organization's current internal web site, note what is *different* from your current internal offering. If you propose to *develop* an internal web site, answer the questions from the perspective of a new service the organization will provide to its employees and possibly its volunteers.

C. Shared Databases

1. Current Shared Databases

A *shared database* is a set of information to which several people have access. For example, libraries used to have card files of their holdings. This paper-based database was publicly available to anyone who came into the library. Most libraries now store and display this information on a publicly accessible computer. Similarly, your agency may have databases that are kept on index cards or in file folders, or people in your organization may have made their own simple databases to track information of interest to them. In all these scenarios, it is difficult for several people to share the information. Under such circumstances, several people often track the same data, and data are "lost" when the person who created a file moves. When information kept in these various repositories changes, someone—or perhaps several people—must change it, either manually in paper files or electronically in multiple individual databases. Finally, security is only as good as the security of the file drawers and individual desktop computers in which the information is stored. These are the reasons why a shared electronic database may be a good idea.

With a shared electronic database, several people can have access to the same data. If the information changes, the change has to be made only once. Security must be maintained in only one central location. And access to data can be restricted to appropriate personnel.

You may discover that your organization has several shared databases, serving different needs. Shared databases constitute a network service area for which an understanding of the organization's business processes is absolutely critical if this service is to function as desired. Often, access to information and the ability to use it quickly and easily is the crux of providing client services. For *each* shared database that your organization currently has, use these questions as a guide to describing it:

- Does your organization currently have any shared databases? How many?

- How is each one used?

- What data are shared?

- Who uses the data?

- Can users get the information they need in a timely way? Do they need to go to multiple sources, for example, to produce a required monthly report?

- From where is the shared database accessed? From the organization's offices, from employees' home offices, on the road?

- What are the current shared database security measures? For example, is the organization HIPPA[1] compliant?

2. Proposed Shared Databases

If you plan to improve your organization's current shared databases, convert small individual databases into shared ones, or develop one or more new shared databases from the ground up, answer these questions:

- What are the specific plans to upgrade or implement shared databases? Will you leave some databases "as is," while improving others?

- How will the proposed shared databases be used differently from the current ones?

    - Does the organization need to consolidate databases to improve efficiency and decrease confusion?

    - Does it need to streamline processes for exchanging information between databases—exporting and importing data?

    - Does it need to improve reporting capabilities? Will individual users need to be able to make their own report layouts for special needs?

- Will the proposed shared databases be used by different people than use it now, and if so, who will those people be? Will the databases be used by a larger audience than is currently possible?

- From where will the proposed database be accessed? From the organization's offices, from employees' home offices, on the road?

- Does the organization need to enhance database security? For example, if your organization is in the health care field, does it need to be HIPPA compliant?

- Which business processes is this technology strategy improving upon?

- How much will the changes cost? (Add these items to your budget reminder sheet [Worksheet 11.1] and be sure to include them in Section XV, Budget.)

- By what time does the organization need these changes? (Add this item to your timeline reminder sheet [Worksheet 11.2] and be sure to include it in Section XVI, Implementation Timeline.)

---

1. The federal Health Insurance Portability and Privacy Act (HIPPA) establishes certain security and privacy requirements. Any organization working with individually identifiable health information must be prepared to meet these requirements.

> **TIPS**
>
> - Be sure to differentiate between database solutions and the software applications used to manipulate them. For example, information about clients is a database solution, even though it is usually called, simply, "a database." The applications Access and Filemaker Pro are database engines, the software on which a specific solution may run.
>
> - Security is vital if the organization plans to share confidential data. Be sure to address specific data security issues and plans for confidential data.

D. E-Mail Services

1. Current E-Mail Services

The e-mail service an organization provides centrally for its network users is different from the generally accessible e-mail programs any individual user might subscribe to to read and send e-mail. In this subsection of the technology plan, you are concerned only with the services that are centrally provided. You will consider individual e-mail reading and sending programs in the section that concerns software (Chapter Fourteen).

If your organization currently has e-mail services, answer these questions:

- How are current e-mail services provided? By an ISP or by the organization's own server?

- How does your organization use e-mail? For general communication or for special purposes?

- Who uses the organization's current e-mail services? Employees, volunteers, clients? Do only certain employees have e-mail? If so, which ones and why?

- From where are the services used? From the organization's offices, from employees' homes, on the road?

2. Proposed E-Mail Services

If your organization plans to implement or upgrade its current e-mail services, use these questions as a guide to describing the planned improvements:

- What are your plans to upgrade or implement e-mail services? Are you changing the type of services provided? Switching from POP to IMAP (your technical expert may need to help you with this answer)? Switching from an ISP to an internal server, or vice versa? Adding capabilities such as more frequent backups or junk mail filtering?

- How will e-mail be used differently than it's currently used?

- Who will use the proposed e-mail services? Different people or more people than use it now?

- From where will the services be used? From the organization's offices, from employees' homes, on the road?

- Which business process improvements do the changes support?

- How much will the changes cost? (Add these items to your budget reminder sheet [Worksheet 11.1] and be sure to include them in Section XV, Budget.)

- By what time does the organization need these changes? (Add this item to your timeline reminder sheet [Worksheet 11.2] and be sure to include it in Section XVI, Implementation Timeline.)

TIPS

- Draw up policies on the proper use of e-mail services, as part of the implementation. (Include these policies in Section XIII, Acceptable Use Policies, discussed in Chapter Twenty-Two.)

- Get outside help from an expert for the more technical aspects of e-mail service description and planning.

E. Other Current and Proposed Network Services

Include subsections as appropriate for any additional network services that your organization currently has or proposes to implement. Be sure to include the current and proposed descriptions for each, as shown in the discussions of Web sites, shared databases, and e-mail. Using the question lists presented earlier, develop similar questions to guide your descriptions. Always keep in mind the basic questions stated in the first list of questions in this chapter.

Examples

Example 12.1: Parents Helping Parents, Inc., of Santa Clara County, a medium-sized family resource center for parents of children with special needs (www.php.com). This integrated description uses both narrative and tables to comprehensively describe the current and proposed public Web site. Note the direct correlation to business process improvements in the table of proposed web site improvements. The addition of budget and timeline references provides a complete picture of this network service. The paragraphs following this table refer back to the organization's strategic goals. Scaled appropriately, this technique will work for an organization of any size. Additionally, this same format can be used to describe other network services.

EXAMPLE 12.1

Parents Helping Parents, Inc.: Network Services

3.1. Public Web Site

3.1.a. Current public Web site

PHP's current Web site is utilized by the community of families caring for and professionals serving families and children with special needs. Based on recent evaluation using Wusage 7.0 we estimate over 2 million pages viewed on our Best/Verio hosted site. Additionally, 50% of our usage is outside the USA. We are not evaluating our Web usage on our in-house Web server at present.

Our Web site is developed and managed internally by PHP staff. The Web master updates, changes, and adds to the HTML portion of the site and develops and updates the Cold Fusion Web interface applications. PHP staff updates the many databases viewable on the Web. There are several databases in which the community may add their resources and events. However, the community-based additions to the Resource Directory and Links Page are screened prior to being available for Web viewing.

Verio, Inc. hosts the HTML portions of our public Web site at up to 250 Megs of disk space which is adequate for our needs. PHP hosts the database server in-house on an HP NetServer E60. A Cold Fusion interface allows public access to several community-based resources including:

- Resource Directory
- Equipment Exchange
- PHP and community event calendars
- Staff phone lists and e-mail links
- Links to other related Web sites

Our usage tracking is performed inconsistently and done internally.

3.1.b. Proposed public Web site

Proposed Web Site Improvements	Processes Supported
On-line training using flash and media technology providing alternate community education in addition to on-site training	3.1.b
On-line chat for specialized groups	3.1.b, 18.4.d, 2.3.f
Add PDF files to our Web site for events and information sheets	3.1.b
Create interactive tools for parents and professionals to use	3.1.b
Obtain monthly metrics for internal and external Web servers	3.1.b
On-line mentor parent database	3.1.b., 2.3.f
On-line Individualized Education Training (Special Ed)	3.1.b

EXAMPLE 12.1

Parents Helping Parents, Inc.: Network Services, Cont'd

We plan to improve our site to better educate families on how to be their child's best advocate in obtaining services to meet their child's special needs and that of their family. Included in improvements will be tools specific to obtaining special education services for children and ensuring parental involvement at all levels. Generally, we would like to expand our client self-service capabilities.

Our new vision includes better meeting the needs of families worldwide. Through live chat, educational media files and on-line mentor parent matching, we will eliminate the geographical boundaries that currently limit our outreach to families. This will especially assist our local families having children with rare conditions.

To achieve the improvements we will research and implement:

- Software to create flash and digital media files of training
- Staff or volunteers to create the digital media
- Video Conferencing
- On-line Information Packets (Education department and other collections of electronic documents)
- Increased bandwidth on existing DSL connection to support increased traffic and file transfer on our Web site
- Increased disk space to accommodate larger files on PHP Cold Fusion Web server
- Acquire software to enable online chatting—voice/text
- Acquire software to create PDF files
- Acquire Web metrics software
- A volunteer has offered to create the mentor database
- Acquire upgrade of PhotoShop 6.0, from 4.0

Activity	Timeline	Budget
Web Metrics	December 2001	No Impact—In-kind donation expected from Ilux.com
Creation and availability of PDF files for events, educational materials and registration forms available on PHP's Web site	December 2001	No Impact—We will acquire this software upon certification and acquire the software via our Adobe donation.
Offer training materials through digital media on Web and CD-ROM	Explore by: June 2002 Implement: December 2002	Unknown at this time
Determine the best hosting solution for the increased services	September 2002	Unknown—*A visit to Exodus was held in March 2001 to explore availability and pricing.* $1,500 monthly for server hosting. Information from multiple Internet Service Providers is being sought.
Offer live chat utilizing voice and text	February 2003	Unknown budget impact
On-line Mentor Database	January 2002	Volunteer Created

Example 12.2: Child Care Coordinating Council of San Mateo County, Inc., a large agency that works on behalf of children, families, and early education professionals (www.thecouncil.net). This nonprofit does not currently have an internal web site, and eloquently describes its need for one.

Example 12.3: Hope Rehabilitation Services, a large, multicounty agency serving people with developmental disabilities (www.hopeservices.org). This nonprofit succinctly describes its current shared databases and provides a proposal for needed data consolidation.

Example 12.4: Girl Scouts of Santa Clara County, a medium-sized, community-based organization that is a chapter of a national organization (www.girlscoutsofscc .org). The tabular organization of the information presented here gives readers a lot of data in a consolidated, easy-to-read format.

Example 12.5: Services for Brain Injury, a small health and human services organization that assists brain injured people to reach their highest level of independent living (www.SBIcares.org). This example describes a specific issue with current e-mail and a proposed solution.

Example 12.6: Girl Scouts of Santa Clara County, a medium-sized, community-based organization that is a chapter of a national organization (www.girlscoutsofscc .org). This description of the ways an extranet can help the organization meet certain business process improvements is thorough and clear.

EXAMPLE 12.2

Child Care Coordinating Council of San Mateo County, Inc.: Network Services

3.2. Internal Web Site (Intranet)

a. Current Internal Web Site (Intranet)

Currently we have no internal-use-only web site. Users share files across the network, but without a browser interface.

b. Proposed Internal Web Site

The Council struggles with effective and timely internal communication, across the board—among staff, management, and program areas. In beginning discussions about prioritizing business processes, the technology team identified "better internal communications" as an area in need of improvement. However, we were stumped about how to approach this as a single, chartable process. In time, better internal communications grew as a cross-cutting issue, and an intranet as one viable solution. We plan to implement an agency intranet, and are currently in the research phase of this project. The technology team is examining the uses and benefits of an intranet as well as exploring the options available for both purchased and hosted solutions. Some of the criteria considered for deciding between a purchased and hosted solution include cost, ease of uploading, creating and controlling content, internal expertise to troubleshoot software, and annual expense of maintenance and upgrades.

The intranet will be used for facilitating internal agency communication, and provide an easy-to-access source of information needed by all employees. Some of the ways we hope to use the intranet include:

- **Headlines or banners** to alert staff of emergencies, technology problems, office closures, or other urgent communication
- **Shared document files** to serve as a central repository for all Council polices, i.e.: Personnel, Human Resources, Administrative, Acceptable Use of Council Technology, etc.
- **Group calendars** for Council-wide events as well as a scheduling tool for our three busy conference rooms
- **Centralized sign-in sheet** that functions as an in/out board
- **Forms library** for the many internal Council forms, with the ability to fill out a form on the intranet and submit it directly to the appropriate recipient
- **Discussion forums** for use by internal teams of employees working on special projects

All employees will be able to access the intranet from their own workstations. The intranet will reside either on our server, if we choose to purchase the software, or at the site of the host company. Likewise the intranet will be maintained either by our internal technology staff or by the host company. An internal team of "intranet editors" will make updates.

The intranet will support several business process improvements, as identified in section 2, including Advocacy, Produce Publications, Receive Clients, Outgoing Mail, Benefits Administration, Hiring, and Web Site Maintenance.

EXAMPLE 12.3

Hope Rehabilitation Services: Network Services

C. Shared Databases

1. Current Shared Databases. Currently Hope has several databases that are shared by a number of individuals and departments. They are, at present:

   a. Paradigm—A donation database in use by the Foundation which resides on the NT server, and is used by approximately 3 members of the department.

   b. Navision—An accounting database used by the Financial department which also resides on the NT server, and is used by 10 users at the central site, as well as about 5 users at remote sites, across a T1 line and by Citrix dialup.

   c. TIM (Total Information Management)—An information management database developed by Hope, used by multiple departments, to collect data on clients, jobs, payroll hours, and more. It is presently deployed as separate copies of the database at remote sites as well as at the central sites, with the intention of bringing the data to a central site for remote access in the long term. It currently outputs reports that are used for exempt client payroll purposes, which are e-mailed to the payroll department to bring into the accounting software and thus generate payroll checks.

   d. Paradox DB—An information management database developed by Skills Center, which is the predecessor to TIM (see 3 above) and is in a different language than TIM. This will be eliminated over time by 2.(2.) below.

   e. HRIS—An HR database that is shared by several users on the Hope central site file server.

   f. Paradox HR—An HR database that is shared by several users on the Skills Center file server, which is a different database than the one in use by Hope's HR. (This is not actually used by Hope and will be eliminated by 2.(1.) below.)

2. Proposed Shared Databases. At this time there are several planned changes to the current shared databases, based on the conversations that have occurred with the department managers for the business process section. The changes are primarily in the nature of simplifying the business processes that are presently duplicating databases with differing software at Hope and at Skills Center. The goal would be to choose a single database software for use at both Hope and Skills.

   1. Agree on a single HR database software and implement it for both Hope and Skills.

   2. Combine the functions of the Skills version of TIM with the new version of TIM, upgrade it to use SQL server. The cost of doing so is undeterminable at this time since it involves not only negotiations with the developers but also between the two groups at Hope and Skills Center. Hope recently sold the rights to TIM to the developers.

   3. Deploy a training database that can be made available to staff throughout the organization.

EXAMPLE 12.4

Girl Scouts of Santa Clara County: Network Services

3.3. Shared Databases

Current shared databases

GSSCC currently has many shared databases. They are used in a number of functions from membership and volunteer records to donor records. Use varies from a few specific people, such as the accounting staff for accounting and payroll databases, and store personnel for store inventory, to a majority of the staff, such as meeting and schedule coordination of the office resources. These databases have onsite access only with one exception: payroll is housed by ADP offsite. Table 3.3.a.1 lists each of our shared databases, how it is used, who uses it and from where.

Table 3.3.a.1.

Database	How used	Who uses it	From where
1. Store Inventory (QS 2000)	Manage inventory	Store Coordinator Customer Service Mgr.	Main Office
2. Equipment loan (Excel)	Manage equipment inventory and access	Customer Service staff	Main Office
3. Volunteers (FileMaker Pro)	Manage training registra-tion, volunteer screening, performance mgmt., recognition processes	Volunteer Services Coordinator Customer Service staff Administrative Assistant	Main Office
4. Membership (WinPCMS)	Manage membership records and analyze membership data	Registrars Membership staff	Main Office
5. Camp Registration (ACCESS)	Manage summer camp registration process	Registrars Outdoor Program staff	Main Office
6. Donor Records (Raiser's Edge)	Manage donors	Advancement staff	Main Office
7. Accounting (MAS 90)	Manage finances	Accounting staff	Main Office
8. Camp Staff (ACCESS)	Manage camp staff personnel records	Outdoor Program staff	Main Office *1
9. Payroll (ADP)	Provide payroll services	Accounting staff	Main Office, and ADP Office *2

*1. This database resides on a computer that is relocated to a remote property 3 months of the year.

*2. This database is housed at ADP and is accessed remotely by our accounting staff for updating.

During the business process analysis, six (6) new database needs were identified. They all represent differ-ent organizational needs. These needs are listed in Table 3.3.a.2 along with what each database would provide, who would utilize it, and where it would be used.

EXAMPLE 12.5

Services for Brain Injury: Network Services

3.4. E-mail services

3.4.a. Current e-mail services

The agency's current e-mail capability was born of necessity, and has been quickly outgrown. Five desktops dial up AOL, and the entire agency has a single AOL account with multiple "screen names." The ISP serving the SBIcares.org domain, Verio, is configured with autoforward capabilities, so SBI staff have e-mail addresses "@SBIcares.org" which are automatically forwarded to AOL. Staff are encouraged to give out their SBIcares.org e-mail address, and discouraged from giving out their AOL address.

3.4.b. Proposed e-mail services

After high-speed access to the Internet is installed (March 2002), use of AOL will cease. Sufficient POP mailboxes will be supplied with our new ISP for all staff who need e-mail. Netscape will be downloaded and installed on every desktop as the primary Web browser and e-mail editor. The choice of Netscape is partly motivated by the observation that Microsoft Outlook is often a conduit to spread viruses. The choice of Netscape is partly motivated by economic choices.

EXAMPLE 12.6

Girl Scouts of Santa Clara County: Network Services

3.5. Other Network Services

3.5a. Current services

GSSCC does not currently have an extranet.

3.5b. Proposed services

GSSCC plans to implement an extranet to facilitate the following business processes: 1, 3, 5, 8, 11, 13, 14, 15, 16, 17, 18, 20, 21, 22, 23, 25, and 29.

The extranet will serve as the portal for remote staff or constituents to the Council's shared databases through the Internet. The extranet will help facilitate the "one-stop-shopping" use of the web site. It will be a secured part of the Council's web site, retaining the same look and feel. The Web Site Manager will design and maintain the extranet. Research will be done to determine if hosting the extranet should be outsourced or kept in house.

All regular employees will have access to the extranet from their workstations or from any remote computer with appropriate access codes. Temporary and seasonal employees will have access to the extranet if it is required for their job performance. Sections of the web site will contain certain information/databases that will be restricted based on a business need to know, e.g., a Board Members section. Secure sections may include but are not limited to Board of Directors, product sales, store, payroll, member databases, and donor records.

Timeline: 10/01–6/02

Budget: $4,000–$8,000

Chapter 13

Equipment Narrative and Table

NOW THAT you have determined what services you currently have and what services you propose to add, this chapter takes you to the next level of detail. In this section of the technology plan (Section V in Resource A) you will describe what equipment your organization currently owns and how it may need to change its equipment mix to better deliver both network services and desktop capabilities to users.

The equipment narrative and table section of the technology plan should include these subsections:

A. Current equipment inventory and narrative

B. Proposed hardware acquisitions

A. Current Equipment Inventory and Narrative

To determine the appropriate equipment inventory and configurations to support your technology strategies, you need to know what your organization currently owns. Many organizations maintain an equipment inventory in some form. If yours does not have an inventory of all its equipment, now is the time to take one.

Include in the inventory desktop computers, laptop computers, peripherals (printers, scanners, external modems, external media drives, and the like), and servers.

Organize the inventory into tables (as shown in Worksheets 13.1, 13.2, and 13.3), and include a narrative section along with the tables to explain oddities, history, the motivation for needing a particular outdated piece of equipment, and other information that may be useful for guiding purchase and upgrade decisions later. Several specific types of information are useful in assessing future equipment needs. They are listed here for each type of equipment you need to inventory. These lists will also help you in filling out the worksheets. Note that the items correspond to the worksheet column heads.

For each *desktop computer and laptop* include this information:

- Item name and model
- Brand
- Central processing unit (CPU) type and speed (for example, "Pentium III, 400MHz")
- Current operating system (OS) name and version
- Amount of memory (RAM) in megabytes (MB)
- Size of hard disk (HD) in megabytes (MB) or gigabytes (GB) and percentage free (or used)
- Network card (NIC) installed (yes or no)
- Internal modem installed (yes or no)
- Other internal peripherals (floppy disk drive, CD drive, CD burner, Zip drive, and so forth) installed in the computer
- Monitor attached to the computer or built in (particularly if it is especially good or bad—for instance, one last old monochrome monitor or a twenty-one-inch screen when everyone else has a seventeen-inch one)

For each *peripheral* include this information:

- Item name and model
- Brand
- Network available (yes or no)
- If not networked, indicate which computer it is attached to
- Other relevant technical specifications (for example, the speed of an external CD-ROM drive or a laser or network printer)

For each *server* include this information:

- Item name and model
- Brand
- Central processing unit (CPU) type and speed (for example, "Pentium III, 400MHz")
- Current operating system (OS) name and version
- Amount of memory (RAM) in megabytes (MB)

- Size of hard disk (HD) in megabytes (MB) or gigabytes (GB) and percentage free (or used)

- Uninterruptible power supply, attached or not

- Backup unit, installed or attached

- Internal peripherals (floppy disk drive, CD drive, CD burner, Zip drive, and so forth) installed in the server

For each item in the computer, peripherals, and servers tables, indicate whether you intend to "keep," "upgrade," or "replace" the item. This note will help you in making purchasing decisions when the time comes to implement your technology strategies. If you are keeping or upgrading an item but plan to move it to a new location (an action sometimes called *cascading*), you may want to make a note of that also, so that you have a record of all your early decisions about what to do with equipment.

If you intend to *upgrade* the item, answer these questions:

- What element of it do you want to upgrade (memory, processor, network cards, disk, and so forth)?

- Which process improvements do the upgrades support?

- What will the upgrades cost? (Add these items to your budget reminder sheet [Worksheet 11.1] and be sure to include them in Section XV, Budget.)

- By what time do you need to upgrade? (Add this item to your timeline reminder sheet [Worksheet 11.2] and be sure to include it in Section XVI, Implementation Timeline.)

If you intend to *replace* the item, answer these questions:

- What will you replace it with?

- Will the item become obsolete, or will it go to another user?

- Which process improvements does replacing support?

- What will the replacements cost? (Add these items to your budget reminder sheet [Worksheet 11.1] and be sure to include them in Section XV, Budget.)

- By what time do you need to replace? (Add this item to your timeline reminder sheet [Worksheet 11.2] and be sure to include it in Section XVI, Implementation Timeline.)

Think about the cost of ownership when deciding whether to keep, replace, or upgrade. How hard is it going to be to maintain older equipment? Will parts be available? In general, it is advisable to stay in the middle of the equipment life cycle, neither *bleeding edge* (so new that its problems are unknown) nor *graveyard edge* (so old that it fails frequently, is not up to the task, or cannot be easily maintained).

Be sure to consider how software decisions will affect the hardware inventory. For example, if you plan on upgrading software but not hardware, will the new software run reliably and efficiently on the old hardware?

TIPS

- Give *minimum* specifications rather than absolute ones. (For example, say, *"at least* 64MB RAM" instead of "64MB RAM.")

- Label table columns. If the table requires more than one page, make sure that these column headings repeat on the next pages.

- Add columns to capture additional information, if needed.

- Number table rows so that people can later refer to specific equipment simply by row number in the inventory. This will also be helpful in the software inventory (Chapter Fourteen), to identify which computers have what software title installed.

- Do not identify machines by their user's names in the final document, *unless* your organization is very small and has only a few computers to inventory. (Refer to the examples to see how a small organization might handle this situation.)

- Consider using Worksheets 13.1, 13.2, and 13.3 to assist with the inventories.

- Use the narrative portion of this plan section to summarize and provide any necessary explanation. Do not just repeat the information listed in the table.

- Establish equipment donation guidelines (minimums and specifications). The less the variety of your organization's equipment and software, the easier it will be to maintain it and train users to operate it.

- Devise a way to allow users to inventory their own systems. This will prevent the full burden of the task from falling on only one person.

Also consider the following things when taking inventory. If your organization is small or does not currently own very much equipment, it may be possible to combine the tables for hardware and software (software is discussed in Chapter Fourteen). If you do so, make sure that the tables remain easy to understand. Your goal is to understand what your organization currently owns so that you can make informed purchasing decisions to implement your technology strategies, and to make it easy for others to understand as well.

B. Proposed Hardware Acquisitions

In the inventory you created in the previous subsection, you identified current equipment that you wish to replace with something new, so the inventory count remained constant. In this subsection, describe *new* equipment, items that will increase your organization's inventory. What does your organization want to or need to acquire that is *different* from its planned upgrades and replacements? For example, does it need to provide equipment for some employees who do not currently have computers? Does it need to purchase additional equipment for new hires? Does it need an additional server to provide new network services?

If your organization has configuration guidelines for equipment purchases and donations, refer to these guidelines as you specify what new equipment you will need. If your organization does not have such guidelines, now is a good time to develop them. Describe the organization's minimum configuration guidelines in narrative before itemizing the proposed hardware acquisitions.

It is generally not advisable to combine the tables for the current hardware inventory and the proposed equipment acquisitions. By keeping them separate you can be very clear about what you have and what you need. This clarity makes it easier to justify the proposed purchases to prospective funders.

Use these questions to guide your discussion of new hardware acquisitions:

- Which business process improvements do these acquisitions support?

- Does the organization have any special equipment needs beyond the minimum configuration guidelines?

- What will the new equipment cost? (Add these items to your budget reminder sheet [Worksheet 11.1] and be sure to include them in Section XV, Budget.)

- By what time do you need the new equipment? (Add this item to your timeline reminder sheet [Worksheet 11.2] and be sure to include it in Section XVI, Implementation Timeline.)

TIPS

- Again, be general. (For example, say, "laptop computer" rather than naming a specific vendor and model.)

- If you need a specific configuration for a special purpose, state it explicitly. (For example, say, "laptop computer with internal modem" to describe the equipment for someone who will connect from remote sites into your organization's network.)

- Give *minimum* configuration specifications rather than absolute ones. (For example, say, *"at least* 128MB RAM" instead of "128MB RAM.")

Examples

Example 13.1: Youth Science Institute, in Santa Clara County, a small natural science museum and educational service organization (www.ysi-ca.org). The equipment inventory table in this example includes a notes column that further describes upgrades or replacements, giving precise upgrade or replacement specifications. Because they are a small organization, they included the names of specific users. This is not advisable in larger organizations.

Example 13.2: San Jose Repertory Theatre, a large arts organization (www .sjrep.org). The equipment inventory table shown here expands the keep/ upgrade/replace column information by adding the options of Eliminate (E) and Cascade (C) (that is, pass along a piece of equipment, an internal hand-me-down), providing information useful for technology deployment activities later on. They also included a "Status" column and an "Acquired" column. The Status column indicates whether the computer is currently being used. The Acquired column includes the date and indicates whether the computer was bought, donated, or custom built. This information is useful in deciding whether to keep, upgrade, or replace.

Example 13.3: Junior Achievement of the Bay Area, Inc., a medium-sized education service organization (www.jaba.org). This organization has added "guiding principles" for new hardware acquisitions to its new hardware acquisitions subsection to provide a context for purchases, donations, and cascading equipment to other users. Although this example was written by a medium-sized nonprofit, the notion of guiding principles may work for an organization of any size.

Example 13.4: Clara Mateo Alliance, Inc., a medium-sized organization providing shelter and supportive services for the homeless (www.clara-mateo.org). This narrative clearly outlines minimum equipment requirements for two categories of users. It is helpful in determining what sort of equipment and minimum configuration is needed and what will be accepted for donation or purchase.

EXAMPLE 13.1

Youth Science Institute: Equipment Table

Table 7. Workstations

VASONA USERS	OS	RAM	HD	CPU	Modem	NIC	Internal Peripherals	Keep/ Replace/ Upgrade?	Replace or Upgrade with:
Geraldine HP Vectra XA	Win 98	32MB	515MB	Pent 166	No	HP Enhanced PCI 10/100TX Interface	Floppy	Keep	Upgrade to Win 98 Upgrade to 64MB
Megan HP Vectra VL	Win NT	32MB	2GB	Pent II 266	No	3 Com Etherlink III 16-bit ISA	Floppy	Keep	Upgrade to Win 98 Upgrade to 64MB
Bonnie HP Vectra XA	Win 98	32MB	2.5GB	Pent 166	V.90 56K	3 Com Etherlink III 16-bit ISA	Floppy 40x CD-ROM	Keep	Upgrade to Win 98 Upgrade to 64MB
Marion Compaq Presario 4402	Win 98	80MB	1607MB	Pent 133	33.6K	NetGear FA310TX Fast Ethernet PCI	Floppy CD-ROM	Keep	Upgrade to Win 98 (Replace 2002)
Anne HP Vectra XA	Win NT 4.0	96MB	2.4GB	Pent 200	56K	3 Com Etherlink III 16-bit ISA	Floppy CD-ROM	Keep	
Ken Aptiva 510	Win 95	32MB	513MB	486	33.6K	None	Floppy CD-ROM	Replace	Replacement TBD (See New Hardware)
Teachers									IBM Multimedia 5288 (See New Hardware)

EXAMPLE 13.2

San Jose Repertory Theatre: Equipment Table

Table 1. Desktops and Laptops

Brand	Name and Model	Quantity	CPU	Status	Date	Acquired	RAM	HD	NIC	CD-ROM	Internal Peripherals	K/R/U/E/C
Hewlett Packard	Brio BA 410	8	Celeron 733MHz	Active	Aug-01	Purchased	128MB	20GB	10/100	Yes		Keep
Hewlett Packard	Brio BA 410	1	P3: 933MHz	Active	Aug-01	Purchased	256MB	60GB	10/100	Yes	CDRW	Keep
Hewlett Packard	Brio BA 410	4	Celeron 733MHz	Active	Aug-01	Purchased	64MB	20GB	10/100	Yes		Keep
Hewlett Packard	Brio BA 400 (SMB)	5	Celeron 500MHz	Active	Feb-00	Donated	128MB	13GB	10/100	Yes		Keep
Hewlett Packard	Brio BA 400 (SMB)	1	Celeron 500MHz	Active	Feb-00	Donated	128MB	13GB	10/100	Yes	HP CD-Writer Plus 9100i IDE	Keep
Hewlett Packard	Brio BA 400 (SMB)	8	Celeron 500MHz	Active	Feb-00	Donated	64MB	13GB	10/100	Yes		Keep
Hewlett Packard	Brio BA 400 (SMB)	1	Celeron 500MHz	Active	Jan-00	Purchased	64MB	13GB	10/100	Yes		Keep
Hewlett Packard	Vectra NT 4.0	1	x86f6 3 step 3	Inactive		Purchased	97712KB	2.4GB	10/100	Yes		Eliminate
Hewlett Packard	Vectra VL5-200	1	Pentium 200	Active	Nov-97	Donated	64MB	2GB	10/100	No		Replace
Hewlett Packard	Vectra VL5-200	4	Pentium 200	Inactive	Nov-97	Donated	80MB	2GB	10/100	No		Eliminate
Hewlett Packard	Vectra VL5-200	4	Pentium 200	Active	Nov-97	Donated	80MB	2GB	10/100	No		Replace

Manufacturer	Model	Qty	Processor	Status	Date	Source	RAM	HDD	Network		Peripherals	Action
Apple	iMac	1	G3 450MHz	Active	Oct-00	Donated	320MB	20GB	10/100	Yes	Zip 100 drive, 3.5" (external)	Keep
Hewlett Packard	Omnibook XE2i	1	Celeron 500MHz	Active	Feb-00	Donated	64MB	13GB	10/100	Yes		Keep
IBM	300 GL	1	Pentium 200	Active	Aug-99	Donated	160MB	6GB	10/100	Yes		Replace
Apple	iBook	1	G3 500MHz	Active	Jul-01	Personal	256MB	20GB	10/100	Yes	Kenyo speakers, Imation Superdisk	Purchase new if position changes
JDR	Micro	1	Pentium 200	Active		Purchased	64MB	6GB	10/100	Yes		Replace
IBM	ThinkPad 365XD	1	Pentium 120MHz	Active	May-01	Donated	40MB	775MB	10/100	Yes	3.5" drive (external)	Keep
Apple	iBook	1	G3 233MHz	Active		Personal	64MB	9GB	10/100	Yes	Zip 100 drive (external)	Purchase new if position changes
Generic		1	K6-3D	Active	Dec-99	Built	128MB	8GB		Yes	56K Modem	Replace
Panel PC	MCR	1	Celeron 500MHz	Active	Aug-01	Purchased	64MB	10GB	10/100	Yes		Keep

---

EXAMPLE 13.3

Junior Achievement of the Bay Area, Inc.: Equipment Narrative

New Hardware Acquisitions

Guiding principles

- Computers (both desktop and laptop) fall into four classes, based on their roles: Server, LAN workstation, remote workstation, and terminal, in descending order of capability.

- Server hardware should be planned based on the specific services to be run on it.

- LAN workstations must be capable of running the current network-ready operating system (e.g., Windows 9x or Windows 2000), the current office productivity suite including word processing, spreadsheet, and database management and reporting (e.g., Office 97 or Office 2000 Professional), the current messaging/collaboration software, and the current enterprise database client application(s).

- Remote workstations must be capable of running an operating system capable of WAN and internet connectivity, Windows Terminal client software (and using all LAN workstation applications in a Terminal session), the current office productivity suite, a Web browser, and messaging software capable of reading messages from the current messaging/collaboration database via a remote-storage protocol.

- Terminals must be capable of LAN or WAN connectivity and capable of running Windows Terminal client software (and using all LAN workstation applications in a Terminal session).

- User desktops and laptops should be upgraded, replaced, or redeployed based on an assumption of a two-year cycle of obsolescence.

- Deployment of desktops and laptops should attempt to match capacity and features to the user's job and ergonomic needs, with the most capable hardware being deployed to the most demanding users. Laptops should be deployed to users with the greatest needs for mobility.

- In no case will donated equipment be deployed or used in any manner inconsistent with a donor's express intention.

EXAMPLE 13.4

Clara Mateo Alliance, Inc.: Equipment Narrative

Appendix H: Minimum System Requirements

Staff Workstations

The minimum operational requirement for all new staff workstations will be the ability to effectively run Windows 2000 Professional and Office 2000 Professional. Currently our smallest computer has a 400MHz Pentium II processor with 32MB of RAM and a 4GB hard drive, and does not meet our criteria. While this will be the minimum requirement for donated equipment, future purchases will be, at a minimum, a 866MHz Pentium III processor, 128MB RAM, 20GB hard drive, CD-ROM drive, and 10/100 NIC card. These requirements will be evaluated during our tech plan review as scheduled in our timeline.

Resident Workstations

The operational requirement for resident workstations is the minimum requirement for donated computers, mentioned above. This minimum requirement will allow us to establish a low end threshold of Windows 95 or 98 for all resident workstations. As equipment is donated it will be evaluated to determine the most current version of Windows that effectively runs on the system. If new licenses are needed we will strive to inexpensively upgrade the computers to comply with the requirements of Windows 2000 Professional. As newer equipment is acquired for staff use, older staff systems will be wiped clean and reloaded with OS and software for the use of residents. This requirement will be reviewed during our tech plan review as scheduled on our timeline.

WORKSHEET 13.1

Hardware Inventory: Computers

Qty.	Item Name and Model	Brand	CPU (Type and Speed)	OS	RAM	HD	NIC (Speed)	Internal Modem?	Internal Peripherals*	Monitor	Keep/ Upgrade/ Replace?
1.											
2.											
3.											
4.											
5.											
6.											
7.											
8.											
9.											
10.											
11.											
12.											
13.											
14.											
15.											
16.											
17.											
18.											
19.											
20.											
21.											
22.											
23.											
24.											
25.											
26.											
27.											

* Floppy, CD-ROM, Zip, and so forth.

WORKSHEET 13.2

Hardware Inventory: Peripherals

Qty.	Item Name and Model	Brand	Network Available?	If Not Network Available, Direct Connected to Which Computer?	Other Relevant Technical Specifications	Keep/ Upgrade/ Replace?
1.						
2.						
3.						
4.						
5.						
6.						
7.						
8.						
9.						
10.						
11.						
12.						
13.						
14.						
15.						
16.						
17.						
18.						
19.						
20.						
21.						
22.						
23.						
24.						
25.						
26.						
27.						

WORKSHEET 13.3

Hardware Inventory: Servers

	Qty.	Item Name and Model	Brand	CPU (Type and Speed)	OS	RAM	HD	UPS? (attached or not)	Backup Unit?	Internal Peripherals*	Keep/ Upgrade/ Replace?
1.											
2.											
3.											
4.											
5.											
6.											
7.											
8.											
9.											
10.											
11.											
12.											
13.											
14.											
15.											
16.											
17.											
18.											
19.											
20.											
21.											
22.											
23.											
24.											
25.											
26.											
27.											

* Floppy, CD-ROM, Zip, and so forth.

Chapter 14

Software Narrative and Table

IN THIS SECTION, as in the previous section, Equipment Narrative and Table, you are investigating your current software inventory and future software needs at a detailed level. You will look at what your organization currently owns, what it proposes to acquire to implement the technology strategies, and how it keeps track of the software licenses it owns.

If you are wondering if it is possible to work on the equipment inventory in the previous section after you work on this section about software, the answer is yes. In fact, you will probably work on both sections at the same time. Your equipment configurations will inform software upgrade and purchase decisions, and your software needs will inform equipment configurations. One reason for this interdependence is that newer software may not run on older equipment. Decisions concerning equipment and software must be made with full knowledge of both areas of technology.

Section VI, Software Narrative and Table, of the technology plan should include these subsections:

A. Current software inventory and narrative

B. Proposed software acquisitions

C. Software license tracking

    1. Current license tracking procedures
    2. Proposed license tracking procedures

A. Current Software Inventory

In this part of the technology plan, provide an inventory of your organization's current software, in table form. Annotate the inventory table as necessary with narrative to explain oddities, history, or other information you wish to capture for both your own and other readers' later understanding. Worksheet 14.1 can assist you in this effort.)

For *desktop computers, laptops, and servers* include this information:

- Software title (for example, Microsoft Office, Adobe Acrobat, FileMaker Pro, and so forth)

- Type of software (OS, End-user, Server)

- Software description, including the following:

  - Operating system software (for example, Windows 98, Windows 2000, Windows ME, Mac OS 9, Linux, and so forth)

  - All programs your agency uses to accomplish their daily work (for example, word processing, spreadsheet, database, desktop publishing, e-mail, and Web browsing software)

  - Desktop security software, including antivirus software

  - Server software

  - Server security software, including antivirus software

  - Server backup software (must match your backup equipment listing in your hardware inventory)

  - Network services software (for example, Web hosting, database server, e-mail server)

- Release or version number

- Operating system the software is compatible with (for example, Windows 98, Windows 2000, Windows ME, Mac OS 9, Linux, and so forth)

- Which computers, laptops, or servers the software resides on (this will help you later when you need to upgrade software on specific computers)

- Number of software licenses (see more about software licenses in the explanation about subsection C)

- Number of licenses needed

- Whether your organization plans to keep, upgrade, or release the title

For *servers* include this information:

- Operating system name (for example Windows 98, Windows 2000, Windows ME, Mac OS 9, Linux, and so forth)

- Operating system version number

- Security software, including antivirus software

- Backup software (This must match your backup equipment listing in your hardware inventory.)

- Network services software (for example Web hosting, database server, e-mail server)

- Count of each title if you have more than one server

- Indication of which server each title is on if you have more than one server

- Whether you plan to keep, upgrade, or replace the title

If your organization plans to *upgrade* the item, answer these questions:

- How does it plan to upgrade? By going to a newer version of the program, installing patches?

- Which process improvements do the upgrades support?

- How much will the upgrades cost? (Add these items to your budget reminder sheet [Worksheet 11.1] and be sure to include them in Section XV, Budget.)

- By what time does the organization need these upgrades? (Add this item to your timeline reminder sheet [Worksheet 11.2] and be sure to include it in Section XVI, Implementation Timeline.)

If your organization plans to *replace* the item, answer these questions:

- What will you replace the item with? A completely different program of a different type? A different title of the same type?

- Which process improvements do the replacements support?

- How much will the replacements cost? (Add these items to your budget reminder sheet [Worksheet 11.1] and be sure to include them in Section XV, Budget.)

- By what time does the organization need these replacements? (Add this item to your timeline reminder sheet [Worksheet 11.2] and be sure to include it in Section XVI, Implementation Timeline.)

TIPS

- Use the narrative portion to summarize and provide any necessary explanation. Do not just repeat the information listed in the table.

- Lengthy explanations of upgrades or replacements should be made in the text, not in the table.

- To indicate which computers have which software titles, refer to the numbered rows in the equipment inventory tables.

- If the table requires more than one page, make sure the column headings are repeated on each page.

- Consider using Worksheet 14.1 to assist the team in this effort.

Consider also the following points when taking software inventory. If your organization is small or does not currently own very much software, it may be possible to combine the tables for hardware and software (see the discussion of hardware in Chapter Thirteen). If you do so, make sure the tables remain easy to understand. The goal is to understand what the organization currently owns so that you can make informed purchasing decisions to implement the technology strategies and also to make that information easily accessible to anyone who reads the plan.

Consider whether decreased technology support and training costs (see Chapters Nineteen and Twenty) would justify standardizing on a given type of software for certain applications. Also consider upgrading everyone to the same version of a given piece of software to minimize technology support costs (Chapter Nineteen).

Be aware that licensed software should not be resold once it has been used to permit an upgrade to the next version. Even if you give this earlier version away, make the recipient aware that it has already been used for an upgrade once and is not eligible for upgrade use again.

PLANNING IN PRACTICE
Consider Software Upgrades Carefully

For Scott Render, chief executive officer of the Santa Clara Chapter of the American Red Cross, it wasn't planning for or acquiring more computers that concerned his staff. It was the treadmill of software upgrades they found themselves on. The organization was already using computers for accounting, donor tracking, and other tasks. Adding functions like an expanded Web site, e-mail, and on-line registration for CPR and first-aid classes went fairly smoothly.

The problem arose when they found that the "planned obsolescence" built into much software forced them to shift from word processing and spreadsheet applications the staff knew and could use easily to newer and different applications. The new applications had a huge amount of potential functionality, but much of it was not essential, and not even desired, by the people who stood ready to provide disaster services on short notice. This made them consider the option of upgrading software carefully when they were working on their technology plan.

The new software was faster in theory. In practice, however, the large memory demands it made on their computers made it slower in use. As Render said, "Sometimes I feel when we upgrade and buy a program, the software requirements require so much memory. So when you go to do things, you find it's actually slower. And you say, yeah, it does a thousand and one things, but I only need it to do ten, and I need to do it with great speed."

At a certain point, however, staff conceded to the need to upgrade. Although they were happy with the existing software, eventually they found themselves unable to open incoming documents and unable to have their outgoing documents opened by other organizations. They also discovered that the applications they were using were written with poor backward compatibility and would not open documents from previous versions. They also lacked compatibility with other popular applications. With specifications coming from a national organization, compatibility between chapters was important.

Despite being happy and comfortable with what they were using, the staff at this agency were forced to switch. Render summed up the situation this way: "[The existing software] does everything that you want. Then you're going to switch over to a different system. And it's not going to do any more for you. It just requires you to learn a different process."

B. Proposed Software Acquisitions

In the software inventory section of the technology plan, you identified the upgrades and replacements needed to implement your technology strategies. In this subsection, you are identifying the *new* software that is needed to carry out the organization's strategies. This new software may include additional copies of and licenses for titles your organization already owns and new titles for your collection of software tools. Your agency's business process improvements should guide and inform the decisions regarding new titles. For example, perhaps your organization plans to add staff and needs to provide them with computers and software, or perhaps it is computerizing a segment of its business that is currently operating with manual processes.

For anticipated acquisitions, describe what you want to acquire. Answer these questions to guide your decisions:

- For what specific reasons are you adding new titles, copies, or licenses?

- Which business process improvements do these acquisitions support?

- Do these acquisitions replace any software currently in use?

- How many copies or licenses do you need?

- How much will the acquisitions cost? (Add these items to your budget reminder sheet [Worksheet 11.1] and be sure to include them in Section XV, Budget.)

- By what time does the organization need these acquisitions? (Add this item to your timeline reminder sheet [Worksheet 11.2] and be sure to include it in Section XVI, Implementation Timeline.)

When determining new software acquisitions, remember to consider including *operating systems* for desktop computers, laptops, and servers.

Also consider *end-user* software for communications (for example, for e-mail clients to enable them to read and send e-mail) and instant messaging; for accessing and browsing the Internet; for word processing, spreadsheet functions, presentations, graphic arts and illustrations, desktop publishing, and Web site authoring; for accessing shared databases; for scheduling and tracking projects; and for security (such as antivirus and desktop security).

Finally, include *server* software for network security, desktop security on the server itself, backup functions, Web hosting, a database engine, and e-mail services, and for supporting other network services required by the technology strategies.

TIPS

- Consider the hardware implications of new software acquisitions. Make sure the organization's existing hardware will support each new application or new system software.

- Be wary of acquiring software from Web-based auctions. Often these packages are not licensable, because they were licensed previously to someone else, or they have limited distribution restrictions: for example, they are for students only, cannot be upgraded, have a limited set of features, or have a limited period of use.

- Be sure to include in the timeline section of the technology plan an appropriate amount of time for configuring and customizing new software, testing it in your environment, and training everyone to use it.

- Be sure to budget for the costs of these activities in the budget section of the technology plan.

- If you are considering changing to a new application for an existing process, take existing expertise into account before choosing a product with a radically different approach or user interface. Making a radical change will greatly increase training costs.

C. Software License and Tracking

Whenever you purchase a package of software, you get a license to use it. Software license terms vary from issuer to issuer. Take the time to understand the usage permissions and limitations that come with the software your organization purchases.

Proper software licensing is important because it is against the law to use unlicensed software. Commercial computer software purchased from suppliers is protected under the Copyright Act (*U.S. Code,* Title 17, secs. 106, 501). Audits are sometimes conducted by the vendor, the Software Publishers Association—the enforcement arm of major vendors—or the Business Software Alliance. Copyright violations can lead to steep fines or even (though rarely) jail time.

For these reasons it is important that your organization keep track of the number and type of software licenses it owns and that it can access these records if asked.

There are several types of software licenses. *Individual* licenses are what typically come with shrink-wrapped products. Often a card is included that the purchaser fills in and mails, though frequently the purchaser is asked to register via the Internet at the time he installs the product. A *site* license gives the purchasing organization the right to use the software on a specific number of systems at a given site. Terms vary from vendor to vendor. An *enterprise* license gives the purchasing organization the right to use the software on a large number of systems. As the name implies, it is intended to cover an entire organization. These licenses are used for large organizations, usually with multiple sites. A *variable* license is issued based on server size or the percentage of registered users. A *named user* license gives only the specified user the right to use the licensed software. A *concurrent* license allows a specified number of people to use the licensed software at the same time.

1. Current License Tracking Procedures

In this subsection of the plan, describe how your organization currently keeps track of software licenses. You can keep track of software licenses by holding onto the actual license that comes with the software package or by keeping the purchase receipts showing proof of ownership or by doing both. Many organizations start out with an ad hoc approach—whoever purchases the software keeps the license or receipt of purchase in a file folder or drawer. Then, as the organization grows, it becomes more formal about keeping track of software purchases. Consider these questions as you complete this subsection:

- What are your organization's current software license tracking procedures? Can you currently locate licenses or proof of ownership for the software the organization has?

- Are the organization's current tracking procedures adequate? If not, why not?

2. Proposed License Tracking Procedures

Having assessed how your organization tracks software licenses, describe how it proposes to track licenses. Consider these questions in describing the proposed tracking procedures:

- Does your organization already have a satisfactory software license tracking procedure in place? If so, you do not need to complete this section. Simply state that the organization's procedure works, and it does not plan any changes.

- What measures will you take to inventory the organization's current licenses?

- How will you track new acquisitions?

- Will any costs be incurred? (Add these items to your budget reminder sheet [Worksheet 11.1] and be sure to include them in Section XV, Budget.)

- By what time does the organization need these new procedures to be implemented? (Add this item to your timeline reminder sheet [Worksheet 11.2] and be sure to include it in Section XVI, Implementation Timeline.)

Examples

Example 14.1: Youth Science Institute, in Santa Clara County, a small natural science museum and educational service organization (www.ysi-ca.org). The use of computer user names across the columns is an easy way to identify which user has what software and version. Also note the introductory statement about taking an annual inventory to keep records current. This approach works well for small organizations in which user names can easily fit across one page.

Example 14.2: Cupertino Community Services, a small, community-based organization (www.CupertinoCommunityServices.org). This example uses counts for each software title rather than user names, and the organization has integrated software license tracking into the same table. This approach will also work for a medium-sized or large organization.

EXAMPLE 14.1

Youth Science Institute: Software Table

Current Software Inventory

Included in our timeline will be the annual evaluation of software to determine if the version needs to be updated in order to stay current and compatible.

Table 10: Software Inventory

SOFTWARE (V = Vasona)	Keep/ Toss/ Upgrade	Anne (V)	Bonnie (V)	Geraldine (V)	Marion (V)	Part-Timer (V)	Teachers (V)	Alum Rock	Sanborn	Vasona Server
Microsoft Office Pro 97	Keep	X	X	X	X	X	X	X	X	
FileMaker Pro 4.1 v1	Toss									X
EXCEED by Trac v3.0	Keep									X
Adobe Illustrator 7.0	Keep	X								
Adobe PageMaker 6.5	Keep	X				X		X	X	
Adobe Photoshop 4.0	Keep	X								
Adobe Acrobat 4.0	Keep							X	X	
Netscape Navigator 4.04	Upgrade	X	X	X						
Internet Explorer	Upgrade	5.0	4.0	4.0	5.0	4.0		3.0	3.0	
AOL	Upgrade	4.0	4.0	4.0				3.0	3.0	
Quickbooks Pro 2000	Keep	X			X					
Site Aid 2.0 (HTML editor)	Keep	X			X					
Cute FTP 2.0 (FTP site manager)	Keep	X								
McAfee VirusScan 95 v2.0.6	Toss			X	X			X	X	

EXAMPLE 14.2

Cupertino Community Services: Software Table

1.1. Current Software Inventory

1.1.a. Table

Current Software Inventory

Qty.	Title	Type of SW (OS, End-User, Server)	Description	Release or Version	Number Licensed	Licenses Needed	Keep/ Upgrade/ Replace
7	FileMaker Pro	End-User	Database	5.5	7	0	Keep
7	Microsoft Internet Explorer	End-User	Internet Browser	5.5 SP1	NA	NA	Keep
7	Microsoft Office	End-User	Office Suite of Products	2000 SR-1 Premium	7	0	Keep
4	Netscape Communicator	End-User	Internet Browser	4.77	NA	NA	Keep
7	Norton AntiVirus	End-User	Virus Scan	2001	0	7	Keep
7	Windows 2000 Pro	OS	Windows 2000 Operating System	2000 Pro	7	0	Keep
1	QuickBooks Pro	End-User	Accounting	2001	1	0	Keep
1	Adobe Photoshop	End-User	Graphics	5.0.2	1	0	Keep
4	Palm	End-User	Scheduling Software	IIxe	4	0	Keep

Example 14.3: Cupertino Community Services, a small, community-based organization (www.CupertinoCommunityServices.org). The narrative in this example covers all categories of software acquisition—operating system, end-user, and server—with concise descriptions of acquisition intentions. Although written by a small community service organization, this approach works for an organization of any size.

Example 14.4: Junior Achievement of the Bay Area, Inc., a medium-sized education service organization (www.jaba.org). In this example, "guiding principles" for new software acquisitions are included in the subsection Proposed Software Acquisition to provide a context for purchasing and installing new software. This parallels what the same organization wrote for new hardware acquisitions (Example 13.3). Although this example was written by a medium-sized nonprofit, the notion of guiding principles may work for an organization of any size.

EXAMPLE 14.3

Cupertino Community Services: Software Narrative

New Software Acquisitions

Operating Systems

We will purchase Windows 2000 Operating System licenses for the two computers kept for the volunteer workstations. Windows 2000, along with licensing, will already be included on the new purchased desktops. Windows 2000 is compatible with Windows 2000 Server, so no additional licensing is necessary.

End-User Software

We will continue to work with the applications that are currently installed on the desktops and will invest in the purchase of the needed licenses. This will occur in both Phase II and Phase III. FileMaker Pro has proven to be sufficient for our database software and we will need a license for everyone who will access it. We will continue to use Photoshop for desktop publishing; therefore we will purchase one fully licensed version. We will also research and purchase Web design software in order to develop and maintain our Web site. Microsoft Office 2000 Standard Edition licenses will also be purchased for every user. We feel it is imperative to invest in 12 licenses for Norton AntiVirus software with a one-year subscription to virus and product updates along with 13 licenses of WinZip. We will utilize the already accessible mail and browser components of Windows 2000 Server (Outlook Express & Internet Explorer) for our mail and Web browsing needs.

We are currently researching alternative accounting software programs that are designed to fill the needs of a nonprofit. This purchase will not occur until Phase III.

Server

We will purchase Windows 2000 Server Operating System once the new facility is completed. We will also acquire Norton AntiVirus Corporate Edition 7.6 for Small & Medium Size Business for the server.

EXAMPLE 14.4

Junior Achievement of the Bay Area, Inc.: Software Narrative

New Software Acquisitions

Guiding principles

- New application software must work on the current workstation/network operating system demonstrably better, on the whole, than the current version/product.

- Interoperability with existing software is highly desirable.

- No software, whether free or licensed, should be installed on JABA-owned machines without the approval of the network administrator.

- As often as practicable, software should be installed new, rather than upgraded. This is especially true of operating system installations.

- The system administrator should maintain, as a documented step-by-step process, a recommended initial software configuration for each machine class. All attempts should be made to apply as many elements as practicable to user-owned machines.

Example 14.5: Cupertino Community Services, a small, community-based organization (www.CupertinoCommunityServices.org). This example succinctly states both the agency's current ad hoc license tracking and its proposed consolidated approach. Note that specific license information is contained in the organization's software inventory table, displayed in Example 14.2.

EXAMPLE 14.5

Cupertino Community Services: Software Narrative

Software License and Tracking

Current License Tracking Procedures

There is currently no license tracking procedure. All licenses are located in various locations.

Proposed Tracking Procedures

The Director of Housing Services will maintain a license tracking spreadsheet. All licenses will be placed in a locked fire safe cabinet located in the Bookkeeper's office. Staff will receive education on the importance of proper software licensing.

WORKSHEET 14.1

Software Inventory

	Qty.	Title	Type of SW (OS, End-User, Server)	Description	Release or Version	OS the Software Is Compatible With	Computers the Software Is On	Number Licensed	Licenses Needed	Keep/ Upgrade/ Replace?
1.										
2.										
3.										
4.										
5.										
6.										
7.										
8.										
9.										
10.										
11.										
12.										
13.										
14.										
15.										
16.										
17.										
18.										
19.										
20.										
21.										
22.										
23.										
24.										
25.										
26.										
27.										

Chapter 15

Network: LAN/WAN Narrative, Inventories, and Diagrams

A LOCAL AREA NETWORK (LAN) is a network that connects computers and peripherals within a limited physical space like a building, part of a building, or a few small buildings in close geographical proximity. It allows multiple computers to share access to network services, to the Internet, or to each other.

A *wide area network* (WAN) is a network that includes at least one component that is geographically remote. A WAN can link several LANs together or simply link a LAN to the Internet. In the simplest terms, if you have an Internet connection, you have a WAN.

In the previous sections of your plan you identified your organization's basic network needs at the user level, including network services, hardware, and software. The purpose of this section of the technology plan (Section VII in Resource A) is to describe the interconnectivity between all of these elements: that is, the network infrastructure that is needed to support all of your organization's network services and user access to tools and each other. The first step is to describe your organization's current LAN and WAN. The next step is to describe your proposed changes to the current infrastructure.

The LAN/WAN section of your technology plan includes these subsections:

A. A description of your current LAN and WAN

B. Current LAN/WAN equipment inventory

C. Current LAN/WAN logical diagram(s)

D. Current site plan diagram(s)

E. A description of your proposed LAN and WAN

    F. Proposed LAN/WAN equipment acquisitions

    G. Proposed LAN/WAN logical diagrams

    H. Proposed site plan

If your organization has more than one site, include descriptions and diagrams for each site, plus one overall diagram to show how the sites will be connected together.

This section of the technology plan is very technical. If you do not have appropriate technical expertise on your staff, you will benefit from the advice of a qualified outside expert.

A. Description of Current LAN/WAN

This subsection provides background and auxiliary information so readers of the plan can better understand the inventory and diagrams that will follow. Write a narrative description of your current LAN and WAN that includes the following information:

- Wiring standards (for example, Cat5, fiber optic, LocalTalk, coax). Note that a single network may use multiple wiring standards. Be specific about which standards are used and for what purposes.

- Network speeds (for example, 10Mbs Ethernet or 100Mbs Ethernet)

- Networking protocols (for example, TCP/IP, AppleTalk, IPX/SPX [Novell]). Note a single network may use multiple protocols. Be specific about where or for what purpose each protocol is used.

- Type of Internet connection and connection speed (for example, the Internet connection type might be modem, DSL, frame relay, T1, or ISDN).

- Description of your organization's ISP relationship.

  - Name of the ISP

  - Number and type of connections to the ISP

  - Protocols you use to communicate with the ISP. This will probably be TCP/IP if you have a basic Internet connection.

  - IP addressing scheme. If you use network address translation (NAT) or dynamic host configuration protocol (DHCP), describe it.

- Description of firewall capabilities

- Description of remote access services (RAS) or virtual private network (VPN) services

TIPS

- Delegate! Find qualified experts to help you complete the most technical aspects of the description.

- Do not feel that you must complete this entire section at one time. Start by supplying what you know and find help to fill in the missing parts.

- If you are not sure about an item, leave a placeholder for it until you can get appropriate advice.

B. Current LAN/WAN Equipment Inventory

Provide an inventory of your organization's current network equipment, in table form. Annotate your inventory table as necessary with narrative to explain oddities, history, or other information you wish to capture for your own understanding later. Both LAN and WAN equipment may be included in a single table. If your organization has multiple sites, you may include all sites in the same table, but be sure to group the equipment for each site together and to label the rows to show the site for each inventory item. Be sure to include all networking-related equipment in your inventory, such as routers, switches, hubs, remote access service equipment, modems or modem pools, and firewalls. Use Worksheet 15.1 to assist this inventory process.

For each item in the table, indicate whether the organization intends to keep, upgrade, or replace the item.

If you plan to *upgrade* the item, answer these questions:

- How do you want to upgrade? By adding memory perhaps or ports?

- Which business process improvements will the upgrades support?

- How much will the upgrades cost? (Add these items to your budget reminder sheet [Worksheet 11.1] and be sure to include them in Section XV, Budget.)

- By what time does the organization need these upgrades? (Add this item to your timeline reminder sheet [Worksheet 11.2] and be sure to include it in Section XVI, Implementation Timeline.)

If you plan to *replace* the item, answer these questions:

- What will you replace it with?

- Which business process improvements will the replacements support?

- How much will the replacements cost? (Add these items to your budget reminder sheet [Worksheet 11.1] and be sure to include them in the budget section of the plan.)

- By what time does the organization need these replacements? (Add this item to your timeline reminder sheet [Worksheet 11.2] and be sure to include it in Section XVI, Implementation Timeline.)

TIPS

- Keep the table entries brief. Lengthy explanations of upgrades or replacements should be made in the narrative.

- For multiple-site networks, group equipment for each site together and indicate the site for which it is intended.

- If the table requires more than one page, make sure that the column headings repeat on each of the pages.

C. Current LAN/WAN Logical Diagrams

To accompany the narrative, provide logical diagrams of your current LAN and WAN. A LAN diagram shows where equipment on the network is placed relative to other equipment, and what type of wiring connects the equipment. For instance, though this is overly simplified, if you have a network with one computer (A) and one server (B), the logical diagram will simply show two boxes, one labeled "Computer A" and one labeled "Server B," with a line connecting the two. At this time you are not yet concerned about where the computers are located physically inside a building, or about the length of the wires that connect parts together.

If your organization has a simple network with just a connection to the Internet, then put the LAN and WAN on the same diagram. If it has a simple WAN, perhaps one consisting of two sites each of which has a simple LAN, the diagrams may all fit on one page. However, if it has multiple sites, then you will likely need to provide several diagrams: one LAN diagram per site plus one diagram to show the overall WAN connectivity between sites and to the Internet. The overriding principle in creating these LAN/WAN diagrams is clarity, both for your own use and for readers' understanding.

In these diagram(s), represent all the equipment that makes up the network. In addition to the network equipment listed in your LAN inventory table, include servers, desktop computers, and networked peripherals, for example printers or a fax server (that is, the hardware listed in the equipment inventory that is connected to the network, see Chapter Thirteen).

TIPS

- Simplify or break apart diagrams into as many pages as needed in order to achieve clarity.

- Use different icons for the different types of equipment. (Software programs that do this sort of diagramming come with libraries of standard icons.)

- Use different types of lines to represent the different wiring standards in use (for example, Cat5 or fiber optic).

- Include a key to the symbols and lines in the diagrams, so readers can identify equipment and wiring types easily.

- If your organization has a lot of computers, *do not* include a box for every single computer on the network. Instead, represent all the computers on one segment, or part, of the network with a cluster of two or three computer icons.

- Do not include buildings or building components, such as walls, in this diagram.

- Make sure dotted lines will print out dark enough to read.

- Do not use color, or use it judiciously, in these diagrams. The diagrams should be understandable even if printed or copied in black and white.

Several good diagramming programs are available for creating LAN and WAN diagrams. If your organization is large with a complex network infrastructure, you might find it useful to invest in such a tool. However, simple networks can be easily hand-drawn or drawn with a good presentation or graphic art program. Find the tool that works for you, your organization, and the amount of diagramming you need to do, both now and in the future.

D. Current Site Plan

A site plan is a physical and geographical diagram of your organization's buildings, including the walls and rooms inside them. For a multibuilding campus, the site plan shows the geographical location of all buildings in the network, including the distance between buildings along the path your wires actually follow from one building to another.

If you have a multisite organization, provide site plans for each site. If you have a multistory building, with networking on each floor, provide a site plan for each floor showing the connectivity between floors.

Include these items in your site plan: location of buildings, rooms, and wiring drops within them; location of server room(s); location of main distribution frame (MDF), the main point from which all wires to all parts of your network originate; location of intermediate distribution frames (IDFs), points that connect to the MDF and then fan out to individual computers and peripherals; location of minimum point of entry (MPOE), where the phone lines come into the building from the phone company; and all distances, including building dimensions, distances from MDF to IDFs, distances from other buildings on the same campus, and distances between floors.

TIPS

- Use icons to indicate the server, MDF, IDFs, wire drops, and other special designations.

- Include a key and scale to define the symbols and distances in your diagrams.

- Check that everything is readable when printed and copied onto an 8½-by-11-inch page.

- Show only as much detail as necessary. Door swings, windows, and other building details are not necessary to understanding the network installation.

- If you have access to building blueprints or building diagrams, and they are readable when reduced to standard letter page size, this will save you some drawing time. You need only mark the distances and network specifics on your reduced copies.

- The same diagramming tools that you may have or may purchase for doing the LAN/WAN diagrams may also work for drawing up the site plans.

E. Description of Proposed LAN/WAN

Now that you have a detailed and well-considered view of your organization's current network, along with all of the other information you have gathered so far, you can take a careful look at how you might need to change, enhance, or expand your LAN and WAN to support your organization's technology strategies.

Describe proposed changes, improvements, or additions to the things named in the current LAN and WAN description. Consider everything that was covered in the description of your organization's current LAN/WAN—network wiring standards, network speeds, network protocols, type of Internet connection, ISP, firewall, and remote access services or virtual private networks. In addition, include these items in your proposed solution:

- Which business process improvements do these changes or improvements support?

- How much will the changes or improvements cost? (Add these items to your budget reminder sheet [Worksheet 11.1] and be sure to include them in Section XV, Budget.)

- By what time does the organization need these changes or improvements? (Add this item to your timeline reminder sheet [Worksheet 11.2] and be sure to include it in Section XVI, Timeline.)

TIPS

- Consider each component of your LAN and WAN and the ways the individual improvements you envision will work together to provide a coherent network solution upon which to implement all of the other technology changes you have proposed.
- Be specific about which business process improvements the proposed changes will support. This will also help you make your organization's case to your board and potential funders.
- Consider each aspect of your network carefully. The overall implementation will be easier if you include everything in the plan and then decide what to implement first and what to postpone. Trying to integrate a critical element later on that was not planned for may be difficult if the infrastructure you created does not support it.
- When you are wiring for your LAN, consider adding more wire drops than you think the organization needs at this time. For example, it is less expensive in the long run to put two wire drops in an office once you have the labor available and the walls and ceiling opened up than it is to install one now and one later.

F. Proposed LAN/WAN Equipment Acquisitions

In the LAN/WAN equipment inventory, you identified upgrades and replacements for current equipment. You also accounted for the cost of these equipment improvements and the time investment in them. Now, in the proposed LAN/WAN equipment acquisitions subsection, describe, in narrative or table form, any new network equipment that will need to be added to your inventory. As you did for the proposed software and hardware acquisitions, answer the following questions:

- What do you want or need to acquire that is different from your planned upgrades and replacements?
- Which business process improvements do these acquisitions support?
- How much will the new equipment cost? (Add these items to your budget reminder sheet [Worksheet 11.1] and be sure to include them in Section XV, Budget.)
- By what time does the organization need this new equipment? (Add this item to your timeline reminder sheet [Worksheet 11.2] and be sure to include it in Section XVI, Implementation Timeline.)

Consider the same types of network equipment that you considered when taking your current inventory. For example, if you do not have a firewall, do you plan to install one? Do you need to connect additional users to a LAN so that you need additional switches or routers? Are you adding a remote site to a WAN so that you need a complete new complement of equipment, including Internet access and upgraded ISP service to the site? If your organization has or anticipates a large, complex network, do you need to acquire intelligent network devices? (In this context, *intelligent* refers to the equipment's ability to automate tasks such as diagnostics, routing, and communicating with several different devices.) If your organization has a multisite network, make sure that you link each proposed piece of equipment with its site.

TIPS

- Be general. (For example, say "24-port switch," rather than giving a specific manufacturer and model.) However, if you know exactly what equipment you need and have the ready means of acquiring it, there is no harm in stating the specifics as long as you document your minimum needs.

- If your organization anticipates significant network growth, an incremental investment in intelligent network equipment is advisable.

- Consider the facilities implications of the planned acquisitions. Such things as the wiring standard (how many feet of wire you can use before signal degradation is likely to occur), wiring closets, physical security, power, and air conditioning may all be affected. Keep notes about items you will need to include in Section IX, Facilities Plan.

G. Proposed LAN/WAN Logical Diagrams

The proposed LAN/WAN diagrams record your organization's plans for the future, providing a complete picture for readers, such as potential contractors to whom the agency has sent a request for proposal (RFP). As a rule of thumb, the components included in the diagrams for a *proposed* network should match those included for the *current* LAN and WAN, including separate diagrams for multiple sites or multiple floors of a multistory building. Although uncommon, an exception to this rule of thumb occurs when you are simplifying and consolidating network segments and equipment. In this case you may have fewer and simpler diagrams.

TIPS

- Review the guidelines and tips for drawing your *current* LAN/WAN diagrams. All the same guidelines and tips apply here.

- Indicate on the diagrams what is new, upgraded, or replaced. Placing annotations on the drawing (for example, "N," "U," or "R" next to the appropriate icon) or using varied icons are ways of making these indications. Make sure the diagram includes a key that indicates what any annotations mean.

H. Proposed Site Plan

In addition to a set of logical LAN and WAN diagrams for your organization's proposed network, you will need site diagrams that show any physical plant changes or new construction. If the organization requires minimal changes, you can start with the same site drawings that you used for the current site plans. If the site changes are extensive, you will need to draw completely new site plans.

Examples of physical site changes include moving the server to a new location, adding wiring to new offices, or adding a site to the organization's WAN. In the last case, you will need a site plan for the new site.

TIPS

- Review the guidelines and tips for drawing your current site plans. All those guidelines and tips apply to the proposed site plans as well.

- If the proposed site changes are small, indicate on the diagrams what is different from the original site plans.

- Major site changes will probably be obvious to readers, so do not clutter the diagrams with unnecessary annotations.

- As you did for your current site plans, indicate the distance of any new wire runs and the wiring standard that will be used.

- When the organization is not changing a physical site, you do not need this subsection of the technology plan. However, make that clear to the reader by stating simply that there are no changes to the site.

Examples

Example 15.1: Presentation Center, a medium-sized interfaith retreat and conference center (www.prescenter.org). This example is of a LAN and WAN equipment inventory and narrative for an agency that is moving from no local area network to a modest network to meet basic collaboration needs. Note that the inventory of the proposed equipment is simply listed in bulleted form. Because its LAN needs are simple, it has no need for a large equipment inventory table.

EXAMPLE 15.1

Presentation Center: LAN/WAN Narrative and Inventory

5. Network: LAN & WAN Equipment Inventory and Narrative

There is currently no LAN or WAN at this site.

5.1. Current LAN & WAN Equipment Inventory

5.1.a. Narrative N/A

5.1.b. Table N/A

5.2. Proposed LAN & WAN Equipment Acquisitions

The following equipment will be acquired for Phase I:

- Router—none
- **12 port, 10/100Mbps switches—FOUR**
- **24 port, 10/100Mbps switches—ONE**
- Hubs—none
- Remote access services—none
- Modems—none
- Firewalls—none
- Other:
    - **802.11b radios (Multifunction Bridges) and antennae (including cable from radio to antenna and mast to support antennae)—FIVE**
    - **Patch panel—FIVE**
    - **Server—ONE**
    - **CAT 5 wiring**
    - **Jacks, boxes, faceplates, and patch cords**

Phase II acquisitions, which are at least a year away, include the following:

- **Router—ONE**
- **Appropriate firewall**
- **Other equipment, at present unknown, which will be needed to establish the WAN**

Example 15.2: Hope Rehabilitation Services, a large, multicounty agency serving people with developmental disabilities (www.hopeservices.org). Because this organization is so large, only excerpts from the LAN/WAN equipment inventory and LAN/WAN narrative are included in this example. The narrative excerpt includes a general overview and description for one of several outlying sites, and typifies how a large, multisite organization might approach documenting complex information.

EXAMPLE 15.2

Hope Rehabilitation Services: LAN/WAN Narrative and Diagram

LAN Narrative & Diagrams

<u>General Discussion:</u> Hope networking currently consists of two primary sites, Fairway Glen and Whittier, which both have independent Microsoft Windows NT4 domains, NT4 servers, and IP/IPX-based local area networks. At each site there is also a legacy Novell Netware 3.12 server, both of which are in the process of being phased out as software is migrated to the NT servers. The two sites are connected by a T1, employing Cisco routers. There is also a T1 connecting a subsidiary site in Santa Cruz (Mattison Lane) and a T1 connection to an ISP for Internet connectivity. There are small NT servers in place, but not in use, at two of the remote sites, Mountain View and 10th Street. A third site, Clove Drive, has one of the small servers in use. All of these small servers have 64MB of RAM and will need to be upgraded to make them capable of serving users. Almost every NT4 server is in a separate Domain.

A. Current LAN

Mountain View

Presently Mountain View has CAT5 cabling in place, though the server is not connected to the cabling, or set up to serve the users there. This is preparatory to installing the server for general use there. When this is done, a 10Mbps 3Com switch will also be installed.

Cable Infrastructure: There are presently 15 drops at Mtn View, all terminating at a patch panel in a phone/electrical closet. All cabling is CAT5.

B. Proposed LANs

<u>Overview</u>

The LANs that are described for the remote sites will all be connected to the Fairway Glen hub by having a DSL connection to the Internet, and then by use of VPN software to provide a secure circuit. In this plan, a total of 8 DSL services will be employed for Hope to connect the 8 remote sites. Additionally, there may be some other costs for setting up the VPN connections that have not yet been defined. At present the cost of maintaining these connections is estimated to be only $1,192 per month for the 8 sites, and free initial installation has been promised.

As each LAN wiring is completed, a wiring diagram will be produced by the wiring contractor, to be kept in the IT files.

Mountain View

Mountain View currently has a complete set of LAN cabling, all CAT5, in place, terminating at a patch panel. A 3Com switch will be mounted on the wall below the patch panel, and 3-foot CAT5 patch cables will be used to connect from the switch to the patch panel. The server will also be set up in this room, and it will be connected to the switch directly. Connections from the switch to a Cisco DSL router will also be made from the switch.

C. New Proposed LANs

SITE	Changes	Business Process Supported	How?	By When Completed	Cost
Mtn View	Finish setup, install patch cables	7,21,22,25,26	Expansion, stability for users	12/15/00	$250.00
Total new cabling costs					$250.00

Example 15.3: Hope Rehabilitation Services, a large, multicounty agency serving people with developmental disabilities (www.hopeservices.org). This example is the LAN/WAN diagram for the large, multisite organization also cited in Example 15.2. It combines both a WAN diagram and LAN diagrams for some of the remote sites. Note that a complete diagram would show all sites across multiple pages.

Example 15.4: Child Care Coordinating Council of San Mateo County, Inc., a large agency that works on behalf of children, families, and early education professionals (www.thecouncil.net). The LAN/WAN diagram illustrated here shows a simple, single-site LAN configuration that can support just a few or many users. The WAN connection is simply a connection to the Internet.

Example 15.5: Unnamed Nonprofit (the name of this nonprofit has been withheld for security reasons), a medium-sized organization. The site plan shown here is clearly presented, with descriptive icons and a corresponding legend. Note that all rooms are labeled as to who occupies the space.

Example 15.6: EMQ Children and Family Services, a large, multisite, social services agency and provider of children's mental health (www.emq.org). This nonprofit has not only multiple sites but also multiple buildings at its main campus. This example shows building sizes, shapes, and locations; interconnectivity between buildings; and wire run lengths. Note the overview table at the top of the site plan, giving the pertinent information in compact form.

EXAMPLE 15.3

Hope Rehabilitation Services: LAN/WAN Diagram

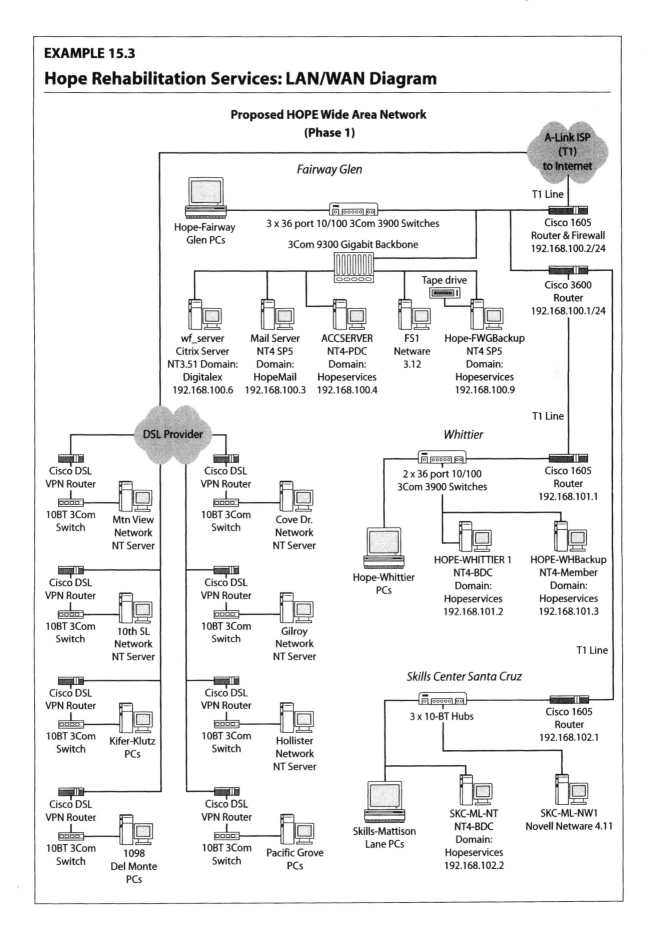

Proposed HOPE Wide Area Network
(Phase 1)

EXAMPLE 15.4

Child Care Coordinating Council of San Mateo County, Inc.: LAN/WAN Diagram

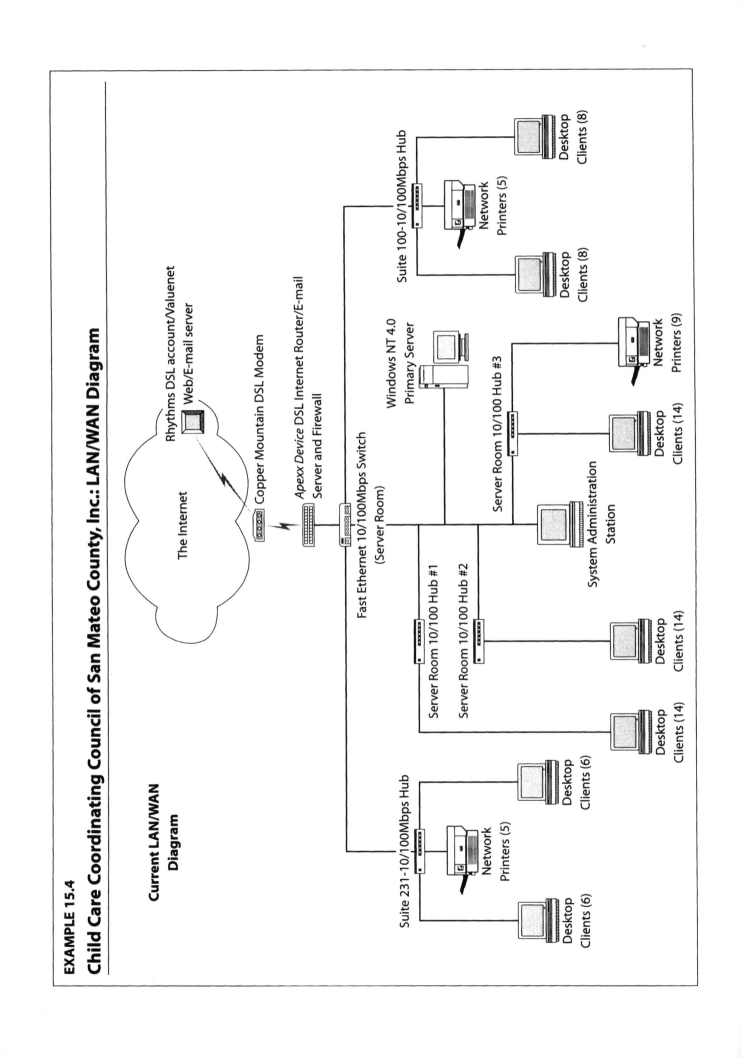

EXAMPLE 15.5

Unnamed Nonprofit: Site Plan Diagram

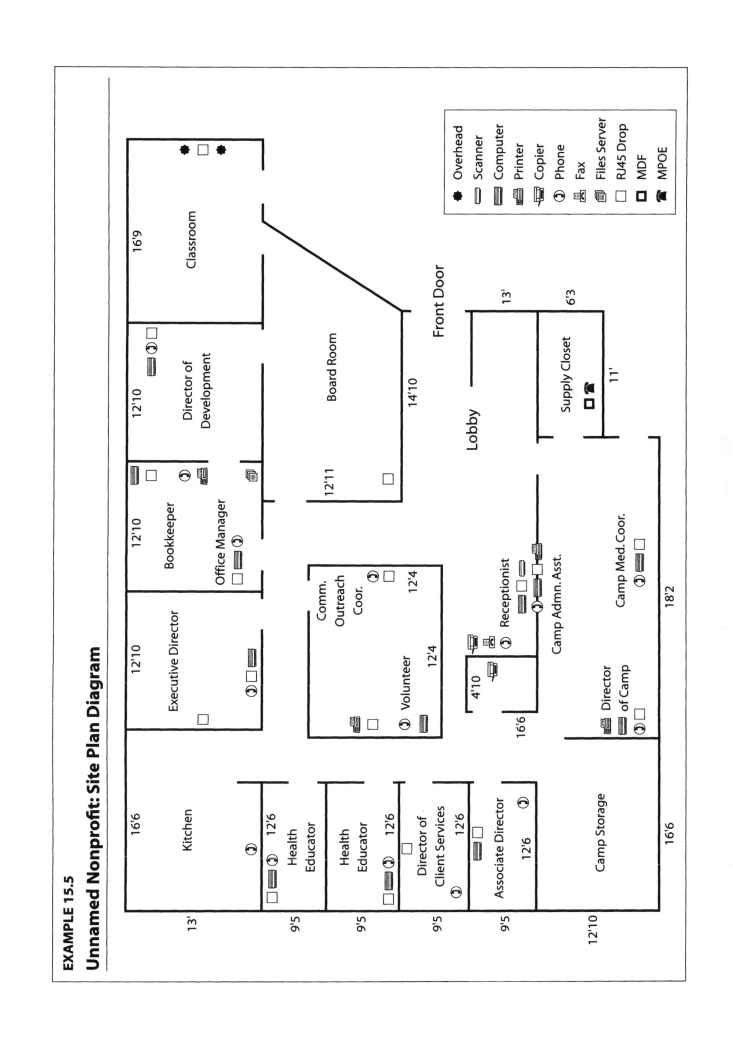

EXAMPLE 15.6

EMQ Children and Family Services: Site Plan Diagram

Campbell Campus Network Overview

| Fiber Optic Cable Runs | | | Stations Connected | | |
Building	Label	Length	Maximum	Current
Learning Ctr	G-F	80'	5	3
Access	G-H	200'	25	5
Hobbit	G-X-B	550'	25	20
Sierra	G-X-C	550'	5	3
Central Supply	G-X-D	550'	2	2
Wright	G	0'	30	25

Key
— Fiber optic cable, buried in conduit
– Fiber optic cable, in conduit inside
A Wire closet

(NOT TO SCALE)

Learning Center — 99 feet — F — 61 feet — To Mall — 45 feet — G — Wright — 46 feet — 42 feet — H — Clinical Services Building — 27 feet — 36 feet — H — Access — 45 feet — 58 feet — 195 feet — 150 feet — 27 feet — Hobbit — 96 feet — 69 feet — B — 39 feet — C — 64 feet — Sierra — 93 feet — X — 21 feet — Central Supply — D — 40 feet — N

WORKSHEET 15.1

LAN/WAN Equipment Inventory: Routers, Switches, Hubs, RAS, Modem/Pools, Firewall, and So Forth

	Qty.	Item Type	Item Name and Model	Brand	Software Version/ Release	Keep/ Upgrade/ Replace?
1.						
2.						
3.						
4.						
5.						
6.						
7.						
8.						
9.						
10.						
11.						
12.						
13.						
14.						
15.						
16.						
17.						
18.						
19.						
20.						
21.						
22.						
23.						
24.						
25.						
26.						
27.						

Chapter 16

Other Technologies

TWO ADDITIONAL CATEGORIES of technologies are considered in Section VIII of the technology plan: assistive technologies and business technologies. *Assistive technologies* comprise the equipment needed to accommodate people with disabilities. *Business technologies* include general business equipment, such items as phones, copiers, pagers, and fax machines. Although the technology plan places a heavy emphasis on network infrastructure and the technology equipment and tools people need to do specific jobs, it is important not to overlook these two additional types of technology. If changes or additions in either of these areas are needed, the impact on your organization's budget and implementation timeline should be clearly documented.

As you do in every other section of the technology plan, describe where your organization is now and where it needs to be. Include these subsections for the other technologies section:

A. Assistive technologies

    1. Current assistive technologies

    2. Proposed assistive technologies

B. Business technologies

    1. Current business technologies

    2. Proposed business technologies

A. Assistive Technologies

1. Current Assistive Technologies

This section provides a place to directly address any special needs people may have when using your organization's equipment and software. You are, in part, responding to the requirements of the Americans with Disabilities Act (ADA).[1] You are also responding to individuals' more general ergonomic needs. For example, do any of the organization's users experience hand or wrist syndromes that might be alleviated by a special keyboard or monitor stand? Does the organization need or want to take any preventative measures by supplying monitor stands or other special items for everyone?

Describe your agency's current strategies for providing assistive technologies. If it does not currently need to provide assistive technologies, simply state that fact.

2. Proposed Assistive Technologies

Describe future strategies for providing assistive technologies if and when it becomes necessary. Consider how accommodating people with special needs will help your organization meet its strategic goals and achieve its mission. Also consider any special ergonomic needs within your current user community. Include the following items in your discussion:

- Which business process improvements do the assistive technologies support?

- How will the organization train employees to use these technologies? (Add this information to Section XII, Training Plan.)

- If you anticipate specific assistive technology needs, what will the cost be? (Add these items to your budget reminder sheet [Worksheet 11.1] and be sure to include them in Section XV, Budget.)

- If you anticipate specific assistive technology needs, by what time must the organization meet these needs? (Add this item to your timeline reminder sheet [Worksheet 11.2] and be sure to include it in Section XVI, Implementation Timeline.)

TIPS

- Gather best practices and lessons learned from other nonprofits about the ways they address and identify appropriate assistive technologies (for many nonprofits, assistive technologies are an integral part of the services they provide to clients; they are far from being solely an employment issue).

---

1. A good resource to help you determine special needs is the ADA Technical Assistance Program. This program, which began in 1992, has built up a vast infrastructure of resources, including numerous ADA publications and videos, materials targeted to specific audiences, training packages, and an unparalleled knowledge of the ADA. The heart of the ADA Technical Assistance Program is its network of Disability Business Technical Assistance Centers (DBTACs). These centers provide public awareness, technical assistance, training, materials, and referrals and are located throughout the country.

- If you have a choice of equipment, consider choosing items with the fewest training issues, even though this may not be the least expensive option in the short run.

- If the agency does not have an immediate or foreseeable need for assistive technologies, state that it will address the matter at such time as the need arises. This tells readers that the organization is aware of the issue.

B. Business Technologies

1. Current Business Technologies

As you have with all other equipment, start by taking an inventory of what your organization currently owns. Look for such equipment as a local phone system (for example, Centrex, which supplies features the organization would otherwise have to get directly from a telephone company), cell phones, pagers, personal digital assistants (PDAs), and stand-alone copiers (as opposed to networked copiers that appear on the LAN/WAN inventory). Use Worksheet 16.1 for guidance. This inventory is quite simple, asking for each item's name and count, equipment type, network availability (yes or no), age or purchase date, and whether the item is leased or owned by the organization.

2. Proposed Business Technologies

What changes or additions to your business technologies does the organization need in order to meet its strategic goals? For example, is it paying for both cell phones and pagers for field personnel when a single integrated unit would do a better job less expensively? Does it need to provide each staff member with a telephone so she can retrieve messages and return calls more quickly and efficiently? As in all the technology plan sections, your discussion should be informed by the business process improvements and be reflected in your budget and timeline planning. In completing this subsection, consider these questions:

- Which business process improvements do these acquisitions support?

- How will the organization train employees to use these technologies? (Be sure to add this information to Section XII, Training Plan.)

- If you anticipate specific business technology needs, what will the cost be? (Add these items to your budget reminder sheet [Worksheet 11.1] and be sure to include them in Section XV, Budget.)

- If you anticipate specific business technology needs, by what time must the organization meet these needs? (Add this item to your timeline reminder sheet [Worksheet 11.2] and be sure to include it in Section XVI, Implementation Timeline.)

TIPS

- Consider multifunction machines. For example, if you need a fax and a copier and a printer, you may be able to purchase a single machine that does it all.

- Be sure local support and maintenance service is available for the equipment you consider.

- Ask other nonprofits about their experiences and recommendations.

- Avoid the "Gee whiz!" factor. Make sure that any "Gee whiz!" features are ones people will really use. For example, a color copier may be great, but does your organization really make so many color copies that the expense is justified? In this example, also consider the costs beyond the initial purchase of the copier, such as color ink cartridges.

- Try to select equipment that limits training issues. For example, will people need assistance to learn to use a fancy copier feature?

Examples

Example 16.1: Parents Helping Parents, Inc., of Santa Clara County, a medium-sized family resource center for parents of children with special needs (www.php.com). This example shows a comprehensive assistive technology section for a medium-sized organization that makes heavy use of assistive technologies.

Example 16.2: American Red Cross, Santa Clara Valley Chapter, a chapter of a national organization (www.redcross.org/ca/scv). This is an excellent example of wording for an organization that does not need to provide assistive technology but is aware that the need may arise in the future.

Example 16.3: Cupertino Community Services, a small, community-based organization (www.CupertinoCommunityServices.org). This example illustrates a simple narrative and companion chart that clearly lays out business technology needs.

EXAMPLE 16.1

Parents Helping Parents, Inc.: Other Technologies

9.1. Assistive Technologies

9.1a. Current assistive technologies

PHP is fortunate to have an Assistive Technology (AT) Department, known as The iTECH Center, with 1 staff member who is certified to perform Assistive Technology Assessments and another in the process of certification. We also have an Assistive Technology Information and Referral staff person as part of a contract we have through The Alliance for Assistive Technology.

When a staff person presents with a need for assistive technology due to a learning disability, visual or hearing impairment, or other condition, our assistive technology staff avail themselves to explore the best solution.

Given the population PHP serves it is critical to be 100% ADA (Americans with Disabilities Act) compliant. Many of the PHP staff and clients have children with mobility issues who require the use of wheelchairs and other mobility devices. PHP has provided the funding for all upgrades to our leased building.

PHP has implemented the following assistive devices and/or accommodations:

- TTY machine to accept calls from hearing impaired clients.
- The ability to check event dates and register for classes on our Web site.
- Links to all staff e-mail addresses are available on the Web site, enabling direct contact.
- Accessible restroom facilities on both floors of the building PHP leases at our own expense.
- Installation of ADA compliant power assisted doors, using available interior and exterior switches.
- Our main entrance areas have been modified to enable wheelchair accessibility. Even our garden area is wheelchair accessible.
- We have 4 disabled parking spaces at the front of our building, consistent with the 1 in 8 spaces being accessible. All are van accessible.
- In 2000, with CDBG (Community Development Block Grant) funding from the City of San Jose and through private donations, PHP installed an elevator to allow wheelchair access to the second floor.
- When setting up new workstations, we follow wheelchair accessible guidelines.
- Our Web site is "Bobby Approved." Bobby is a Web-based tool that analyzes Web pages for their accessibility to people with disabilities.
- A Web-based "Equipment Exchange" database for people to find or buy and give away or sell assistive devices.

9.1b. Proposed assistive technologies

PHP will continue to call upon our assistive technology staff to accommodate staff and the community. We are in the process of expanding our AT department resources and resources to offer the best technology available for trial prior to purchase to decrease the budget impact on the agency.

Another business plan is in development for the Assistive Technology Department. See Appendix F.

EXAMPLE 16.2

American Red Cross, Santa Clara Valley Chapter: Other Technologies

Assistive Technology

The Chapter does not currently require any assistive technologies. The need for assistive technology is continually undergoing evaluation. Assistive technology could be added at any time in response to a specific Chapter need.

EXAMPLE 16.3

Cupertino Community Services: Other Technologies

Business Technologies

Current business technologies

The majority of CCS's office equipment has been donated.

The current phone system has limited capabilities. All calls are received by the receptionist and are transferred to the appropriate staff. Callers wishing to leave a direct message to a staff must hang up and call a different number. Our voice-mail boxes are provided by Community Technology Alliance, a local nonprofit. We have 7 phones and 6 voice-mail boxes that are shared among 10 staff. Staff accessing voice-mail messages must dial out to the system that contains the voice-mail.

Our donated fax and leased copier are also inadequate for our potential growth due to their continual breakdowns. We currently have only one small shredder, located in the Executive Director's office.

An adequate pager is used by the Housing Services Program Director to respond to emergencies throughout the housing programs.

Current Business Technology Inventory

Qty	Type of Equipment	Item Name and Model	Network	Age	Lease or Own	Notes
1	Phone System	Phone	No	5 yrs	Own	Basic & inadequate
1	Fax	Fax	No	3 yrs	Own	Constant breakdowns
1	Copier	Copier	No	2 yrs	Lease	Constant breakdowns
1	Shredder	Shredder	No	1 yr	Own	Small unit
1	Pager	Pager	No	1 yr	Own	Adequate

Table 8: Business Technology Inventory

Proposed business technologies

The acquisition of new business technologies will occur with the completion of the new facility, in Phase II: Transition. A new telephone system will be acquired to meet our needs. We are currently working with the **Heart of Cupertino** contractor and Pacific Bell to determine the best system. Each office space and potential office space will have at least one phone hookup. The new system will allow for adequate voice mailboxes and the capability to add additional boxes as necessary. The receptionist will be able to transfer a caller to staff or his/her voice-mail box. Staff will also be able to access voice-mail directly from the system. This will directly address our process improvement goal **e. Improve telephone communication.**

Additionally, we will acquire better fax machines for both upper and lower levels in the new facility. We will acquire two copiers: a better model for administrative use, which will be located on the top floor, and a small copier will be available for small jobs on lower level.

Other Technologies Inventory

Qty.	Item Name and Model	Type of Equipment	Network Available?	Age or Purchase Date	Lease or Own?	Notes
1.						
2.						
3.						
4.						
5.						
6.						
7.						
8.						
9.						
10.						
11.						
12.						
13.						
14.						
15.						
16.						
17.						
18.						
19.						
20.						
21.						
22.						
23.						
24.						
25.						
26.						
27.						

Chapter 17

Facilities Plan

FACILITIES INCLUDE such things as wiring, electricity, air conditioning, locks on doors, building maintenance and upkeep, and modifications to the physical building, such as adding a door to a doorway that did not previously have one. Your proposed LAN and WAN configurations may require that some changes be made to your organization's site, or you may simply need to make changes in its facilities to support the current network. This section of your technology plan (Section IX in Resource A) will include these subsections:

A. Upgrades required

B. Impact of upgrades

A. Upgrades Required

Determine whether any upgrades to your organization's facilities are needed in order to implement the proposed network infrastructure. If your organization has multiple sites, check each site to determine the impact network improvements will have on it. Then describe all upgrades required to meet the agency's projected needs. Be sure to consider these questions:

- Is the *electricity* supply adequate and stable enough to support all of the anticipated servers, desktop computers, peripherals, and network equipment?

- Do you have enough *electrical circuits* to accommodate all of the equipment, plus a copier (which may require a separate circuit) and lunchroom appliances (which may require a separate circuit)?

- Do you have adequate *air conditioning* for servers in a locked room?

Computers, especially servers, are more sensitive to heat than people are.

- Do you need to install new or additional *network wiring?* If so, where must it be installed?
    - At different sites?
    - To additional places within one site?
    - To connect two or more sites?
- Do you need to improve the *physical security* of servers, network equipment, and other sensitive equipment? For example, will simply adding a lock to the door to the server room improve security?
- If your organization's office space is in a multitenant building, can outsiders access that space through a false ceiling? How can you *secure* your equipment and data in such an environment?
- Do you need to consider *natural disasters?* For example, in an area prone to earthquakes you need to anchor equipment racks and equipment to the building structure. Likewise, in an area prone to floods, you need to ensure that equipment is placed high enough to avoid water damage.

TIPS

- If your organization is in an older building or one that has been neglected, get an electrician to check out the power system.
- Similarly, get an HVAC expert to check out air-conditioning options.
- Be aware that servers need continuous air conditioning, twenty-four hours a day, even if heating and air conditioning are turned off in the rest of the building or office space during nonworking hours.
- Position equipment racks so that both the front and back are accessible for servicing.

B. Impact of Upgrades

Your planned upgrades could have significant impact on your organization's building, and require special permissions to carry out. Many of your upgrades may also have significant impact on both your budget and your timeline. Equipment purchases and installations need to be carefully timed in relation to the completion of facilities work. Consider these questions:

- Which business process improvements do these upgrades support?
- Can you easily punch holes in walls to pull wires through and install outlet jacks?
- Can you gain access to a false ceiling and run wire across it?

- Do you need to place wire runs outdoors to get to another building on your organization's campus? What are the permit requirements for this? Will the wiring need to run above ground or underground?

- Do you need to install conduit anywhere?

- Are there any fire code issues, such as required plenum air space, required plenum cable, or regulations that prohibit punching through building firewalls?

- Can people in your organization do the work or can your organization hire people directly, or is your organization required to go through its landlord?

- If your organization must go through its landlord, what documentation must you provide for the project and in what time frame? Will you have a long lead time to start work?

- How will having to work through the landlord affect the overall technology plan timeline?

- How much disruption will the upgrades cause to ongoing business?

- How much will the upgrades cost? (Add these items to your budget reminder sheet [Worksheet 11.1] and be sure to include them in Section XV, Budget.)

- By what time does the organization need these upgrades? (Add this item to your timeline reminder sheet [Worksheet 11.2] and be sure to include it in Section XVI, Implementation Timeline.)

TIPS

- Hire professionals to do the wiring. This expense will pay off in lower maintenance and repair costs.

- If you plan to use volunteer help to do the wiring, hire at least one professional to organize the work and oversee the volunteers so that you get the result you really want. For liability reasons, among others, you should not assign volunteers to such tasks as punching holes through walls or crawling through ceilings.

Examples

Example 17.1: Hope Rehabilitation Services, a large, multicounty agency serving people with developmental disabilities (www.hopeservices.org). This example shows the facility plan plus the impacts for eight sites, condensed into a table on a single page.

Example 17.2: Clara Mateo Alliance, Inc., a medium-sized organization providing shelter and supportive services for the homeless (www.clara-mateo.org). This example, from a small, single-site organization, presents facilities needs in a well-organized narrative.

EXAMPLE 17.1

Hope Rehabilitation Services: Facilities Plan

Facilities Plan

A. Upgrades Required to Meet Projected Needs (by site)

Site	Electricity	Air Conditioning	New Wiring Implications	Physical Security
Fairway Glen	Upgrade to 208v AC for total UPS requirements.	Has own air conditioning that is adequate.	May be fire code issues that need to be addressed.	Security is OK, locked room with coded security door.
Whittier	Upgrade to 208v AC for total UPS requirements.	Has own air conditioning that is adequate.	OK, recabling will be done to specifications.	Security not so good; servers are in file room available to any staff who need access to files. Will be building a wall and in-stalling a coded locked door.
Mountain View	May need clean reserved safe circuit outlet at server site.	Have rerouted air-conditioning duct for direct AC to server room (former utility room with phones and electrical).	None, all wiring completed.	Security OK, may want to put coded lock on door to server room.
10th St.	May need clean reserved safe circuit outlet at server site.	Building AC is OK, will be adequate for needs.	None at this time for projected wiring.	Security will be OK. Closet will be built to speci-fications with locked door.
Clove Dr.	May need clean reserved safe circuit outlet at server site.	Building AC is OK, will be adequate for needs.	None at this time for projected wiring replacing old.	Security will be OK. Closet will be built to speci-fications with locked door.

EXAMPLE 17.2

Clara Mateo Alliance, Inc.: Facilities Plan

10. Facilities Plan

10.1. UPGRADES REQUIRED TO MEET PROJECTED NEEDS

10.1.a. Electricity

Although the number of on-site personal computers in active use will increase from 22 to 37, the existing electrical capacity appears to be adequate to handle those units. However, the room where we would position our server and backup will need to be upgraded with the addition of two 20 amp 110 V circuits and an air vent from the air-conditioning system, as well as a hookup for a portable air-conditioning system.

10.1.b. Air Conditioning

While our site has air conditioning, the landlord controls its use. Currently the air conditioning runs during nights and weekends, but is shut down during critical usage periods by our landlord. Because of this, we will purchase an air-conditioning unit for the server closet and monitor ambient temperature in the closet for safety purposes.

10.1.c. Implications of New Wiring

Currently we do not have network wiring in the building; however, the entire building has false ceilings, which will simplify wire runs. To ensure compliance with fire codes, we will install plenum cable for any runs where fire hazard might be an issue. No outdoor wire runs will be necessary, since we are located in one building. At this point we do not think we need to add conduit before punching holes for wire runs and drops; however, this will be part of our request for proposal for installation of the CAT5 Wiring.

10.1.d. Physical Security

The doors to the server closet will remain closed and locked. Staff can get access to this room through the Operations Manager or the Associate Director. For emergencies, our landlord/police have keys to all our doors and a spare key will be kept in the Executive Director's safe. There is no alarm system: the need for one is currently under discussion. In addition we will increase our insurance to ensure replacement cost of equipment.

10.2. IMPACT OF UPGRADES

We will select a licensed electrical contractor to install the additional alternating current circuits needed for server room/closet at our own expense.

Experienced CAT5 installers will perform the installation of wire runs and drops, including punch downs in equipment rack installation, if necessary. Installation will be at our own expense.

The facilities upgrades are essential to all aspects of the technical plan, and support all the planned business process improvements. The installation of the CAT5 wire and server will probably occur during the September through November 2001 time frame. The AC electrical upgrade will occur by the end of May 2001.

Section 16, Budget, and section 17, Timeline, contain the dates and cost for acquiring this technology.

Chapter 18

Security Plan

SECURITY IS an issue that comes up many times in the technology plan. However, Section X, Security Plan, is the point in your technology plan when you present an overall unified view of your organization's security arrangements. What you say in this section ties together the threads of your proposals for software, hardware, network infrastructure (LAN/WAN), and facilities with respect to security.

Technology may or may not make data more vulnerable. For example, if your receptionist notes donations on a paper log, then leaves the paperwork on his desk when on a break, that information is vulnerable. Likewise, if the information is put in a password-protected database on the computer but the receptionist leaves that record open on the screen when he takes a break, the data is also vulnerable. There is no such thing as absolute security, whether your agency's information is stored in paper files or on the computer, but this section of your technology plan documents how your agency plans to mitigate security breaches as much as possible.

Three kinds of security—information, physical, and system—are documented here:

Information security protects confidential information from data theft. Protecting any confidential information gathered by your organization is critically important. Confidential information may range from client information to the credit card numbers of donors. In particular, if your organization is subject to HIPPA requirements (see Chapter Twelve), it will need to take special measures to be in compliance.

Physical security protects equipment against theft and physical tampering.

System security protects network systems against software intrusion from viruses, worms, Trojan horses, and the like.

In the technology plan, discuss all three types of security for all the types of equipment and network services your organization has. Include these subsections:

A. Current security arrangements

B. Proposed security plan

A. Current Security Arrangements

Describe the security measures your organization currently has in place.

For *server* security consider these issues:

- Physical location. Are servers out in the open or behind a locked door? Are they as protected as possible from natural disasters such as floods and earthquakes?
- Access to shared databases.
- Access to e-mail accounts and e-mail messages.
- Access to server accounts and privilege definitions.
- Antivirus measures, including frequency of definition updates.
- Backup procedures, including frequency of backing up and the media used for storage.
- Frequency and types of software updates, such as service packs, patches, or bug fixes.

For *desktop* and *laptop* security consider these issues:

- Desktop password protection for desktop computers that may store confidential or sensitive information or that are in a publicly accessible area.
- Startup password protection, so that if a computer or laptop is lost or stolen it will present a barrier to use.
- Antivirus software, including frequency of definition updates.
- Backup procedures, including frequency of backups.
- Software updates, such as service packs, patches, or bug fixes.
- Physical security. Are your organization's computers locked to desks? Are they as protected as possible from natural disasters such as floods and earthquakes?
- Current disaster recovery plan. For example, in the event of a fire or natural disaster, how will you recover your data?

For *network equipment* security consider these issues:

- Physical security. Is network equipment easily accessible or behind a locked door? Is it safe from a natural disaster such as a flood or an earthquake?

- Firewall. Is one installed and appropriately configured?

  For *Web site* security consider these issues:

- Physical security if your organization hosts its own Web site.

- The security your Web hosting service provides if your organization does not host its own Web site.

- If staff post data from a shared database, who has access to what data and how is that access limited?

- Firewall. Is one installed and appropriately configured?

- Current disaster recovery plan. For example, in the event of a fire or natural disaster, how will you recover your data?

TIPS

- If you organize your description by type of equipment and service, as the previous lists are organized, then discuss the three categories of security (information, physical, and system) for each type of equipment and service.

- If you organize your description by category of security (information, physical, and system), then discuss each equipment type within each category that applies. Choose the method that seems most appropriate to you.

B. Proposed Security Plan

Determine what you are trying to protect and from whom. Carefully assess your organization's current security measures and identify any holes or vulnerabilities. For example, are virus definition updates downloaded and installed on a frequent and regular basis or somewhat haphazardly? Does the server and network equipment room have a door that locks, but no one ever bothers to lock it and the key is lost anyway? Are laptops used by personnel in the field brought into the office to have virus updates and software updates installed or to have files backed up? Construct your own scenarios by asking "What if . . ." for each of the issues in the bulleted lists you just considered when addressing current security arrangements.

Describe where improvements could be or should be made. Consider these questions in your analysis:

- Which business process improvements do these measures support? Note that the relationship between business process improvements and security may be somewhat indirect because most security precautions are simply part of good business practices. You should, nevertheless, consider the question. For example, if your organization handles very sensitive data, such as patient records, security is absolutely mission critical to your agency and relates strongly to your business processes. However, if your organization does not handle any confidential data, and has no plans to do so, then devising and implementing numerous security plans to protect information confidentiality is of no particular use and will only use up valuable resources.

- Does your organization have a disaster recovery plan? In the event of a fire or natural disaster, will your data be safe and recoverable?

- Is training needed on new security software and procedures? (Add this information to your discussion in Section XII, Training Plan.)

- How much will the proposed security plans cost? (Add these items to your budget reminder sheet [Worksheet 11.1] and be sure to include them in Section XV, Budget.)

- By what time does the organization need these proposed security plans? (Add this item to your timeline reminder sheet [Worksheet 11.2] and be sure to include it in Section XVI, Implementation Timeline.)

Security is a trade-off between the degree of security you want and what you can afford. Remember, there is no such thing as absolute security. You can, however, take the best precautions possible given your organization's environmental and resource constraints. Here are some tools that can help your organization to take these precautionary measures:

Passwords. Passwords are usually the first line of defense against unauthorized intrusion to systems. However, many people use passwords that are obvious and easy to crack. Such things as a spouse's, pet's, or child's name are easy to guess, as are street addresses and telephone numbers and descriptive terms like "admin." Using passwords like these provides little protection. Encourage users to be creative about their passwords. Think also about how often you will require users to change their passwords and whether or not they should personally choose them or have the passwords assigned to them. The trade-off is that if passwords must be changed often and are assigned, users are more likely to write them down so as not to forget them, especially if the passwords are complicated strings of letters and numbers that people find impossible to remember. Passwords should be memorized, not written down. A note tacked onto a monitor or put in a pencil drawer, for example, makes it easy for anyone to discover the password.

Antivirus software. Installing this software is one of the easiest security measures to take against intrusion by viruses, worms, Trojan horses, and other bad software. However, for optimal protection, virus definitions must be updated frequently and regularly. This procedure can be automated by configuring equipment to perform the updates automatically at night when usage is low. Alternatively, you can configure computers to automatically update when they are first turned on in the morning.

Laptop security measures. Laptops need special security measures and procedures because they are designed to travel with a user and therefore may not always be under the organization's immediate protection. Requiring the user to log on with a user name and password when the computer is started up provides some deterrent to unauthorized access. Procedures that require laptop users to regularly update virus definitions and software and make backups are also a good idea. Or institute a policy that requires users to bring their laptops into the office on a regular basis to take care of these maintenance tasks.

Backups. Back up hard disks regularly on all servers. Instituting backup procedures for data stored on desktop computers and laptops is also advised. Establish a regular backup tape rotation if you are using a tape backup solution. Provide for off-site media storage of periodic major backups. Then, if a disaster occurs on site, your organization will not lose all its data.

TIPS

- If security improvements related to new equipment are needed, the improvements should be made when the new equipment is deployed, not later.

- Develop a disaster recovery plan if you do not already have one.

- Be aware that one advantage of allowing an Internet service provider (ISP) to host your Web site is that the ISP is responsible for security and the Web site host is isolated from your network, reducing your security concerns for that network.

- You do not need a firewall if dial-up access to ISP accounts is the only access to the Internet allowed on your organization's network.

Examples

Example 18.1: Junior Achievement of the Bay Area, Inc., a medium-sized education service organization (www.jaba.org). This example clearly describes security measures in a narrative format, with the proposed security focused only on identified needs.

Example 18.2: Parents Helping Parents, Inc., of Santa Clara County, a medium-sized family resource center for parents of children with special needs (www.php.com). This example shows current and proposed security measures side-by-side, in tabular form. Note also the specific mention of protection categories.

EXAMPLE 18.1

Junior Achievement of the Bay Area, Inc.: Security Plan

Security Plan
Current security arrangements
Servers

The JABA server is located in a locked space in the main office. The door is keyless entry, requiring an access code. Access to JABA data and accounts requires all users to log onto a workstation as well as log in to the database applications. The servers' local drives are backed up during the early morning. The RE database engine is shut down for the duration of the backup, which runs daily, in the early morning, Monday through Friday. These tapes are kept on site and overwritten weekly. A series of tapes made in the early morning on Saturdays are taken off site Monday evenings, stored at the responsible staff member's home, and brought in again in rotation, being overwritten approximately monthly. JABA has just received Norton AntiVirus software and plans to install immediately on the terminal server. The mail service is protected by Norton AntiVirus for Exchange.

User computers

The JABA main office is located in a secure office building with adequate security, with the office space requiring a key. JABA does not lock down workstations with cable or other physical security device. Laptops are taken home with the employee or locked away at the end of the day. Laptops are lent out to JABA telecommuters with the expectation that they will use the laptops only for work purposes, and will return them should they secure employment elsewhere or have purchased their own. JABA has just received Norton AntiVirus software and plans to install immediately. Means of automating updating virus signatures on user computers will be investigated, but laptops and LAN-attached workstations, being too rarely connected to the LAN, will probably require some user attention. Remote workstations and laptops are configured with a batch file to archive recently modified files to a ZIP file when Windows starts. The backup file is stored on a separate physical hard drive, if available. Laptop users are also encouraged to save all of their files to their share on the file server periodically.

Network equipment

Network equipment is located in the same secure space as the server. There is no firewall protection at this time.

Web site

Because JABA has its own server, the physical security of the JABA Web site is not compromised. However, with the rise of nonprofits as target for hackers, JABA has recognized the necessity of a firewall to ensure the security of the entire network.

Proposed security plan
Firewall

JABA has been in communication with vendors and donors, with little success, to obtain a firewall for the JABA network. JABA hopes to obtain a firewall through the resource bank. The timing of this implementation will therefore probably depend on the availability of resource bank hardware. Of all new implementations discussed in this technology plan, the installation and configuration of the firewall are the most likely to require the services of an outside consultant. Such services would probably be contracted for no more than the installation, configuration, and testing of the firewall. Consulting services were budgeted as a contingency item for fiscal year 2000–2001. The estimated retail hardware cost to install a firewall with VPN support on the JABA site would be $2,669.

EXAMPLE 18.2

Parents Helping Parents, Inc.: Security Plan

11. Security Plan

11.1a. Desktop Computers

Current	Proposed
Desktop Protection: We are transitioning to Windows 2000, offering improved security. PHP's LAN requires passwords to gain access though Windows 98, provides less security to the desktop files and applications.	Windows 2000 installed on all PCs by June 2001.
Virus Protection: Antivirus software is installed all desktops. Once a month, we update the "DAT" files in order to maintain proper protection against new viruses that may be circulating around our Intranet and Internet, or in response to any new major virus alert.	All mail packets from the gateway will arrive through a hardware virus filter to maintain a virus free Intranet. Acquire service by December 2001. Users will continue to have virus protection on their desktops.
Theft Prevention: We lack a consistent prevention method for publicly placed machines. Most offices have locked office doors and laptops are always stored in those offices in a desk drawer.	In any public area desktops and laptops secured with cable/locking mechanisms will be attached by January 2002.
Backup Procedures: PHP staff are encouraged to save their files to the specified network drive to be included in an automatic nightly tape backup. Most staff save files of significant value to the shared drive. Tapes are changed daily each morning. Tapes are overwritten every 10th day. We also occasionally use a Zip drive to save a group of files. Tapes are kept with the IS department staff as we have no other off-site location to store our data.	None planned.
Software Updates: Service Packs for our Windows 2000 work-stations are updated as they are released. Other software such as the Office 2000 line is updated as patches are released.	None planned.

Chapter 19

Technology Support Plan

SECTION XI of the technology plan is divided into two parts. The first part documents how you will support your organization's technology, and the second part documents how you will maintain it over time. *Support* is the ongoing work required after something is installed (for hardware) or implemented (for software) to ensure that the system can continue to be successfully employed by users. *Maintenance* is the ongoing work required after something is installed or implemented to keep the environment running smoothly.

The key to a successful technology support plan is to always remember that technology is there to serve the end-users, not for the end-users to support the technology. Whenever there is a choice of actions in a support matter, choose the one that will make the end-user's life easier, not the support technician's. This is important to keep in mind while describing your organization's current and proposed end-user support and maintenance procedures.

This section of the technology plan follows the same pattern as previous sections. First, you will document how your organization *currently* conducts technology support and maintenance, and second, you will propose how it will conduct support and maintenance in the *future*.

This section of your technology plan should include these subsections:

A. Current end-user support

B. Proposed end-user support

C. Current periodic maintenance

D. Proposed periodic maintenance

A. Current End-User Support

End-user support typically involves answering user questions and resolving any bugs or issues that arise from either hardware or software. It is sometimes difficult to determine the cause of a problem when it is first reported. It may take a few rounds of investigation to gather enough information to provide a solution to the user. The manner in which the problem is first reported and the manner in which investigation proceeds are important both for finding a solution and for meeting the needs of the user. The sequence of steps to be followed by an end-user or technical support person to resolve a user's problem is called an *escalation path*. The escalation path begins with the simplest things to try, such as rebooting the computer, and moves on to increasingly complicated things to try and progressively more expert people to contact until the problem is resolved.

In this section, describe your organization's current end-user support procedures and escalation path. Remember to address both local users (those who use the network on site) and remote users (those who access the network off site: for example, staff working from home or clients accessing the organization's Web site). Consider these questions:

- What should end-users do when they first encounter a problem? For example, they might check to see that all the cords are attached firmly and plugged into the appropriate places and then reboot the system.

- Whom do users call when they have a problem that they cannot fix themselves? For example, does the organization have an *accidental techie*—someone whose regular job is not related to technology support but who is relied on for her technical expertise—whom people frequently call for help?

- Whom does that person call when she cannot solve the problem? These are your first- and second-level resources.

- How is problem resolution communicated back to the end-user who first reported the difficulty?

- Are problems ever left "pending," with no way to close the loop and provide resolution?

- Can end-users reach a live human being when they report a problem, or are they connected to a voice-mail system or an e-mail name?

- If end-users cannot reach a human being, how are they assured that their problem report was received?

- Does the organization maintain a log of all problems reported, progress on finding solutions, and final resolutions?

TIPS

- An escalation path can be concisely presented in flowchart format, starting with "User reports problem," ending with "User receives resolution," and showing all the steps in between and who takes what actions toward resolution.

B. Proposed End-User Support

You will probably identify areas for end-user support improvement fairly quickly. Use the list of questions just posed to help determine whether changes are needed. Also consider these additional factors:

- Do you need to improve problem reporting procedures?

- Do you need to improve problem report record keeping?

- Do you need to acquire any software or hardware tools to aid in problem tracking, diagnosis, and repair or in evaluation of system health?

- Do current procedures accommodate remote sites and personnel working in the field?

- Will any new hardware or software you propose to acquire present any special end-user support issues? For example, software that is used by just a few people or maybe only one person may require specific technical knowledge for its support.

- Which business process improvements do these changes support? Note that the relationship between business process improvements and technology support may be somewhat indirect because most technology support procedures are simply part of good business practices. The question, nevertheless, needs to be addressed. For example, it is inadvisable to devise a plan to handle requests from workers in the field simply because you might have such a situation in the *far distant* future.

- How much will the proposed improvements cost? (Add these items to your budget reminder sheet [Worksheet 11.1] and be sure to include them in Section XV, Budget.)

- By what time does the organization need these changes? (Add this item to your timeline reminder sheet [Worksheet 11.2] and be sure to include it in Section XVI, Implementation Timeline.)

TIPS

- *Written* escalation procedures are recommended so that every end-user can have a copy to use when the need arises.

- Problem report tracking logs are a useful tool for tracking when problems are reported, by whom, what steps are taken to resolve them, and what resolution is found. Although such logs may be kept by hand, maintaining them on-line in a database can prove very useful when you need to analyze problem trends and data or look up old problems for some reason.

C. Current Periodic Maintenance

The term *periodic maintenance* covers all the tasks undertaken to keep equipment in good working order. Describe your organization's current periodic maintenance procedures, including virus definition updates, virus scans, software patches and bug fixes, software version upgrades, scheduled printer maintenance, and disk defragmentation.

For each item include the following information:

- A brief description.

- Who does it.

- When the person does it.

- On what equipment it is performed. There may be differences in procedures for servers and desktop or laptop computers.

- How it is done for remote sites.

D. Proposed Periodic Maintenance

You will probably identify areas for periodic maintenance improvement fairly quickly. Use the list of questions posed earlier to help you determine whether changes are needed. Also consider these additional factors:

- Do you need to improve your periodic maintenance procedures?

- Should you establish set schedules for certain types of maintenance, such as virus scans or disk defragmentation?

- Do you need to acquire any software or hardware tools to aid in carrying out periodic maintenance?

- How are remote sites or personnel working in the field serviced?

- Will new hardware or software you propose to acquire present any special maintenance needs?

- Which business process improvements do these changes support? Note that the relationship between business process improvements and periodic maintenance may be somewhat indirect because most maintenance procedures are simply part of good business practices. You should, nevertheless, consider the question.

- What will the proposed improvements cost? This is particularly important to make note of if you plan to purchase software or hardware tools to help with maintenance or if you need to add personnel to service remote sites. (Add these items to your budget reminder sheet [Worksheet 11.1] and include them in Section XV, Budget.)

By what time do you need the changes? For example, should you establish a regular virus definition update schedule immediately? (Add this item to your timeline reminder sheet [Worksheet 11.2] and include it in Section XVI, Timeline.)

TIPS

- Maintenance fees are usually a wise investment for any hardware or software that you do not plan to heavily modify and that has a life span of greater than one year.

- *Written* maintenance procedures are recommended.

- Think about establishing formal *service level agreements* with your vendors.

Also take the time to consider these support and maintenance staffing issues. IT support and maintenance can be staffed in several ways. Medium- to large-sized organizations usually have at least one full-time IT staff member, and some nonprofits even have IT departments. In some cases, usually at the smaller organizations, the more technology-proficient staff members assist with support and maintenance, adding these tasks to their existing job (that is, they become accidental techies). If you have accidental techies in your organization, it is advisable to formalize their role so that their workloads can be accommodated to the additional responsibilities. Many organizations outsource their IT support and maintenance, relying on consultants. This is effective for small to medium-sized organizations, but larger organizations are likely to need full-time staff in house.

Other sources of support and maintenance staff are volunteers and students. Use these resources judiciously. Volunteers often like to learn and practice new skills, but make sure that they work within your guidelines and procedures and that they have accountability, even if it is not fiscal (see Chapter Eight). If your organization chooses to enlist volunteers and students, it is advisable to have one full-time staff member to oversee their work and provide direction so that organizational technology support standards can be maintained.

Examples

Example 19.1: San Jose Repertory Theatre, a large arts organization (www.sjrep.org).
This example illustrates both current and proposed escalation paths in flowchart form, so the changes are easy to spot.

EXAMPLE 19.1a

San Jose Repertory Theatre: Technology Support Plan

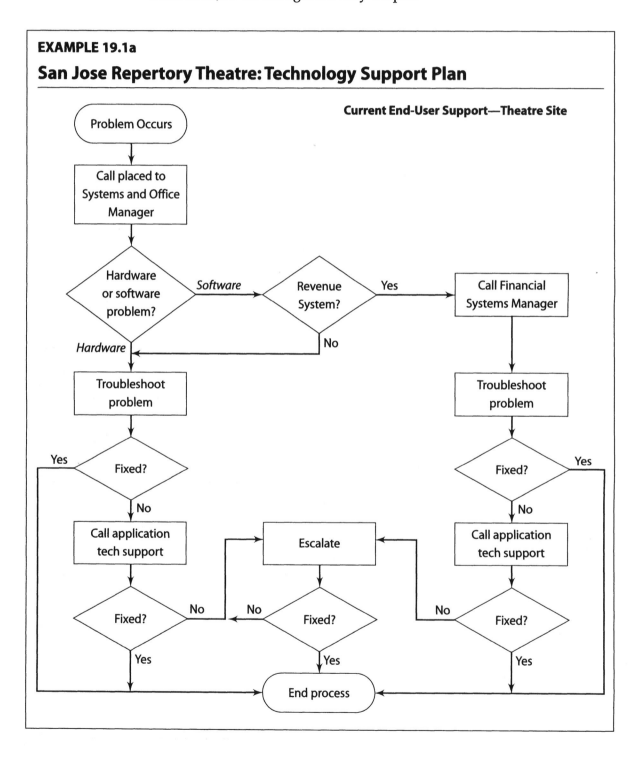

EXAMPLE 19.1b

San Jose Repertory Theatre: Technology Support Plan

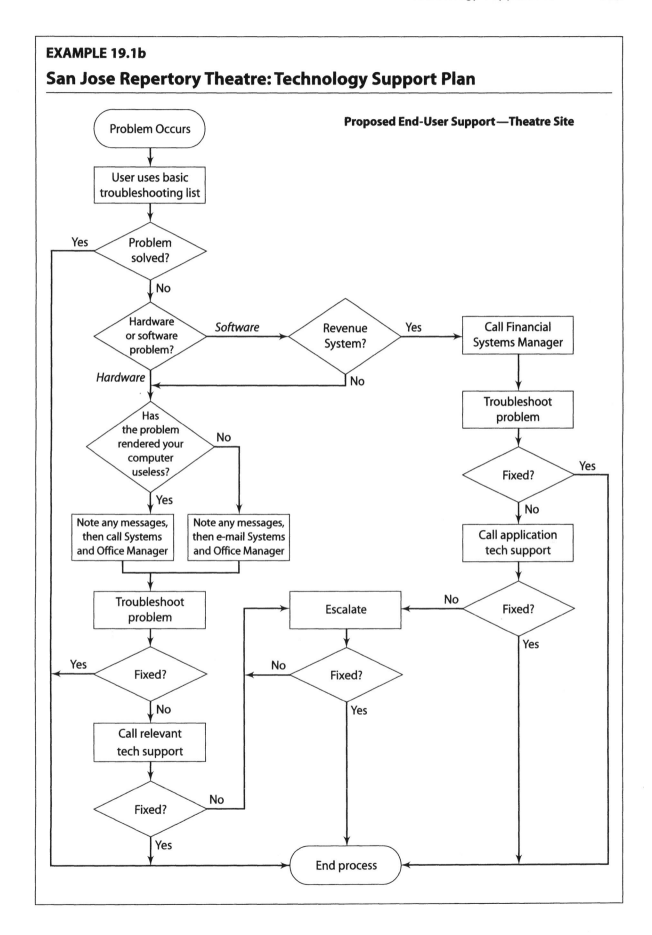

Example 19.2: Cupertino Community Services, a small, community-based organization (www.CupertinoCommunityServices.org). This example shows current and proposed end-user support in narrative form.

EXAMPLE 19.2

Cupertino Community Services: Technology Support Plan

Current End-User Support

Support Procedures

Currently, the CCS staff has a wide range of computer skill levels. Basic troubleshooting proves to be a problem for several staff. For this reason, the two staff most comfortable with computers spend a large amount of time as accidental IT professionals. Should these staff members be unable to cure the situation, CCS's IT Consultant will be called.

Proposed End-User Support

Support Procedures

CCS's accidental techies (the Housing Services Program Director or the Executive Director-AT) and the IT Consultant will compile troubleshooting guidelines and provide training to each staff. The training will begin with basic operations and troubleshooting. Each staff will have a clear set of procedures to follow, with clear instructions of who and when to call for assistance.

When a problem occurs, the staff will conduct preliminary troubleshooting. If the problem is not solved, the staff will call the AT.

The AT will determine the type of problem. In the case of software related problems or questions, the AT will try to solve the problem. If a higher level of support is required, the AT will contact the vendor to obtain software support on the product. All software purchased will come with support except for the MS Windows 2000 operating system. If the problem cannot be fixed, it will be escalated to the IT Contractor.

If the problem is hardware related, and the AT cannot fix it, the AT will contact the IT Consultant to assess the problem(s). He will contact the vendor or manufacturer for warranty or support on the product. All new computers and monitors to be purchased will carry a 3-year on-site warranty.

The IT Consultant will make regular monthly maintenance visits, at which time the AT will provide an update of all noncritical problems encountered in the previous month. However, if during the month the AT determines that a problem is critical and requires attention, the IT Consultant will be contacted immediately.

The users will keep a standard log for their workstation of each unusual occurrence that was resolved.

Example 19.3: San Jose Repertory Theatre, a large arts organization (www.sjrep.org). This example gives periodic maintenance information in a clear narrative.

EXAMPLE 19.3

San Jose Repertory Theatre: Technology Support Plan

10.3. Current Periodic Maintenance

Due to the size and locations of the company, periodic maintenance is not carried out on a regular basis. When problems occur, Scandisk is run immediately and temp files and cookies cleaned out from Microsoft programs and Netscape. As most workstations do not have their antivirus engines activated due to conflicts with other (shared database) programs, updates are not installed. Defragmentation of local disks to optimize space is carried out periodically, especially if it is known that programs have been installed or removed and problems are observed.

Software patches and service packs are currently installed only when serious problems have occurred that require outside vendor support (who perform any installations necessary), or when any network hardware is added. Firewall firmware patches have been installed every six months since its installation in Fall 2000.

Printers do not presently undergo any periodic maintenance, but support vendors are used when problems arise.

10.4. Proposed Periodic Maintenance

We aim to service all desktop computers' maintenance needs on both permanent sites through quarterly visits. (It is foreseeable that memory upgrades for desktops will usually be added at the time of purchase.) We would like to see printers serviced once a year, before our regular performance season opens.

Service packs for software programs, operating systems, and the firewalls will be installed twelve times a year, and the Norton AntiVirus package comes with a two-year automatic software and virus definition update option that we expect to buy.

We also intend to update productivity, office, and graphics software once a year, or as needed.

Chapter 20

Training Plan

TRAINING IS the companion to good support for technology users. Effective training for your organization's users is critical to their successful use of technology. Even with state-of-the-art equipment and up-to-date software, your organization's investment may go to waste if its users do not know how to use the capabilities offered. Those for whom training may be important are employees, volunteers, clients, new hires, new volunteers, accidental techies and peer experts (technology support training), and technology support staff (advanced technology support training).

An organization may benefit from providing training on numerous topics, covering the spectrum from basic computer use through use of highly specialized software. The methods of providing training are also numerous, ranging from using in-house expertise to sending personnel to special courses presented by vendors.

Section XII, Training Plan, of the technology plan will cover all these areas, and should include these subsections:

A. Current training methods and practices

B. Proposed training methods and practices

A. Current Training Methods and Practices

In this subsection, describe how training is provided to your organization's various users. Explain what training the organization currently provides, and how it determines what training is needed. Consider these questions:

- Does the organization survey its users to find out what training they think they need? Or does it provide standard training classes to everyone?

- Are users expected to do some basic troubleshooting on their own computers? If so, do they know what to look for? What do you expect them to be able to do?

- Does the organization provide training on software commonly used in the organization? For example, does the organization use a set of word processing templates for letters, memos, and other business communications that users need to know about?

- Does the organization provide training on hardware commonly used in the organization? For example, how do new hires get their server account user names and e-mail names, and how do they log on to the server? Can users change the toner cartridge in a printer?

- Do users know how to use the features on such general office equipment as the photocopier or fax machine?

- Do users need to know the policies for entering data, querying, and creating reports in a shared database, so that consistency is maintained across all users?

- Does the organization have specialized software that only a few people need to know how to use? How do these users receive any specialized training they need?

- Does the organization plan for a certain amount of training annually for its technology support staff so they can keep up with technology developments?

TIPS

- Remember to include informal training, such as peer mentoring, in your documentation.

- Be honest about your current training practices. It is not uncommon for an organization to have training needs that have not yet been addressed. By stating the needs up front now, you will be able to avoid obscuring your needs later on.

B. Proposed Training Methods and Practices

Many problems that arise when implementing technology can be solved with good training. Without training, productivity may lag and frustrations may increase. Without training, making the technology changes posed in your plan may become a cause of stress rather than of improvements. In this subsection, you are documenting the current training practices that meet training needs satisfactorily and then determining the training practices that need to be implemented or improved. Remember, new hardware or software will usually require that people receive additional training before they can use these tools effectively.

When evaluating your organization's training practices, keep in mind the many ways in which people learn. Some do well in formal classroom settings, whereas others do better one-on-one with a peer. Still others may prefer learning by reading the user manual. Use both the list of questions from the previous subsection and an understanding of learning styles as guides as you plan the ways you might improve training. In describing your proposed training methods and practices, also consider these additional questions:

- Do current training procedures, methods, or topics need to be modified in order to accommodate users who currently receive little or no training? For example, perhaps all new hires need to be trained in the same basic information about your organization's technology.

- Can the organization improve the way it determines who needs what type of training? For example, might user self-evaluations reveal where pockets of inadequate training or user frustration exist in your organization?

- Will new training needs be created by new technology acquisitions?

- Are there topics on which little or no training is available when it should be?

- How much training can be handled efficiently and effectively in house?

- Does the organization need to hire a professional trainer on a full-time or occasional basis?

- Can the organization send people to outside classes or seminars? How often might it need to do this?

- Will training videotapes or CD-ROMs or computer-based training meet the needs of some people?

- Is a consultant needed to develop some standard in-house training courses?

- Do users at remote sites or personnel in the field have the same access to training as staff at the organization's central location?

- Which business process improvements do these acquisitions support? Note that although good training methods and procedures are part of good business practice, the relationship between business process improvements and training may also be explicit and direct. For example, you may need to improve the time it takes to perform data entry for new clients. The solution may be to improve training on data entry procedures. Even when the relationship is not so obvious, it is still advisable to consider the question.

- What will the proposed training improvements cost? For example, what might you spend hiring a consultant to develop some in-house courses? (Add these items to your budget reminder sheet [Worksheet 11.1] and include them Section XV, Budget.)

- By what time do you need the training improvements? (Add this item to your timeline reminder sheet [Worksheet 11.2] and include it in Section XVI, Implementation Timeline.)

TIPS

- Consider computer-based training. Software vendors often include guided tours of the software on the product CD.

- Consider collaborating with other nonprofits to share a trainer when the organizations' users need similar training. Many trainers offer per person discounts for larger groups of trainees.

- Determine whether a series of short presentations—for example, over lunch—could cover some training topics adequately. Often people need to know only a couple of things to move forward, or they may prefer to learn only two or three new things at a time.

- Think about how you can prioritize your training proposals so that you implement the ones that will deliver the most impact first.

- Consider using a *training plan matrix* to help you organize the process of identifying training needs. Worksheet 20.1 offers such a matrix for you to fill in. Be sure to begin by adapting the column and row heads to your organization's personnel and their training needs.

Example

Example 20.1: Presentation Center, a medium-sized interfaith retreat and conference center (www.prescenter.org). This example provides comprehensive training information. Included is a fun chart showing all staff members' computer skill levels; a table summarizing the types of training, who will be involved, and who will train; and a narrative about types of training for different categories of users.

EXAMPLE 20.1

Presentation Center: Training Plan

12. Training Plan

12.1. Current Training Methods and Practices

Currently Presentation Center has no specific computer-training plan. Employees are hired with the job description designating specific computer skills, if applicable. Because the Center has no current network, computer skills required have been limited to familiarity/experience with Microsoft Office (primarily Word and Excel), PeachTree Accounting, and DonorPerfect. The reservations process is made up of Word documents for contracts and correspondence and simple Excel spreadsheets for schedules and calendars. No specific orientation is given to employees for computer use.

Ongoing training for staff is limited to individual requests for workshops or tutorial software programs. There is no systematic computer education. The Center has no formal on-site tech support; individuals simply ask other employees for basic help. See Section 12 End-User Support Plan for current troubleshooting procedures.

12.2 Proposed Training Methods and Practices

The Center is in the process of determining necessary computer skills for each job position. The following chart shows the desired skill set for each employee and includes the software components that will be part of the Technology Plan.

This Training plan will be evaluated as the individual software components are acquired and put into use. In some cases this person has not yet been identified. As new employees are hired, they will be trained on the necessary programs. Some positions will require that a new hire already have a certain set of skills. Further training will be provided as needed, as described in 13.2.a.

TRAINING

Key: ✧ = Needs skill ▦ = Has skill ☺ = Super-User

Legend used below: **N** = Needs skill, **H** = Has skill, **S** = Super-User, blank = no entry

Training Topics	Director	Administrator	Secretaries	GSC	Finance	Development Dir.	Development Asst. (C)	Development Asst. (M)	Food Serv. Mgr.	Lead Cook	Prep/Dish	Housekeeping Mgr.	Housekeeper	Laundry Serv.	Maintenance Mgr.	Maintenance Asst.	Groundskeeper	Clerical Volunteers
1. Basic Operation	N	H	S	H	H	H	H	H	H	N	N	N	N	N	H	N		H
2. Basic Troubleshooting	N	H	S	H	H	H	H	H	H	N	N	N	N		H	N		
3. Word Processing	N	S	H	H	H	H	H	H	H			N			H	N		H
4. Spreadsheet	N	S	H	N	S	H	H	H	H			N			H	N		H
5. Presentation Graphics	N	S			N	S	H											
6. Accounting Software—input					S													
7. Accounting Software—access					N	N		N										
8. DonorPerfect—input						S	H											
9. DonorPerfect—access only		N				H		N										
10. Reservations Software—input	N	N	N	S														
11. Reservations Software—access	N	N	N	N	N	N	N	N	N	N	N	N	N	N	N	N		
12. Intranet communication	N	N	N	N	N	N	N	N	N	N	N	N	N	N	S	N		
13. Internet (Phase II)	H	H	H	N	N	S	H	N	N			N			H			
14. External E-Mail (Phase II)	H	H	H	N	N	S	H	H	H			N			H			
15. Server/Cube/Network Admin.		N				N	N											

EXAMPLE 20.1

Presentation Center: Training Plan, Cont'd

The following table summarizes staff training for each skill area noted on The Training Assessment Needs Table.

TABLE 9: TRAINING SUMMARY

Types of Training to Be Provided	Who Will Be Involved?	Who Will Train?
1. Basic Operation: • How to turn on a computer • How to open specific program or software	All designated staff required to know this skill (see Table 8)	• In-house training by Super-Users • Volunteer trainers
2. Basic Troubleshooting: • Identifying basic operation problems (on/off, printing, etc.)	All designated staff required to know this skill (see Table 8)	• In-house training by Super-Users • Volunteer trainers
3. Word Processing (Microsoft Word): • Creating • Formatting • Saving • Printing a document	All designated staff required to know this skill (see Table 8)	• Formal training class for staff with no previous experience • Volunteer trainers • In-house training by Super-Users • Tutorial software
4. Spreadsheet (Microsoft Excel): • Creating a spreadsheet • Basic formulas • Basic formatting	All designated staff required to know this skill (see Table 8)	• Volunteer trainers • In-house training by Super-Users • Tutorial software
5. Presentation Graphics (Microsoft PowerPoint): • Creating a presentation • Formatting • Printing slides and handouts • Inserting graphics and charts	All designated staff required to know this skill (see Table 8)	• Volunteer trainers • In-house training by Super-Users • Tutorial software

WORKSHEET 20.1

Training Plan Matrix

People to Train

Topics to Train on	1. Executive Director, CEO	2. Executives	3. Admins, Secretaries	4. Clerical	5. Volunteers	6. Finance	7. Development Office	8. Tech Support	9.	10.	11.	12.	13.	14.	15.
1. Basic Operation															
2. Basic Troubleshooting															
3. Word Processing															
4. Spreadsheet															
5. Presentation Graphics															
6. Accounting Software															
7. Payroll Software															
8. Donor Tracking															
9.															
10.															
11.															
12.															
13.															
14.															
15.															
16.															
17.															
18.															
19.															
20.															
21.															
22.															
23.															
24.															

Chapter 21

Evaluation and Continuous Improvement Strategy

YOUR TECHNOLOGY PLAN describes a course of action in relation to technology so that your organization can improve the ways it does business and ultimately achieve its strategic goals. Once you embark upon implementing the strategies outlined in the technology plan, check periodically to see whether the path your organization is on is still the right one or whether course corrections are needed. (This relates to the Study and Act parts of the Technology Implementation Cycle discussed in Chapter Two.)

The purpose of this section of the technology plan is to plan for these checkpoints. By building them right into the plan, you provide for periodic evaluation of progress to date on process improvements, a review of the technology plan for current viability, and a strategy to update the technology plan, if needed.

Section XIII, Evaluation and Continuous Improvement Strategy, of your technology plan should include these subsections:

A. Process improvement review

B. Technology plan review

C. Technology plan update

A. Process Improvement Review

Determine and document how and when you will review the organization's process improvement progress. Consider these questions:

- How often will you evaluate your business process improvements? Quarterly, semiannually, annually? Note that it is advisable to review process improvements no more than once per quarter and no less than once per year. (Once you schedule dates for these reviews, relative to the time you begin implementation and take the baseline measures of the measures of success, add these dates to your timeline reminder sheet [Worksheet 11.2] and include them in Section XVI, Implementation Timeline.)

- What will the review vehicle be? Some possibilities are board meetings, project team meetings, manager reviews, or special process review meetings.

- What will the review parameters be? Ask, "Have we done what we said we would in the timeframe, within budget, and meeting our measures of success?"

- Use the measures of success defined earlier to determine whether the organization is making progress.

- Will you need to give intermediate progress reports to the board, project teams, or other people? (Add these items to your timeline reminder sheet [Worksheet 11.2] and include them in Section XVI, Implementation Timeline.)

TIPS

- Focus on only a few related processes at a time (for example, processes related to donors and funding).

- If a process is particularly complex, focus only on it, to make sure you cover it adequately.

- Remember to ask the people involved with the process—the owner and key contributors—whether they see progress and what needs improvement. This will be subjective input, whereas the measures of success are objective input. You need both these types of data to form a rounded view.

B. Technology Plan Review

Determine and document how and when you will review the organization's progress on implementing the technology strategies in the technology plan (see also Chapter Twenty-Nine). Consider these questions:

- How often will the organization evaluate its technology plan? Monthly, quarterly, semiannually?

(Once you schedule dates for these evaluations, relative to the time you begin implementation, add these dates to your timeline reminder sheet [Worksheet 11.2] and include them in Section XVI, Implementation Timeline.)

- What will the review vehicle be? Some possibilities are board meetings, project team meetings, manager reviews, and special process review meetings.

- What will the review parameters be? For example, you can look at acquisition, deployment, budget, or timeline. Ask, for example, "Are we where we thought we would be with respect to the budget?"

- Will you need to give intermediate progress reports to your board, project teams, or other people? (Add these items to your timeline reminder sheet [Worksheet 11.2] and include them in Section XVI, Implementation Timeline.)

TIPS

- Use your implementation schedule and milestones (see Chapter Eleven) to measure progress during implementation.

- Document suggested changes to the technology plan as they are made. If you decide not to make a change, document that too and describe why that decision was made.

C. Technology Plan Update

Determine and document how and when the organization will update its technology plan. Consider these questions:

- Are changing organizational needs affecting your original technology strategies?

- Are changing technologies affecting your original technology strategies?

- Who will be responsible for determining what changes to technology strategies are appropriate in the new environment?

- Who will be responsible for updating the technology plan?

- At what time do you expect the organization will need to formally revise the plan? Note that the technology plan review should closely coincide with the strategic plan review. (Add this information to your timeline reminder sheet [Worksheet 11.2] and include it in Section XVI, Implementation Timeline.)

TIPS

- Your agency's technology plan is a living document. It documents a slice of time. Many things about your organization and its environment, including technology itself, change continually, and therefore the technology plan will always need regular revision.

Examples

Example 21.1: Mission Hospice, Inc., of San Mateo County, a medium-sized hospice care and services organization (www.missionhospice.org). This example uses a table to concisely present all pertinent data for the evaluation and continuous improvement of the business process improvement and the technology plan.

EXAMPLE 21.1

Mission Hospice, Inc.: Evaluation and Continuous Improvement Strategy

XVI. Evaluation & Continuous Improvement Strategy

The formal review process is described in the following table:

Component	Frequency	Review Vehicle	Review Parameters
Process Improvement Review	• Quarterly	Performance Improvement Committee: • already established • composed of board members, staff members of all disciplines, volunteers • already meets quarterly • uses FOCUS-PDCA methodology for improvement process	• Measures of success as delineated in Section IV • Other measures as decided by the Performance Improvement Committee • Meeting the timeline • Staying within the established budget
Technology Plan Review	• At least monthly during deployment • Quarterly thereafter	• Technology Committee (Section III) *(Note: The new system administrator to be hired will be part of the Technology Committee.)*	• Acquisition • Deployment • Timeline • Budget • Staff comfort/usage • Hospice software availability
Technology Plan Update	• Quarterly, to discuss organizational and technological changes • More often if an urgent need arises	• Technology Committee (Section III) *(Note: The new system administrator to be hired will be part of the Technology Committee.)*	• Assign the writing of updates to the plan

Table 14: Evaluation & Continuous Improvement Strategy

Example 21.2: Services for Brain Injury, a small health and human services organization that assists brain injured people to reach their highest level of independent living (www.SBIcares.org). This example shows a narrative presentation of review and update plans for evaluation and continuous improvement.

EXAMPLE 21.2

Services for Brain Injury:
Evaluation and Continuous Improvement Strategy

12. Evaluation & Continuous Improvement Strategy

12.1. Process Improvement Review

Business processes are under continual review as part of the normal functioning of the agency. That said, business processes and associated documentation will be reviewed and updated every month while we are implementing the new processes. Once the new processes are functional, reviews will take place quarterly. Staff and the Technology Committee will conduct all review processes.

The parameters which will be reviewed begin with the measurements found in Section 2.5, Measures of Success. Each measure will be monitored to determine the level of success attained, and the business process with technology strategies will be modified and fine-tuned as needed. The agency's business process will be reviewed periodically as part of the CARF process, and more parameters for review will be dictated by that process.

An annual review of commercial/off-the-shelf database solutions will be conducted to determine if total cost of ownership can be lowered from the current cost of the "homegrown" database. Total cost of ownership of the database, including any required configuration of a commercially available database package, will form the sole criterion for deciding to move to such a solution.

12.2. Tech Plan Review

This Technology Plan will be reviewed every six months, in June and December, by the Technology Committee. The purpose of the review will be to monitor the progress of implementation of this plan. Any variances between the plan and the implementation will be addressed and new updates to this Tech Plan will indicate any new tasks identified, including timeline and budget considerations.

12.3. Tech Plan Update

The first Tech Plan Review, in June of 2002, will be unique because it is likely to involve new planning for the probable move into a new facility. The schedule of this move may force a Tech Plan Review prior to June of 2002. In any case, the Site Plan for the new facility will drive the structural changes to this plan. There is only a small likelihood that the new facility will cause any changes other than LAN/WAN and Site Plan changes.

Aside from this one-time update, the plan will be updated on an annual basis, in June by the Technology Committee. Such update will incorporate any Business Process, Technology Strategy, or technology implementation improvements identified during the Tech Plan Review process.

Chapter 22

Acceptable Use Policy

THE ACCEPTABLE USE of the technology in your organization's environment is a matter of business policy. An organization needs to inform its people about the type of behavior it expects of those using technology in its workplace and about the consequences for abusing technology privileges. The policy that provides this information is called an *acceptable use policy* (AUP), and an organization's AUP occupies a separate section in its technology plan.

If your organization already has a written acceptable use policy, it is appropriate to review it from time to time to make sure the policies are keeping up with changes in the organization's technology environment.

If your organization does not have a written acceptable use policy, now is a good time to develop one. Make sure your organization's AUP is in written form, and that it is accessible to the entire user community, including employees, volunteers, and clients who may use the organization's technology.

Some organizations include a review of the AUP during new hire orientation and volunteer orientation, and ask people to sign a statement that they have read and understood both the policy and the consequences for abuse. The degree of formality the organization chooses to adopt in informing people about and enforcing its AUP should be aligned with the way it approaches other organizational policy matters. Because of this, many organizations assign responsibility for the AUP to the human resources function, including it in the employee handbook and other places where organizational policies and procedures are recorded.

Your acceptable use policy section, Section XIV in Resource A, should include these subsections:

A. Rules for technology use

B. Consequences for abuse

A. Rules for Technology Use

Describe the rules that will govern technology use in your organization by employees, volunteers, and clients. Consider addressing these items:

- Using the organization's equipment after-hours.

- Downloading sexually explicit or illegal pictures or off-color jokes.

- Downloading software (a hazard because it might introduce a virus into the organization's system).

- Running a private business with the aid of the organization's equipment or performing other similar activities.

- Installing nonstandard software (which makes technical support more difficult).

- Using e-mail for personal communication. (It is advisable to treat this activity just as you would treat someone's use of the organization's telephone to make a doctor's appointment. If you allow one, you must allow the other, for consistency.)

TIPS

- Try to state policies in terms of actions that might expose the organization to litigation, actions that might cause embarrassment, and actions that might contribute to significant technology support problems.

- Consider what can be gained from allowing people to use the organization's technology for some personal reasons, such as sending and receiving personal e-mail or playing computer games, before instituting a policy against this use. New users, in particular, will spend more time using a computer if they can also use it for personal reasons. This is likely to make them more comfortable with the technology and possibly even inspire creative ideas for using technology to facilitate their work.

- Do not try to define every single thing that is allowable or not allowable. Allow some room for user discretion and a "code of honor."

- Consider the organization's mission, vision, and culture when developing the AUP; make sure it is in line with the spirit of how your organization operates.

- Consider asking employees and volunteers to sign a form stating that they have read and understood the AUP.

B. Consequences for Abuse

Describe what consequences will result and what actions will be taken if the organization's rules for technology use are abused.

TIPS

- Make a distinction between small or single-time breaches and major or ongoing ones. For example, there is a big difference between someone who downloads a software update once and someone who persistently downloads music files. In the latter case, significant disk space and network capacity are consumed.

- Consider the consequences of actions that cause damage to hardware, software, or information. Separate the accidental from the deliberate.

Examples:

Example 22.1: Junior Achievement of the Bay Area, Inc., a medium-sized education service organization (www.jaba.org). This example illustrates that much can be stated in a simple, succinct way. This nonprofit has maintained brevity by relating the acceptable use policy back to its already existing policies and procedures.

EXAMPLE 22.1

Junior Achievement of the Bay Area, Inc.: Acceptable Use Policy

Proposed Acceptable Use Policy

Junior Achievement of the Bay Area, Inc., holds its staff responsible for complying with all local, state, federal, and international laws, all JABA and Junior Achievement, Inc., basic beliefs, human resources policies and other employment policies, and the dictates of prudence and common sense, as they apply to the use of JABA computing and network resources. Such resources include, but are not limited to, computers, data storage, e-mail, and LAN and Internet services. Users are reminded that JABA computing resources are limited and are maintained for the purpose of achieving JABA's mission; any use thereof that does not further the mission is superfluous at best and an abuse of donor resources at worst. Any abuse of computing resources is subject to such action as may be deemed appropriate and consistent with JABA's employee handbook of policy and procedures.

Example 22.2: San Jose Repertory Theatre, a large arts organization (www .sjrep.org). This example provides a longer, well-developed acceptable use policy that sets out a number of use categories. Note the brevity of the description of the consequences for abuse.

EXAMPLE 22.2

San Jose Repertory Theatre: Acceptable Use Policy

13. Acceptable Use Policy

This acceptable use policy is integrated in our Employee Handbook, signed by each person upon commencing employment at the Rep. (Volunteers have no need of access to technological equipment at present.) As updates are settled, all members of staff are required to re-sign their agreement to it. Last revision: September 2001. This policy may be periodically reviewed and additionally modified as technological advances are made, and as industry-based, organizational, and legal circumstances dictate.

13.1. Rules for Technology Use

Computer Use

To maximize the benefits of its computer resources and minimize potential liability, San Jose Repertory Theatre has created this policy. All computer users are obligated to use these resources responsibly, professionally, ethically, and lawfully.

Use of computer resources for any of the following activities is strictly prohibited:

- Sending, receiving, downloading, displaying, printing, or otherwise disseminating material that is sexually explicit, profane, obscene, harassing, fraudulent, racially offensive, defamatory, or otherwise unlawful.
- Consciously disseminating or storing commercial or personal advertisements, solicitations, promotions, destructive programs (that is, viruses or self-replicating code), political information, or any other unauthorized material.
- Wasting computer resources by, among other things, sending mass mailings or chain letters, spending excessive amounts of time on the Internet, playing games, engaging in on-line chat groups, printing multiple copies of documents, or otherwise creating unnecessary network traffic.
- Violating any state, federal, or international law.

You are given access to a desktop computer and our computer network to assist you in performing your job. You should not have an expectation of privacy in anything you create, store, send, or receive on the computer system. The computer system belongs to the company and may only be used for business purposes. Without prior notice, the company may review any material created, stored, sent, or received on its network, or through the Internet or any other computer network. Additionally, computer files (documents, data, or programs) may not be duplicated or otherwise altered for personal gain, even after leaving the company.

Computer resources are not unlimited. There is finite bandwidth on the network and limited storage capacity. Employees should be aware of their duty to conserve these valuable resources. Active conservation includes, but is not limited to, archiving files to storage media (floppy disk, Zip disk, recordable CD, etc.) on a regular basis.

Downloads & System Settings

Because audio, video, and picture files require significant storage space and bandwidth on the network, files of this sort may not be downloaded unless they are business-related. For business-related file downloads (including copyrighted materials) from the Internet or other sites, approval should be obtained from the Systems & Office Manager before the commencement of any file download. Computer or network settings may be changed only by prior agreement with the Systems & Office Manager.

EXAMPLE 22.2

San Jose Repertory Theatre: Acceptable Use Policy, Cont'd

Technology Acquisitions

Provisioning for San Jose Repertory Theatre technology (except as regards stage production technologies), whether purchased, donated, or by other means contributed, should receive approval from the Systems & Office Manager before acquisition in order to ensure continuity of standardization and compatibility within the existing computer environment. This pertains to any and all hardware devices and peripherals including, but not limited to, digital cameras, scanners, printers, disk drives and speakers, and any and all software programs and applications.

Personal Property

Use of employee owned computers and other computer/electronic peripherals are not covered by the Rep's liability insurance policy. San Jose Repertory Theatre assumes no responsibility for the loss, damage, or theft of any personal belongings of any employee. Unauthorized connecting or attaching of any personal equipment to San Jose Repertory Theatre's computers, networks, or systems is prohibited. If your personal computer is approved for business use, please be aware that San Jose Repertory Theatre reserves the right to peruse company files as necessary.

Please refrain from adding any personal software to your company computer (i.e., games, screen savers, or wallpaper) as it may cause conflicts within the system and affect normal computer function. Please refer any questions to the Systems & Office Manager.

Security

All San Jose Repertory Theatre computer system users have a responsibility to ensure company computer files (documents and data) are kept secure through the implementation and confidentiality of network and/or computer and application passwords.

No person shall access a computer, or files on that computer, belonging to another employee unless the owner of said computer has granted prior permission.

No unauthorized access to the server room is permitted. Admission, if deemed necessary, may be gained through the Systems & Office Manager.

Guidelines for Employee Use of E-Mail

You should never consider your electronic communications to be either private or secure. E-mail may be stored indefinitely on any number of computers, including that of the recipient. Copies of your messages may be forwarded to others either electronically or on paper. In addition, e-mail sent to nonexistent or incorrect usernames may be delivered to persons that you never intended. When using the e-mail system, please comply with the following guidelines:

THINK BEFORE SENDING A MESSAGE. It is very important that you use the same care and discretion in drafting e-mail as you would for any other written communication. Anything created or stored on the computer may be reviewed by others.

SENDING UNSOLICITED E-MAIL (SPAMMING). Without the express permission of their supervisors, employees may not send unsolicited e-mail to persons with whom they do not have a prior relationship. Employees should delete all chain e-mail and all non-business related mass e-mail (including virus warnings and jokes) immediately upon receipt and refrain from forwarding them to any other employees.

EXAMPLE 22.2

San Jose Repertory Theatre: Acceptable Use Policy, Cont'd

ALTERATIONS. Never alter the "From:" line or other attribution-of-origin information on your e-mail. Anonymous or pseudonymous messages are forbidden.

E-MAIL RETENTION. Unless directed to the contrary by your supervisor, employees should discard inactive e-mail after sixty (60) days.

VIRUS DETECTION. Files obtained from sources outside the company, including disks brought from home; files downloaded from the Internet, newsgroups, bulletin boards, or other on-line services; files attached to e-mail; and files provided by customers or vendors may contain dangerous computer viruses that may damage the company's computer network. Employees should never download files from the Internet, accept e-mail attachments from outsiders, or use disks from noncompany sources, without first scanning the material with a company approved virus checking software. If you suspect that a virus has been introduced into the company's network, you must notify the Systems & Office Manager immediately.

Telephone

The telephone system is a vital part of our business. Employees should not make or receive personal calls during work hours. Occasionally, personal responsibilities may require some calls, but excessive use and unauthorized long distance calls, as determined by the Rep, are strictly prohibited.

Privacy

The Rep's business premises, including all computer, telecommunication, and related equipment used in connection with San Jose Rep operations, are the sole and exclusive property of the Rep. The Rep reserves the right to inspect at any time, without prior notice, any and all of its property. This includes, without limitation, records or information maintained by any employee at any location (such as a desk or file cabinet) and in any form (such as data stored on computer or transmitted through an e-mail system). As a result, employees should not maintain personal information on Rep premises or store or transmit personal information using Rep equipment or facilities.

13.2. Consequences for Abuse

Failure to abide by any of the above guidelines and policies could result in action directed by San Jose Repertory Theatre's current practice, up to and including but not limited to, disciplinary proceedings or discharge from employment at the Rep's sole discretion.

Chapter 23

Budget

DEPENDABLE BUDGET figures are necessary for successful technology deployment. Without a realistic budget, the organization may run out of funds halfway through the project due to unanticipated costs. Likewise a huge overestimate may give the appearance of unnecessarily exaggerated figures.

Your budget (Section XV in Resource A) should include this basic information:

- *All* expenses mentioned in previous sections. Anything your organization needs to spend money on should be put into this budget (you can do this more easily and accurately if you have been keeping track on a budget reminder sheet).

- The start and end dates of your organization's fiscal year.

- Costs for consumables. Consumables are things that people and machines use up and that need to be replaced, like paper and toner.

- Salaries for technology-related personnel, both current and proposed. In particular, does the organization need to increase staff to support technology in any way?

Differentiate between capital and expense items, if this is appropriate for your organization:

Capital items. These are items that usually have a high purchase price and a long life or that require insurance (for example, some computers and printers, large software packages like a major database, or high-end networking equipment). From an accounting standpoint, the key factor in determining that an item is a capital expense is that it is depreciable or insurable.

Expense items. These are usually small items, low-end equipment (some computers and peripherals), monthly fees (the line for your Internet connection), consulting and outsourcing fees, most software, equipment upgrades, ISP fees, training costs, consultants' fees, and maintenance fees.

Some organizations do not differentiate between capital items and expense items. Be sure to work with your finance or accounting staff to understand the right way to present budget figures for your organization.

PLANNING IN PRACTICE
Getting the Best Value for the Nonprofit Money

Jim Madden, the systems manager for Andover Newton Theological School, was always on the lookout for a good value. He wrote, "I keep my tax exempt certificate in my wallet, and I will glance at items (while shopping personally) that I might need for the School. I always read through the discounted bookshelves at computer stores. Most of these are for older equipment, or older software, which is what we have! This saves the school from purchasing expensive first-run books for equipment that we just do not have yet. Also, it saves on the sales tax, to have the exemption certificate handy."

This kind of attention to the financial details is essential for a small nonprofit that measures its entire IT budget in the hundreds or thousands of dollars, and rarely in the hundreds of thousands. Madden, describing his typical nonprofit budgeting process, said: "I consider myself an excellent planner. I like to plan for all the foreseeable (the next fiscal year) projects at budget time. Budget for them, get my budget cut, then re-plan with the remaining funds for the next year. I set funds aside for contingencies, as well, and spend them as frugally as my tolerance for pain allows."

Remember to think about the total cost of ownership (TCO) of an item. Although there are many different ways to calculate TCO, a good rule of thumb is that the initial acquisition and deployment of technology accounts for only 20 percent of its total cost. The rest of the costs are incurred in such areas as support, ongoing maintenance, consumables, and training. Balance the short-term and long-term costs. Is it possible for your organization to pay more money up front and save money in the long run? (See Chapter Three for additional information on TCO.)

Section XV, Budget, of your technology plan should include these subsections addressing periods of time in your fiscal years:

A. Remainder of the current fiscal year, if you plan to begin implementing your plan immediately

B. Next full fiscal year

C. Additional fiscal years as appropriate

TIPS

- Include at least three columns for figures in your budget spreadsheet: *quantity* (how many you want), *price per unit,* and *extended price* (quantity × price per unit). Include sales tax in this calculation.

- For every budget line item, include data in all three columns, and let the spreadsheet do the arithmetic. (Doing calculations by hand leaves more room for error.)

- Make sure all the budget items are extended properly. Once again, it's better to let the spreadsheet do the arithmetic.

- If the item is a monthly fee, then the price per unit is the cost per month, and the quantity is 12 (the number of months for the year), unless your budget is for part of a year, in which case the quantity would be less.

- On each budget, state the dates that the budget covers.

- If applicable, include the costs of hiring temps while staff are participating in training.

- Include the costs of consumable items, especially for printers. Ink cartridges can get very expensive. (You may find a look at the cost of a year's worth of ink cartridges compelling enough to change your printer strategy to heavy-use ink cartridge-style printers with laser technology.)

- Include tax and shipping costs, where applicable. Include columns for these on your spreadsheet to make it obvious. (If you do not know exact tax and shipping amounts, make a reasonable guess based on the amount of the local sales tax as a percentage of cost and on past shipping history.)

- Make sure that implementation phasing is reflected in the budget. Budget breakdowns by year need to match your implementation phases.

- Consulting fees are perhaps the hardest item to budget for, because of the difficulty of determining whether you will need a consultant for a certain task and, if you do, what the rates will be. You will need to take your best guess.

- Provide a column in which to cross-reference sections of the plan. This will make it clear where the numbers come from and help you avoid missing a critical item or entering something twice.

- Provide a column for notes. You can annotate that vague consulting number here, for example.

- Make sure that the costs are reasonable, not too high or too low. Get a couple of estimates and average them if you are unsure of an amount.

- If your organization anticipates receiving donated goods and services, still include in your budget what it would cost if you were paying for these goods and services. This prepares you in case the donations do not come through. It also helps you describe your total savings if the donations do come through. Some organizations find it useful to create two budgets—one with the anticipated donations included and one without.

- If your organization is faced with maintaining older equipment, consider intangible costs like the possibility that downtime will increase or that parts may be hard or impossible to find.

- Consider using Worksheet 23.1 as a guide for the building of your budget.

Examples

Example 23.1: San Jose Repertory Theatre, a large arts organization (www .sjrep.org). This example shows a multiyear budget with an executive summary and introductory narrative.

Example 23.2: Presentation Center, a medium-sized interfaith retreat and conference center (www.prescenter.org). This example is an executive summary of a multiyear budget that includes cost per each unit category and extended amount for each budget year, as well as a total project budget for all years.

EXAMPLE 23.1

San Jose Repertory Theatre: Budget

14. Budget

Our fiscal year runs from September 1st to August 31st. Each budget allocation is determined in the spring of each year by the Executive Committee, with final figures approved by April, for the upcoming year.

Annual operating income is generated from a diversified base with 50 percent coming from ticket sales and the remainder coming from corporate, government, foundation, and individual grants and contributions. Capital purchases, depreciated over the reasonable life of the item, are generally purchased with special restricted funding, either from designated grants or from the organization's temporarily restricted capital facility fund.

Currently the annual budget for technology related expenses is approximately 3.5 percent of the annual operating income. The majority of the budget covers support costs for the network, hardware, and major software packages, Web site, systems management staff, as well as license acquisition, etc. Increased annual budgets as well as additional capital purchase funding will be necessary to meet the needs of this proposal and the projected budgets.

14.1. Remainder of Current FY, Next Full FY, Successive FY's

The attached budget proposal allows for a general three-phase schedule of equipment replacement and upgrade to match the needs of a fast-growing company: the first is that of immediate procurement for legal and daily routine purposes, the second being general network infrastructure and lastly, of fine-tuning and the completion of projects still in their research stage at present. The budget proposal provided for an annual cost of living increase of 3% on annual continuing expenses items to account for future inflation and price increases.

Executive Summary

	3 year	FY 2001–2002	FY 2002–2003	FY 2003–2004	Financial Year 9/1/xx–8/31/xx
Total Capital Expenditures	$9,100.00	$9,100.00	$—	$—	
GRAND TOTAL CAPITAL	$9,100.00	$9,100.00	$—	$—	
Total Support and Maintenance Expenses	$1,255.00	$395.00	$410.00	$450.00	
Total Office and Productivity Software Expenses	$7,710.00	$6,450.00	$620.00	$640.00	
Total Networking	$20.00	$20.00	$—	$—	
Total Internet Services	$7,000.00	$7,000.00	$—	$—	
Other Technology Expenses	$9,300.00	$3,000.00	$3,100.00	$3,200.00	
GRAND TOTAL EXPENSES	$25,285.00	$16,865.00	$4,130.00	$4,290.00	
Salaries	$14,836.32	$4,800.00	$4,944.00	$5,092.32	
GRAND TOTAL SALARIES	$14,836.32	$4,800.00	$4,944.00	$5092.32	
COMPLETE BUDGET TOTAL	$49,221.32	$30,765.00	$9,074.00	$9,382.32	

EXAMPLE 23.1

San Jose Repertory Theatre: Budget, Cont'd

Capital Expenditures

Category	#	Cost/Each	Extension w/Tax	Category Subtotal	Total	FY 2001–2002	FY 2002–2003	FY 2003–2004	Explanation and Details	Plan Section Reference
Computer Equipment Desktop Computers Subtotal	13 ###	$700.00	$9,100.00	#REF!		$9,100.00			Based on HP Brio BA4I0	4.2
TOTAL CAPITAL EXPENDITURES					#REF!	$9,100.00			Sum of "Account Subtotals" for Capital	

Support and Maintenance

Category	#	Cost/Each	Extension w/Tax	Category Subtotal	Total	FY 2001–2002	FY 2002–2003	FY 2003–2004	Explanation and Details	Plan Section Reference
Maintenance Contracts SBS Keystroke Subtotal	1 ###	$395.00	$395.00	#REF!		$395.00	$410.00	$450.00	Annual support fee	16.4d
Software for Support/ Maintenance Workstation Utilities/Diagnostics Subtotal	0 0									
TOTAL SUPPORT AND MAINTENANCE EXPENSES					#REF!	$395.00	$410.00	$450.00	Sum of "Account Subtotals" for Supt/Mtce	

Office and Productivity Software

Category	#	Cost/Each	Extension w/Tax	Category Subtotal	Total	FY 2001–2002	FY 2002–2003	FY 2003–2004	Explanation and Details	Plan Section Reference
Office/Administration Adobe Photoshop 6.0 PC Subtotal	9 ###	$650.00	$5,850.00	#REF!		$5,850.00			New software license	5.2b
Software Support Fees Gigabytes Subtotal	12	$50.00	$600.00	$600.00		$600.00	$620.00	$640.00	Time & materials	16.4
TOTAL OFFICE AND PRODUCTIVITY					#REF!	$6,450.00	$620.00	$640.00	Sum of "Account Subtotals" for Prod SW	

Networking

Category	#	Cost/Each	Extension w/Tax	Category Subtotal	Total	FY 2001–2002	FY 2002–2003	FY 2003–2004	Explanation and Details	Plan Section Reference
Networking Box of connectors	1	$20.00	$20.00			$20.00			Scene shop wiring	8.1c
Subtotal	1			$20.00						
TOTAL NETWORKING					$20.00	$20.00			Sum of "Account Subtotals" for Networking	

Internet Services and Connectivity

Category	#	Cost/Each	Extension w/Tax	Category Subtotal	Total	FY 2001–2002	FY 2002–2003	FY 2003–2004	Explanation and Details	Plan Section Reference
Internet Services Internet/*PASS* gateway T6 license & software	1	$7,000.00	$7,000.00			$7,000.00			One-time, including training	3.3b
Subtotal										
TOTAL INTERNET SERVICES AND CONNECTIVITY					#REF!	$7,000.00			Sum of "Account Subtotals" for Internet Svc & Connect	

Other Technology Expenses

Category	#	Cost/Each	Extension w/Tax	Category Subtotal	Total	FY 2001–2002	FY 2002–2003	FY 2003–2004	Explanation and Details	Plan Section Reference
Technology Professional Development Courses & seminars	2	$1,500.00	$3,000.00			$3,000.00	$3,100.00	$3,200.00		
Subtotal	2			$3,000.00						
TOTAL OTHER TECHNOLOGY EXPENSES					#REF!	$3,000.00	$3,100.00	$3,200.00	Sum of "Account Subtotals" for Other Technology Expenses	

Salaries

Category	#	Cost/Each	Extension w/Tax	Category Subtotal	Total	FY 2001–2002	FY 2002–2003	FY 2003–2004	Explanation and Details	Plan Section Reference
Salaries Web master	12	$400.00	$4,800.00			$4,800.00	$4,944.00	$5,092.32		16.3
TOTAL SALARIES					$4,800.00	$4,800.00	$4,944.00	$5,092.32	Sum of "Account Subtotals" for Salaries	

EXAMPLE 23.2

Presentation Center: Budget

Presentation Center Technology Budget

Fiscal Year: September 1 to August 31

Executive Summary

	FY 2000–2001	FY 2001–2002	FY 2002–2003	TOTAL Project
Total Capital Expenditures	$1,220	$55,005	$400	$56,625
GRAND TOTAL CAPITAL	$1,220	$55,005	$400	$56,625
Total Support and Maintenance Expense	$58	$4,692	$3,592	$8,342
Total Office and Productivity Software Expense	$695	$1,345	$2,545	$4,585
Total Internet Services	$360	$360	$3,360	$4,080
Other Technology Expenses	$4,886	$11,462	$8,917	$25,265
GRAND TOTAL EXPENSES	$5,999	$17,859	$18,414	$42,272
Salaries	$ -	$ -	$ -	$ -
GRAND TOTAL SALARIES	$ -	$ -	$ -	$ -
	$7,219	$72,864	$18,814	$98,897

Notes: *Presentation Center's fiscal year runs September 1–August 31.*

According to Presentation Center fiscal policy, the entire networking project, aside from ongoing support and maintenance, will be considered a capital expense

Capital expenditure = $500+

WORKSHEET 23.1

Technology Budget

Executive Summary

Total capital expenditures	$
GRAND TOTAL CAPITAL	$
Total support and maintenance expenses	$
Total office and productivity software expenses	$
Total Internet services	$
Other technology expenses	$
GRAND TOTAL EXPENSES	$
Salaries	$
GRAND TOTAL SALARIES	$

Capital Expenditures

Category	Quantity	Cost/Each	Extension	Tax	Shipping	Category Subtotal	Total	Tech Plan Reference	Explanation and Details
Computer equipment									
Line item			$						
Line item			$						
Subtotal						$			
Printers									
Line item			$						
Line item			$						
Subtotal						$			
Network hardware									
Line item			$						
Line item			$						
Subtotal						$			

WORKSHEET 23.1, Cont'd

Capital Expenditures

Category	Quantity	Cost/Each	Extension	Tax	Shipping	Category Subtotal	Total	Tech Plan Reference	Explanation and Details
Other hardware (over $_____ per item)									
Line item			$						
Line item			$						
Subtotal						$			
Network software									
Line item			$						
Line item			$						
Subtotal						$			
Major software packages									
Line item			$						
Line item			$						
Subtotal						$			
TOTAL CAPITAL EXPENDITURES							$	SUM of account subtotals	

Support and Maintenance Expenses

Maintenance contracts									
Line item			$						
Line item			$						
Subtotal						$			
General maintenance support hardware									
Line item			$						
Line item			$						
Subtotal						$			

Parts and equipment (under $_____ per item)		
Line item	$	
Line item	$	
Subtotal		$

Upgrades/other (under $_____)		
Line item	$	
Line item	$	
Subtotal		$

Network software tools		
Diagnostic tools—servers	$	
Server operating systems	$	
Subtotal		$

Software for support/ maintenance		
Workstation utilities/ diagnostics	$	
Virus detection	$	
Subtotal		$

TOTAL SUPPORT AND MAINTENANCE EXPENSES	$	SUM of account subtotals

Office and Productivity Software Expenses

Office/administration		
Workstation software	$	
Upgrades to current software	$	
Subtotal		$

Volunteer		
Workstation software	$	
Upgrades to current software	$	
Subtotal		$

WORKSHEET 23.1, Cont'd

Office and Productivity Software Expenses

Category	Quantity	Cost/Each	Extension	Tax	Shipping	Category Subtotal	Total	Tech Plan Reference	Explanation and Details
Software support fees									
Line item			$						
Line item			$						
Subtotal						$			
TOTAL OFFICE AND PRODUCTIVITY SOFTWARE EXPENSES							$	SUM of account subtotals	

Internet Services Expenses

Category	Quantity	Cost/Each	Extension	Tax	Shipping	Category Subtotal	Total	Tech Plan Reference	Explanation and Details
Internet services									
Service provider			$						[Per mo. chg. for 12 mos.]
Phone lines			$						[Per mo. chg. for 12 mos.]
Web site development			$						
Web site maintenance			$						
Web site hosting			$						
Subtotal						$			
TOTAL INTERNET SERVICES EXPENSES							$	SUM of account subtotals	

Other Technology Expenses

Category	Quantity	Cost/Each	Extension	Tax	Shipping	Category Subtotal	Total	Tech Plan Reference	Explanation and Details
Consumables									
Ink for printers			$						
Printer parts			$						
Special papers			$						
Removable media			$						[Floppies, Zip drive, Jaz disks, CD blanks]
Tapes for drives			$						
Cleaning supplies			$						
Line item			$						
Line item			$						
Subtotal						$			

Technology professional development

Workshops and seminars	$	
Conferences	$	
Subtotal		$

Consulting fees

Line item	$	
Line item	$	
Subtotal		$

TOTAL OTHER TECHNOLOGY EXPENSES	$	SUM of account subtotals

Salaries

Salaries

Technicians	$	
Help desk	$	
Network manager	$	
Web master	$	
Other	$	
Other	$	
Subtotal		$

TOTAL SALARIES	$	SUM of account subtotals

Chapter 24

Implementation Timeline

A TIMELINE is a tool to manage the implementation of technology strategies. It helps you stay focused and moving forward by outlining how you will get from your current state to a future state. It is a tracking device that outlines what tasks need to happen, the duration of the tasks, when the tasks need to be completed, and by whom. With a timeline, you can keep track of your progress and make adjustments when needed.

If you propose a very large, complex technology strategy that will take a several months to implement, or if you propose a large number of technology strategies, consider breaking implementation into phases. Working in phases will give you more frequent opportunities to measure results and emphasize the idea of continuous progress. Thus you are more likely to have results to show at process improvement and technology plan review checkpoints (see Chapter Twenty-One).

A commonly used style of timeline is the Gantt chart. A Gantt chart organized by date is very useful for seeing the big picture, including how tasks relate to each other in time. To build a timeline for Section XVI of your technology plan:

- Define the tasks

- Put activities in date order

- Find the dependencies: that is, what needs to happen before something else can take place

- Estimate the duration of all timeline items, setting estimated start and end dates and milestone completion dates for each activity

- Lay out the tasks on a horizontal grid in which calendar units go across the page and tasks are listed down the left-hand side in date order

TIPS

- Use one of the several excellent project management application programs that are available for creating a Gantt chart. These programs are available in a range of prices.

- Alternatively, build a Gantt-style chart using a widely available program such as spreadsheet software. Example 24.1 illustrates using a spreadsheet to create a Gantt-style chart.

- Group tasks together by technology strategy or by implementation section to see how that part comes together over time.

- Group tasks strictly in date order to see everything that needs to start, be worked on, and end at around the same time. This view will give y a clear picture *of task congestion*, allowing you to reevaluate task timing.

- Include a column to cross-reference the related sections in the technology plan.

Finally, when scheduling people for tasks on the timeline, make sure they have provided adequate input into the duration and deadline estimate. Anyone assigned a task must know about the assignment and agree to both the task and the time allotted to that task, before the information is published to others.

A timeline should include the following items:

- *All* timeline items noted on the timeline reminder sheets (Worksheet 11.2)

- Action items assigned to people

- Major purchases, including dates by which the organization should

    - Make the purchase decision ("drop dead" date)

    - Select the vendor

    - Cut the purchase order

    - Receive the purchase

    - Implement or deploy the purchase

    - Prepare user training

    - Deliver user training

- Grant applications, including dates on which the organization expects to

    - Prepare the grant request

    - File the grant request (a milestone)

    - Wait for action on the request

- Receive funds or an in-kind grant

- Deploy funds or an in-kind grant

- Enact contingencies should the proposal be rejected

- Prepare user training

- Deliver user training

- Review the process, including when status reports are due to the board or others

- Review implementation progress and evaluate process improvements

- Update technology plans, including review dates, revision dates, and when status reports on progress are due to the board and others

▐ **TIPS** ▌

- Keep track of milestones and tasks to complete on timeline reminder sheets. This will greatly simplify timeline preparation. It is much more difficult to go back through the plan hunting for items to put on the timeline than to keep track as you go along.

- Include time for training, implementation, installation, and debugging.

- Account for other staff priorities that must be accommodated during the same time frame.

- Allow for vacations, holidays, and sick time.

- Add a "fudge factor" to all the time estimates. Tasks frequently take longer than you think they will. One rule of thumb is to add 20 percent to the time that you think a task will take. However, when determining your own fudge factor, consider what you know about how others estimate tasks, your agency's culture and ability to handle unscheduled events, and the complexity of each task.

- Consider the impact of a schedule slip. What and who will be affected? Have a contingency plan prepared in case something is not ready on time, and ask the people who would be affected for their input on this plan. Because they are close to the topic, they will have good ideas for handling schedule difficulties.

- Do not schedule in increments smaller than half a day; otherwise the timeline will be too detailed to present a clear picture.

- Do not schedule an important task at the same time that your organization has other important tasks going on.

Examples

Example 24.1: Services for Brain Injury, a small health and human services organization that assists brain injured people to reach their highest level of independent living (www.SBIcares.org). This example is a simple Gantt-style chart prepared with a spreadsheet program, using shaded cells to mark time elements. Note also that this timeline shows project phases.

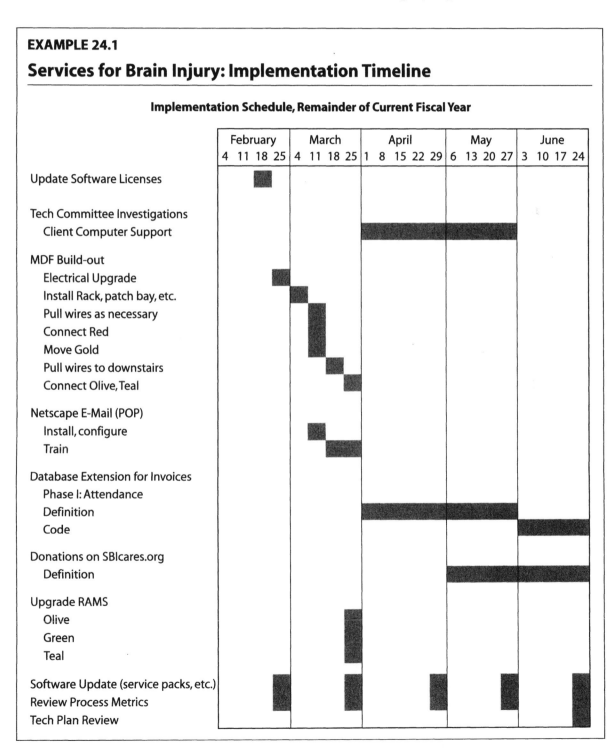

EXAMPLE 24.1

Services for Brain Injury: Implementation Timeline

Implementation Schedule, Remainder of Current Fiscal Year

Example 24.2: Child Care Coordinating Council of San Mateo County, Inc., a large agency that works on behalf of children, families, and early education professionals (www.thecouncil.net). This example was created using project management software and includes a legend for abbreviations used in the chart. This level of detail could also be achieved with a spreadsheet program.

Example 24.3: Hope Rehabilitation Services, a large, multicounty agency serving people with developmental disabilities (www.hopeservices.org). This example demonstrates an advanced use of project management software. Note the use of the various timeline icons to show different types of progress, task durations, and task dependencies, the latter shown by the arrows.

EXAMPLE 24.2

Child Care Coordinating Council of San Mateo County, Inc.: Implementation Timeline

Legend

A	Advertise
C	Configure
CC	Create Content
CD	Convert Data
D	Decision
F	Functional
H	Hire
I	Install
M	Meet
P	Purchase
R	Research
S	Submit
T	Train

Timeline columns span two fiscal years: **2001–2002** (May–Jun) and **2002–2003** (Jul–Jun).

Item	Key Staff	MAY	JUN	JUL	AUG	SEP	OCT	NOV	DEC	JAN	FEB	MAR	APR	MAY	JUN	JUL	AUG	SEP	OCT	NOV	DEC	JAN	FEB	MAR	APR	MAY	JUN
Software																											
Help Desk Software	Rebecca-R,D,P,I,F	R		D,P	I	T,F																					
Benefits Mgmt./HR Software	Nancy-R,D; Rebecca-P,I,F				R	D,P	I	F																			
Web Development Software	Cassie-R,D; Rebecca-P,I,F				R,D,P	I,F																					
Project Management Software	Cassie-R,D; Rebecca-P,I,F							R,D,P	I,F																		
Event Management Software	Cassie-R,D; Rebecca-P,I,F				R,D,P	I,F																					
Adobe PageMaker Software	Rebecca-P						P																				
Mapping Software	Sally-R,D; Rebecca-P,I,F								R	D,P	I,F																
Subsidy Management Software	Selma-R,D,C,T; Rebecca-P,I,C,CD,F	R	D	P	I	C		T	CD,F																		
Dependencies: SQL Server																											
Network Upgrade																											
SQL Server	Rebecca-D,P,I,F		D	P	I,F																						
Resource & Referral Software	Donna-R,D,C,T; Rebecca-P,I,C,CD,F																R	D,P	I	C	T	CD	F				
MIP Accounting Software	Eric-C,T; Rebecca-I,CD,F					I,C	CD	T	F																		
Dependencies: Windows 2000																											
Office 2000	Rebecca-P,I						P				I																
MS Visio 2000	Rebecca-P						P																				
Intranet Software	Rebecca-P,I,C,T,F																R	D	P	CC	T		F				
Library Catalog & Circulation SW	Donna-R; Rebecca-P,I,T,F												R,P	I	T,F												
Windows 2000	Rebecca-I	I																									
Windows 98 2nd Edition	Rebecca-I					I																					
Add E-Mail Option to CSP	Rebecca-C,F						C,F																				

EXAMPLE 24.3

Hope Rehabilitation Services: Implementation Timeline

Hope Rehabilitation Services
Information Technology Department
Wired For Good Technology Plan

A. Implementation Time Frames
1. LAN Site Preparation/Installation

ID	❶	Task Name	Duration	Start	December 19	26	December 3	10	17	24	January 31	7	14	February 21	28	4	11	18	March 25	4
1	▦	LAN site preparation	1 day	Wed 11/22/00																
2																				
3	▦	FWG LAN upgrade	38 days	Wed 11/22/00																
4	✓	FWG electrical upgrade	1 day	Wed 11/22/00																
5	▦	Move hubs & servers down	1 day	Sat 12/2/00																
6	▦	Move patch panels & reterminate	2 days	Fri 1/5/01																
7	▦	FWG set up LAN switches	1 day	Sat 1/13/01							◆ 1/13									
8																				
9	▦	Whittier LAN upgrade	36 days	Wed 11/29/00																
10	▦	Decommission Novell 3.12 server	1 day	Wed 12/6/00																
11	▦	WH electrical upgrade	1 day	Thu 1/4/01																
12	▦	Build security wall/cage	3 days	Mon 1/8/01																
13	▦	Transport donated rack to WH	1 day	Wed 1/10/01																
14	▦	Earthquake stabilize WH rack	1 day	Wed 1/10/01																
15	▦	WH move hubs & servers down	1 day	Sat 12/9/00																
16		Install patch panel	1 day	Mon 12/11/00																
17	▦	WH network wiring U/G	12 days	Mon 12/4/00																
18	▦	WH set up LAN switches	1 day	Mon 12/18/00																
19	▦	Move WH servers to rack	1 day	Sat 1/13/01							◆ 1/13									

Task ▬▬▬ Split ············· Progress ▬▬▬ Milestone ◆ Summary ▬◀──▶▬ External Tasks ▬◀──▶▬ Project Summary ▬◀──▶▬

Project: LANs Setup
Date: Thu 1/11/01

Chapter 25

Appendixes

APPENDIXES PROVIDE supplemental information that will help readers better understand your organization and technology plan. All appendixes are optional and should be included only if they are applicable.

Technology plans commonly include these appendixes:

A. *Glossary.* Contains brief definitions for terms and acronyms specific to the organization's industry or to the organization itself that outsiders and those new to the organization may not know.

B. *Consulting contracts.* Contains copies of consulting contracts the organization currently has.

C. *Support and maintenance contracts.* Contains copies of any current or proposed contracts for equipment or software maintenance.

D. *Technology job descriptions.* Contains job descriptions for any technology jobs the organization currently has or plans to establish. Technology jobs are those for which the technology plan identifies substantial technology responsibilities. Consider including descriptions for positions such as help desk technician, network manager, IT director, support technician, and others applicable to your organization.

Additional appendixes could contain anything that is too long or too distracting to leave in the body of the plan: for example, the flowcharts for business processes; the organization's basic troubleshooting guide; other relevant parts of organizational policies and procedures manuals; the organization's computer skills assessment form; minimum system requirements for technology purchases and donations; detailed versions of plans, logical flowcharts, organizational charts, and the like that have been summarized in the body of the plan; or a history of the versions of the technology plan.

TIPS

- Write down terms that may need defining as you develop your technology plan. It is easier to do this than to try to find them when the document is nearly complete.

- Alphabetize your glossary. Terms that begin with a number should be grouped at the beginning, in numeric order.

- Alphabetize the job descriptions so they are easy to find.

Examples

Example 25.1: Girl Scouts of Santa Clara County, a medium-sized, community-based organization that is a chapter of a national organization (www.girlscoutsofscc .org). The appendix shown here provides a comprehensive bird's-eye view of technology impacts on business processes. The chart allows readers to easily assess where the impact of changes will be felt most. Although too detailed to include in the main text of the plan, it is helpful as supplemental material because it gives background information for key decisions in the plan.

Example 25.2: Parents Helping Parents, Inc., of Santa Clara County, a medium-sized family resource center for parents of children with special needs (www.php.com). The appendix shown here is a well-written job description for an IT director, and illustrates the type of description that is most helpful when seeking IT personnel.

EXAMPLE 25.1

Girl Scouts of Santa Clara County: Appendix

19.8. Appendix H: Business Process Chart and Maps

The following chart outlines all Business Processes with the corresponding technology impact. They are listed in the same order as the Business Strategy table 2.7, with the numbering in the second column.

At a glance, one can see the listed processes crossed with the affected technology. An "N" signifies a new technology while a "U" means an upgrade to an existing technology.

Following this chart, in the same numbered order are the process maps [not shown here]. Some process maps have been combined on the chart as they address identical technology needs. The business process that they refer to is identified in the title.

Business Process	#	Public Web Site	Shared Database	Intranet	Extranet	E-Mail	Desktop	Peripherals	Server	OS	EU	Server	LAN	WAN	Site Plan	Assistive Tech	Office Equip	Facilities	Security	End-User Support	Training	NOTES
							Hardware			Software												
Gift Process & Managing	1	N	U		N						U	U							N	U	U	*Needs to be further investigated
Registering a Member/Unplaced Girls	3	U	U		N			N	N	N	N	N		N					N	U	U	*Legal issues Option for remote, see reports
Program Registration	4		U	U					N		N		U						N	U	U	
Product Sales	5	N			N														N		N	
Creating a Publication	6							N			N											
Communicating with Volunteers	7	U				U		N	U				U							N		
Managing the Board	8	N			N				N		N								N	N	N	
Informing Public	9									N	N	N										
Hiring Staff	11	U	N	U	N	U			U		N		U						N	N	N	
Time-Off Request Record Keeping	12																				N	
HR Info Management	13	U	N	U	N				U	N	N	N	U						N	N	N	
Managing Knowledge	14	U	U	U	N				U				U						N	N	N	

EXAMPLE 25.1

Girl Scouts of Santa Clara County: Appendix, Cont'd

Business Process	#	Public Web Site	Shared Database	Intranet	Extranet	E-Mail	Desktop	Peripherals	Server	OS	EU	Server	LAN	WAN	Site Plan	Assistive Tech	Office Equip	Facilities	Security	End-User Support	Training	NOTES
							Hardware				Software											
Training Staff	15	N		N	N								U								N	
Informational Content, Design, & Structural Changes to Web Site	16	U		U	N			N														
Reporting Computer Problems	17	U	N	N	N						N	N		N							U	
Bulk Mailing	18	N		N	N								U				U		N			
Management Report	19			U									U						N		U	
Outcome Evaluation	20		N		N								U						N	N	N	
Preventative Maintenance System/ Unplanned Breaks & Repairs	21		N	N	N		N				N	U	U	N					N	N	N	
Property Reservations	22	N	U	N	N		N		U		N	U	U	N								
Purchasing & Inventory Control	23	U	N	U	N				U		N		U	N					N	N	N	
Posting Volunteer/ Processing Inquiries	25	U	N	U	N	U							U						N		N	
Volunteer Screening	26	N																	N			
Staffing Training Classes	27																				U	* Move to WinCAS
Training Registration & Record Keeping/ Program Catalog	28	U	N						U			N		U					N		U	

EXAMPLE 25.2

Parents Helping Parents, Inc.: Appendix

18.5. Appendix D: Technology Job Descriptions

18.5a. IT Director

Department: Information Systems

Job Summary: Manages a multiserver, 50 user NT 4.0 network using Microsoft Exchange. Possesses excellent knowledge of desktop and database applications including MS Office, with an emphasis on Access 2000. Oversees all data management, including our client/donor database and statistical data collection. Oversees department staff.

Specific Functions:

Staff Supervision: Supervise department staff including database specialist, technical support specialists, receptionist, and volunteers. Perform annual employee reviews.

Program Development: Expand and enhance the available technologies to meet the needs of the staff and the PHP community. Develop Web applications to better serve a global community.

Quality Assurance: Overall responsibility for the quality of data collection and technical support delivered to staff and volunteers.

Fiscal Management: Develop annual budget and ensure budgetary guidelines are followed.

Information Management: Responsible for all types of information management as needs arise and as requested by CEO.

Materials Management: Maintain accurate inventory of software, licensing, and computer hardware. Ensure that staff are knowledgeable on the use of equipment and comply with guidelines for acceptable use.

Program Marketing: Collaborate with other PHP staff, including Development Director, CEO, and the PHP Board to promote PHP programs and enlist community support whenever possible. Present the agency in a positive light when in the community.

Program Management: Responsible for accomplishment of program goals parallel to the PHP strategic vision and mission. Compliance with timelines and deliverables related to the goals and objectives developed annually.

Qualifications:

BS in Computer Science or Microsoft Certified Engineering Certification and 2 years experience in related field

- Good knowledge of Microsoft NT Systems Administration
- Understanding of TCP/IP Protocol
- Command of Web tools including Front Page 2000, Cold Fusion desired, raw HTML
- Good organizational abilities
- Attention to detail
- Strong written and oral communication skills
- 3 years management experience

Chapter 26

Preparing the Document

YOUR TECHNOLOGY PLAN will be used and read by many different individuals, both internal and external to your organization, so it is important to design the plan for readability. A plan that is easy to follow and understand will be used. It will also be easier to update at a later time. The previous chapters have included a number of ideas for making the plan content clear. This chapter offers some final suggestions and tips on preparing the document.

Proofreading

As you are proofreading, make sure you check the plan for completeness and consistency. Check specifically for the following items:

- Is every section included?

- If you chose not to include a section or subsection, have you explained why that section is unnecessary?

- If you have not made a clear decision on a particular course of action, have you articulated how you will get to the decision?

- Have you checked for consistency between sections? For example, does what is in the narrative match what is in the budget and timelines?

- Is the arithmetic in the budget correct?

- Is the writing style consistent throughout? (With multiple authors there will be multiple styles at first.)

- Have the spelling and grammar been checked by a word processing program?

TIPS

- Have someone read your technology plan from beginning to end to make sure it sounds as though a single person wrote it, even if several people have contributed to it.

- At least one person who has not been involved in developing the technology plan should read the final document before you reproduce it. This person is looking primarily for those things "everyone" knows but that will be unclear to an outsider. Provide all reviewers with a copy of the Tech Plan Review Checklist (Resource C) as well.

- Consider using the Tech Plan Review Checklist (Resource C) yourself.

Publishing Niceties

Cover Page

The cover page should include your organization's name (short and long forms), the document's name ("Technology Plan"), and the date of most recent revision. Do not use graphic images unless they will print cleanly. Including your organization's logo on the cover page provides a nice visual. It is also helpful to include the agency's Web site address.

Table of Contents

The table of contents should include all section headings, including appendixes. For readability, use leaders (the sets of dots that lead the reader's eye from the text to the page number). After creating the table of contents, check the page numbers in the table of contents against the actual page numbers to ensure correctness.

Section Headings

Number section and subsection headings to at least two levels. The numbering makes it much easier to refer readers to another part of the document.

Tables, Figures, and Drawings

Make sure that the text contains references to all tables, figures, and drawings. If the figure is next to the text that discusses it, the connection may be made by saying simply, for example, "In Figure 1 . . ."

Headers and Footers

Include the name of your organization in page headers. That way it will appear on every page. The footer should print at least a page number on every page. If you must insert hand-drawn pages into the middle of the document, then insert that number of page breaks (to make blank pages) into the text file at the appropriate place so that all pages will be correctly numbered after printing. For example, if there are four hand-drawn pages, insert four page breaks. After printing, substitute the drawings for the blank pages.

Fonts

Use a twelve-point font for the main text. Consider using a serif font (one with "feet" and other short, angled lines at the ends of the letter strokes). Common serif fonts are Times New Roman and Palatino. Sans serif fonts (ones without feet and other short, angled lines), such as Geneva or Helvetica, can create eye fatigue when they are the dominant font used. These fonts are typically used only for brief items, such as titles and headers.

Spell and Grammar Check

Spell check and grammar check everything, especially any last-minute changes. Depending on the software you are using, you may need to check the tables and text separately. Also be sure to look carefully at all the text inside the graphics to make sure there are no misspellings or misuses. Exercise caution in selecting "suggested changes" for both the spell and grammar checks. Word processing software often suggests completely incorrect substitutes because it cannot discern contextual meanings.

Printing

If you are distributing the plan to multiple readers, such as vendors or funders, consider saving some paper with doubled-sided printing.

Do not use color printing. Though color can make some pages easier to understand, such as the network diagrams, most people still do not have color copying readily available to them. The charts that make sense in color will most likely not translate well to black and white.

Consider using divider pages with tabs, or perhaps colored paper, to mark the beginning of each section of the technology plan.

Binding

It is more practical to use a three-ring binder to hold your technology plan than to bind it (with spiral binding, for example). This makes it easier to update sections of the plan as needed. It also allows readers to pull out sections and correlate them with other sections—cross-referencing the budget and the timeline, for example. Use binders that have outer transparent pockets so that you can slip a copy of the cover page over the front cover and spine of each binder.

Part Four

What's Next?

AFTER THE technology plan is written, the next step is implementing it. The same project management techniques used for developing the plan, discussed in Part Two, should be employed for its implementation. In addition, three other important issues related to managing the implementation process are discussed in this part of the book.

Chapter Twenty-Seven offers insights into change management as it relates to technology implementation. One key distinction that change managers must bear in mind is the difference between *change* and *transition*, transition being the ultimate objective.

Chapter Twenty-Eight is an overview of the process of securing funding and in-kind resources for technology implementation. Although there are not many differences between securing funding for technology and obtaining it for other organizational needs, this chapter presents some useful ideas and strategies.

Finally, the technology plan is a living document, one that should be used and updated continuously. Chapter Twenty-Nine addresses the importance of revisiting your technology plan and describes when and how to go about this task.

Chapter 27

Managing Organizational Change

INTRODUCING TECHNOLOGY brings major change. When an organization decides to implement new technology it is asking its employees and key stakeholders to adapt to new tools, processes, and policies that are likely to be very different from the ones they have grown accustomed to. More than this, it is committing itself to a culture that encourages and supports change. Many will embrace chance openly; others will resist it (and some will exhibit their resistance openly, and others may keep it to themselves). Many will embrace some changes but not others.

It is important to understand that there is a difference between *change* and *transition*. A *change* occurs at a single point of time. Something old stops and something new begins. A *transition* happens over time. It occurs mainly through an internal process in individuals as they reorient and refocus their ways of thinking and feeling.[1] Although implementing new technology will create changes, it cannot create transition. The objectives of organizational change proposed in your technology plan will occur only when a critical mass of people complete their individual transitions. To achieve the desired organizational change, you must help staff and other key stakeholders go through the transition process. One element of this task is recognizing that individuals occupy varying points on the transition continuum and that you need to take the time to bring everyone along.

The technology plan itself is a great help in managing this transition. It establishes readiness by defining the need for change and describing the vision for the future. When the process of developing the plan includes involving many people in information gathering and decision making, that

---

1. See Bridges, W., *Managing Transitions: Making the Most of Change* (Cambridge: Perseus Books, 1991).

helps people with their transition. This is why developing the plan with a team that is representative of the entire organization, including staff, board, volunteers, and other key stakeholders, is so critical. People who are a part of the planning for change are likely to embrace the change when it occurs, and the more of these people there are, the more likely it is that the change will be widely embraced. Then the people who embrace the change can help bring others along.

For example, say that one of the technology strategies outlined in your technology plan is to create a centralized database for managing donor contact information. Up until now, donor contacts have resided in the executive assistant's Rolodex. The problem is that others who need this information, such as the development director and program managers, do not have easy access to the assistant's desk, and the process of asking the assistant for the information disrupts the work of both the development director and the program managers on the one hand and the assistant on the other. In this case the development director and program managers probably embrace the idea of having a centralized database. However, the executive assistant may not because it requires some extra work—learning how to use the database as well as entering all the contact information. Additionally, this change creates anxiety for the assistant because centralizing the database may mean that anyone in the organization can add, alter, or delete contacts, something defined as part of the assistant's responsibilities in the past. From this point of view, creating a centralized database involves more issues than convenience and efficiency; it represents a change to the assistant's job, which can feel threatening to the assistant.

An important way to help the assistant through this transition is to involve him in the decision-making process—not only to decide whether or not there should be a database but also to determine the criteria for selecting database software, for identifying data that need to be in the database, and for choosing methods of entering data. With this kind of participation, instead of the change happening *to* the assistant, he is actually a part of the change. Further, the assistant can help others make the transition by reminding them where they can find the contacts, instead of personally giving them the contact information when they ask. Finally, the executive assistant can become an advocate for the change, actively communicating the reasoning behind it and the improvements the change represents.

Communication is the most important element in managing organizational change. In fact nothing helps people's transitions more. Communication should be frequent and delivered through multiple methods. There is practically no such thing as overcommunicating—the more informed people are, the better prepared and able to embrace change they are. The communication should be two-way, consistent, honest, and from the heart.

A critical piece of your communication strategy is to remind people why the change is occurring and at the same time acknowledge that something is ending in order for something new to begin. Honor the past way of doing things. Help people understand why this way of doing things needs to change, but do it without denigrating the old way. Instead, define what is going to be different as a result of the change and whom it is going to affect. Acknowledge the groups and individuals who are going to be affected and have to go through a transition as a result of this change. Who is going to need to let go of what? For example, continuing the example of creating a centralized database, the old way of tracking donors is ending in order for the new way to begin. You can honor the old way by acknowledging and communicating the excellent work of the executive assistant and at the same time including the assistant in the decision-making process. Acknowledge that this is a transition not only for the executive assistant but also for the development director and program managers as they too grow accustomed to a new way of processing and accessing donor information.

The technology plan is an excellent communications tool that can generate understanding of the reasoning behind changes while also acknowledging the past and generating excitement for the future. Your communications should

- Define the need for change

- Describe the vision for the future

- Share research data (for example, pass around results of surveys, articles, relevant Web site addresses, and the like)

- Create a sense of urgency (by explaining why the change needs to happen in the planned time frame)

- Supply regular progress reports

- Describe the impact the change will have on existing services

- Acknowledge the impact the change will have on individuals, even on those who want the change.

The remainder of this chapter offers tips for managing change once the technology plan is complete. Keep these tips in mind as you are developing the plan as well, so that you do not create unrealistic technology strategies.

TIPS

- Facilitate a shared vision by arranging for technology demonstrations at other nonprofits or local corporations. Match your organization's staff with their counterparts at the demonstration site. Encourage them to have frank conversations about the benefits and pitfalls of implementing the demonstrated technology.

- Share success stories—best practices and lessons learned; do not focus just on results but on the process as well.

- Figure out the frame of reference of those who are resisting change. Listen to their language; learn about their cultural inclinations and biases. What is the fear or concern behind the resistance? (Refer back to Chapter Four for more information.)

- Make changes slowly and thoughtfully, especially to avoid excessive cost and resource constraints. However, build credibility for new technology projects by starting with one you can finish quickly.

- Once you have decided to make a change, publish a schedule of when the change will occur, and keep to it as much as possible. This will help people avoid undue anxiety from anticipating a change but not knowing when it will occur.

- Give people a taste of feeling empowered by technology. Provide a technology solution that they can easily use immediately, no matter how small. This will help to capture their imagination.

- Acknowledge that change is never easy, even when the change represents something positive.

- When barriers pop up, such as technology breakdowns or a need for training, respond immediately so that people do not have a chance to get mired in their frustration.

- Increase the staff's comfort with technology by making the most of what is already in place. Provide training on existing hardware and software so staff know how to implement it to its fullest. As staff abilities grow, so will staff use of technology.

- Support people in becoming champions who carry the vision forward.

- Implement changes first with those most comfortable with technology and having the least resistance and fear. They will be the most tolerant of any residual kinks in the new system and helpful in straightening them out. Once the system functions optimally, these same staff can act as coaches and assist with the rollout to the remaining staff.

- Recognize that as one part of the system becomes more productive and capable, that may put more strain on another part. Returning to the database example, implementing a donor database will make it more convenient for the development director and program managers to get the information they want, but it will put more strain on the executive assistant who has to enter the information, taking time away from the assistant's work on other important tasks for the organization.

- Make sure that adequate resources are in place to carry out the change, including staff, equipment, budget, and training.

- Post the project timeline where everyone can see it so they can get a clear idea of what needs to be accomplished as well as follow the progress.

- Finally, make sure people celebrate all small and large accomplishments!

Chapter 28

Funding and In-Kind Donations

WHAT RESOURCES are available to increase nonprofits' ability to implement their technology plans? What are the challenges? This chapter addresses some of the strategies to explore when you are determining the means to implement your technology plan, in terms of both funding and in-kind donations and discounts.

Funding

As with any of your organization's fundraising activities, many strategies can be used when seeking funding for the implementation of your technology plan. The first is to approach the same funders you would apply to for operational support. This makes sense because technology has a systemic impact on the entire organization and because many of the things technology will be used to improve are internal business processes. However, just like finding funding for operational support, finding funding for technology in this context can be challenging. For funders, supporting organizational infrastructure does not have the same allure as supporting something program specific or service oriented. The good news related to this challenge is that there is growing interest among funders in providing grants for infrastructure, calling it funding for *capacity building* or *organizational effectiveness.* There are even foundations and federal initiatives that have been formed specifically to provide funding for technology-based initiatives. You can often find these initiatives by searching for funders who are addressing the *digital divide* (a term that is commonly used to describe the gap between the technology haves and have-nots).

Another challenge when seeking funding for technology as part of the organization's infrastructure is that by positioning technology as a standalone operational issue you can inadvertently make it seem as though technology is the goal rather than a strategy for achieving organizational goals. This is misleading for everyone involved and can send a mixed message, especially after you have spent significant time developing a technology plan that *does* align technology use with organizational goals.

Because funders traditionally prefer to provide grants for programs and services that directly meet client needs, it is often a more effective strategy to seek donations for technology in the context of your organization's program funding. This way, the use of technology is embedded in your proposal as one way to meet program goals. Technology simply becomes a line item in your overall program budget, rather than something funded as a separate issue.

Pulling language directly from your technology plan is helpful when employing this strategy, because in that plan you have articulated how technology supports the organizational agenda of providing programs and services to clients. Although you may meet success by generalizing to funders about the ways technology will affect programs and services organization-wide, you may have better luck if you focus on a specific organizational goal and technology strategy from your technology plan, one that is directly related to providing services to your clients—for example, providing clients with easy access to information and referrals through the agency's Web site.

PLANNING IN PRACTICE

Using Technology Plans to Leverage Donations

For Pam Brandin, executive director of the Peninsula Center for the Blind and Visually Impaired, a technology plan opened the door to the donation of an entire wireless network. If the agency had not had a plan, she would not have been going over it with a board member. If they had not been going over the plan together, he would not have mentioned a possible referral to a company that might help implement the plan. The detailed plan gave the center creditability and let this company see exactly what its commitment would be. This facilitated the large donation of a full computer network, including technical support. Brandin estimated that this donation was worth $100,000 a year. The center effectively made back the money it had spent in staff time creating the plan, with interest!

Sister Patricia Marie Mulpeters, executive director of the Presentation Center, was also able to use a technology plan to leverage additional donations. The retreat center had a donor who was already planning to make a contribution. Mulpeters asked if this donor would make an additional $5,000 donation for a server. The donor did. Because the center had a detailed technology plan and could ask for exactly what it wanted and needed, Mulpeters found that it was easier to get donations.

AIDS Community Research Consortium executive director Michael Edell felt that a technology plan had the potential to be a flagship for other fundraising opportunities. He discovered that it can attract more money. By leveraging his plan he was able to turn one group of donated computers into donations of more computers. Edell described the process this way: "Most large corporations understand the need for technology. And if their mission, if their corporate giving missions, are aligned to some of your needs, then they are all on the bandwagon to help. . . . There's potential for you to find partners you didn't know existed or partners that were not willing to give you money before [for] other needs but are willing to do it now for these."

Felicia Sullivan, director of Interactive Media and Community Outreach at Lowell Telecommunications Corporation, a community media center, found that going through the strategic planning process helped the organization determine that decentralizing its basic computer training and moving it out into the community would alleviate the stress on internal resources. This re-visioning helped the organization secure federal funds to build what is now the Lowell Community Technology Consortium. "By focusing on community development and thinking beyond our organization we have been able to do so much more, and not on our own," Sullivan said. "I also see that as our partners move out of the initial mind-set of 'we need a computer lab' or 'we need to teach computers,' they begin to see how the technology they have in place feeds into their larger programmatic goals. All of a sudden the light clicks on, and they realize that they are not running a computer class but rather an after-school program. Or they see how the computer lab becomes not an added activity for, say, their ESL training but an integral part in energizing their students." According to Sullivan, once this jump happened, many of the partners were able to place technology purchases within the context of their program budgets and have become comfortable making the case why the resource is needed for the success of the program.

Many nonprofits employ the strategy of funding new technology by including it in their capital campaigns. This is an idea that works well, especially for an initial technology implementation with a sizable budget for the technology purchases, and for an organization that is moving to a new site, launching a new building, or renovating a current one. Beware, however; capital campaigns usually imply that funding they raise is needed only once, at a specific period of time, to achieve a major goal for the organization. This can be a problem in the funding of technology, as it does not account for the funds needed for ongoing support, maintenance, and training over time.

TIPS

- Access grant libraries and databases to determine which foundations, corporations, governmental agencies, or other funders provide funding for technology.

- Use key words such as *technology*, *digital divide, capacity building*, and *organizational effectiveness* in your search.

- Check with local foundations, such as community foundations, to see whether they have any technology initiatives.

- Check to see whether funders who focus on your organization's specific service area have ever given grants for technology initiatives or, conversely, whether they have any policies against funding for infrastructure.

- Investigate opportunities to partner or collaborate with other nonprofits.

In-Kind Support

Donations for implementing your technology plan need not be only in the form of cash. In fact it is often easier to procure in-kind donations or discounts from corporations, vendors, and individuals. The key to securing appropriate in-kind donations and discounts is clearly articulating what your agency needs and is able to support. Technology is an area in which it is unwise to accept a donation of goods or services without first assessing whether it meets your organizational needs. This is because it is often more expensive to integrate outdated or mismatched hardware and software with your existing system and to support it than it is to purchase compatible items in the first place, even at high retail costs.

Your technology plan is useful in securing in-kind donations and discounts because the plan articulates your organization's technology needs, the reasoning behind its technology decisions, and the ways it is going to support the technology over time. In-kind contributors, in particular, are cautious about providing equipment to organizations that do not have a technology plan, realizing that the total cost of ownership of the equipment they give could be far more than an organization is prepared to absorb. Showing potential contributors your technology plan, or initially at least indicating that you have one, can give you a leg up because it not only provides a description of what you need and how you will support it but also illustrates your commitment to using it in a way that supports your mission.

Here are some additional tips on how to secure in-kind donations or discounts for equipment.

TIPS

- Approach local corporations and vendors. Organizations are more likely to contribute to nonprofits based in their own communities, where their employees and customers live.

- Approach national corporations as well. Many major corporations have some sort of *community investment* program, sometimes called *community relations, public affairs,* or *corporate philanthropy.* Grant guidelines for both cash grants and in-kind donations can usually be found on the company Web sites (often in the section called "About the Company" or just "About").

- Do not give up if a company's guidelines say that it contributes only to educational institutions. Unless they specifically state otherwise, many companies will extend their educational offerings to nonprofits.

- Look for other opportunities to partner with the company or vendor, providing ways for the prospective donor's employees to get directly involved in your organization (even if that involvement has nothing to do with technology). Many companies prefer supporting community organizations that have their employees personally invested as volunteers.

- Post your technology needs on your organization's Web site and in its newsletter. Make sure you post the minimum standards you are willing to accept. Having a policy in place that describes clear criteria for acceptable donations and then publicizing that policy will reduce the risk that a well-meaning patron will offer to donate something that does not meet your needs.

- Make sure your grant application tells the funder how and when you will measure the impact of the technology on your organization and, where possible, on your clients.

Chapter 29

Revisiting the Technology Plan

A UNIQUE quality of a technology plan is that just when you think it is finished it becomes out of date. Because it is not only a document that outlines strategy but also one that outlines processes and procedures, you will find that you are constantly adding or changing pieces as you go along. For example, as you acquire new hardware and software you have to update your inventories, and if you hire a consultant, you may want to add her contract to an appendix.

For most nonprofits the first thing that changes in the technology plan is the timeline and budget. Even with the best-laid plans, one cannot account for all the variables. For example, it is not uncommon for the funding picture to change from that which was planned, making it difficult to implement something new in the time frame outlined. Adjusting the timeline and budget is normal and should not cause you undue concern—as long as you remember to account for the impact this adjustment will have on the rest of the plan. However, try to adjust the timeline and budget sparingly. If you are constantly making changes in these areas, people will stop honoring deadlines, which will create difficulties in achieving success in implementing your organization's technology plan. A good rule of thumb is to revisit the technology plan no more than once per quarter and no less than once per year.

When you are forced to make timeline and budget changes to the plan, actively communicate these changes in order to manage staff, volunteer, and board expectations. Those who are eager for the technology strategies to be implemented in the time frame originally planned are bound to be disappointed. They will need to adjust their own time frames, both in terms of their current work and in terms of their process of transitioning to the new way of doing things. Provide tangible assurances, including the adapted plan, so that the sense of momentum is not lost.

Of course not everything in the plan becomes obsolete immediately. The business strategy section in particular should remain fairly constant unless other organizational changes (probably unrelated to technology) occur, such as a decision to change programs or program goals. These parts of the technology plan should be revisited in conjunction with your organization's strategic plan on at least a yearly basis.

Fortunately, evaluation and continuous improvement is built right into your technology plan. Refer back to Section XIII of your technology plan (discussed in Chapter Twenty-One) to review your strategy for this effort. Determine the stage your organization has reached in the implementation cycle (see Chapter Two). Is it still in the *do* stage, implementing the things outlined in the technology plan, or has it implemented enough to *study* the changes that have been made, including whether or not the changes have had the desired effect? Remember to *act* on what you learn in the study stage, and then come right back to the *plan* stage.

Revisiting your technology plan does not mean starting from scratch. Instead, regather your technology planning team, adding or subtracting members as necessary, and review each section, starting with the business analysis section. Go back to the five-step business analysis process outlined in Chapter Eleven. Determine which strategic goals are still relevant and which are not, and if not, why not. Articulate new strategic goals that your organization may have developed during the strategic planning process. Reevaluate the agency's major business processes, delete those that are no longer relevant (again, if they are not, determine why not), and add any new ones now in place. Consider whether there are new or additional ways to improve both the new and the ongoing business processes and identify those improvements that can best be accomplished by using technology. Finally, identify technology strategies that can facilitate these processes.

Then go back to each subsequent section of the plan and make the alterations necessitated by this business analysis review. Make sure as you do this that you conduct the research necessary to make sure the organization is not ignoring a new technology that may better serve its needs. However, when considering changes to these sections of the technology plan, examine all the implications. For instance, are the changes in technology absolutely necessary at this point in time? Will you need to change your network infrastructure or desktop computers? Will staff have to be trained? For example, perhaps a new version of the office software used by your organization came onto the market six months ago. It promises to be improved in ways that you can see would be useful for your organization. However, you also should ask these questions about it: Does it require more memory on the desktop computers? Will you have to upgrade any computers to run it? Are the improvements ones that staff will require training to learn how to use? Also evaluate whether six months on the market is long enough for all the bugs to have been worked out of this new version. Depending on your answers to all these questions you may decide to wait to upgrade the office software. If that is the case, make sure you document that decision in your technology plan, noting on your timeline when this issue will be readdressed.

After one year (or whatever period your timeline sets), it is unlikely that you will have implemented all the technology strategies originally outlined in the technology plan. Additionally, a year is probably not long enough to determine whether or not these strategies have been effective. Although many changes will have practically instantaneous results, such as improving communications by using e-mail, realize that because of the variables associated with implementing new technology, such as bugs in hardware and software systems or delays in getting staff appropriately trained and acclimated, it can often take several years before an organization is able to see the results of implemented technology changes. If this is the case in your organization, make sure you document these findings when you revisit your plan, and adjust the timeline and budget accordingly.

Depending on how much your organization has changed and the effectiveness of the technology strategies it has already implemented, you may or may not need to make significant changes to your technology plan each time you revisit it. Regardless, it is important that your technology plan remain a living document—not something that sits on the shelf, but something that is routinely pulled out, used, added to, deleted from, and reevaluated.

Part Five

Resources

PART FIVE presents five resources that will assist you in preparing and implementing a technology plan for your nonprofit organization. Resource A presents a comprehensive outline for a technology plan, Resource B shows the symbols most commonly used on flowcharts, and Resource C contains a technology plan checklist that you may use to ensure that your plan is complete before you print it and distribute it. Resource D is a glossary of terms that you are likely to encounter while preparing a technology plan. And, finally, Resource E offers selected sources for obtaining more information about nonprofit technology and technology planning, the use of technology to assist people with disabilities, the funding of nonprofit technology, and change management.

Resource A

Comprehensive Technology Plan Outline

Main Section	Subsection	Content
I. Front Matter	A. Cover Page	Include: • Organization name (full name, abbreviation if any). • Document name ("Technology Plan"). • Date of creation.
	B. Table of Contents	Guidelines: • All sections and pages numbered consecutively. • All drawings and figures page numbered. • All tables and charts labeled and page numbered. • All appendixes listed, labeled, numbered individually (for example, "Appendix A: Consultant Contract"), and page numbered consecutively with rest of document.
	C. Executive Summary	Provide an overview of the technology plan. Possible items to include: • A brief statement of what your organization is about, staffing level, and annual budget. • Major changes you are planning for your organization (not necessarily related to technology). • Time frame covered by your technology plan (which fiscal years). • Major business areas you strive to improve with technology. • Major technology strategies you are planning. • Overall budget for your technology plan.
II. Introduction	A. Mission Statement	Provide your organization's mission statement.
	B. Brief Description of Organization	Briefly describe your organization for the external reader. Possible items to include: • Primary purpose of your organization (health and human services, arts and culture, youth development, and so forth). • When founded. • Number and type of clients served.

Main Section	Subsection	Content
		• Number of full-time equivalent employees. • Number of volunteers. • Number of office locations. • Geographical service area. • Current fiscal year (FY) budget. • Structure (departments and reporting relationships).
	C. Technology Planning Team	For each member provide: • Name. • Title. • Phone number(s). • E-mail address(es). • Organizational position or company affiliation. • Role on the planning team, that is, any technology background, financial background, and so forth. • Role in creating the technology plan. Indicate which member is the project manager and who is responsible for keeping the plan and contact information up-to-date.
III. Business Analysis NOTE: Subsections C through F can be very nicely presented in table format.	A. Strategic Goals	State your organization's strategic goals explicitly and in business terms, not technology terms.
	B. Current Business Processes	• Describe each business process in narrative text, flowchart, or table form. For each business process answer these questions: • What tasks are performed? • In what order? • Who does what tasks? • Who is the owner? • Who are the key contributors, and what is their contribution? • What data are taken in, and when do these inputs occur? • Where are reports created, for whom, and containing what? • Why are things done this way? NOTE: This may be significant. • Describe any significant uses of technology in the current processes. NOTE: Number the business processes for cross-reference in later sections, and if you decide to use a chart format, include a key that defines chart symbols.
	C. Process Improvement Goals	Describe your organization's goals for improving these business processes without regard to technology. Answer these questions: • Which processes do you want to improve? • Why do you want to or need to improve these particular processes? • How do you want to improve them? NOTE: You may identify improvements that do not require the use of technology! However, include only those processes that can be improved by technology in this section.

Main Section	Subsection	Content
		NOTE: Number the process improvement goals for cross-reference in later sections.
	D. Technology Strategies	Identify each process improvement that you think can benefit from the application of technology as a full or partial solution. • Be specific: for example, "two new servers," "higher speed Internet connection," "new database." For each technology strategy you come up with identify: • The processes that are affected. Whose work is affected? • Why this strategy is a good one for improvement. Who will use it? • Anticipated date needed (add to timeline reminder sheet).
	E. Measures of Success	Describe how you will measure success in the process improvements to which you apply technology: • Think quantitatively—you want something measurable at multiple points in time, not a milestone. • Avoid use of vague terms such as *better, satisfied customers, good turnaround time.* • Surveys are an acceptable measurement instrument as long as you take an initial one to use as a baseline to measure against later. • When will you take these measures? (Add to timeline reminder sheet.)
IV. Network Services NOTE: Include at least these four main subsections. You may see the need to include additional subsections: for example, for an extranet or other services not listed here that may be provided over your organization's LAN or WAN or via its servers.	A. Public Web Site (contains two subsections)	1. Current Public Web Site Answer these questions: • Does your organization have a public Web site? • Where or how is it hosted? • How is it used? • Who uses it? • How is it maintained and updated? 2. Proposed Public Web Site Answer these questions: • What are your plans to upgrade or implement a public Web site? • How will it be used that is different from current use? • Who will use it who is different from the people who use it now? • From where will it be used? • How will it be maintained and updated? • Which business process improvements do the changes support? • What will this cost? (Add to budget reminder sheet.) • By when do you need these changes? (Add to timeline reminder sheet.)
	B. Internal web site (contains two subsections)	1. Current Internal web site (Intranet) Answer these questions: • Does your organization have an internal-use-only web site? • Where or how is it hosted? • How is it used? • Who uses it? • How is it maintained and updated?

Main Section	Subsection	Content
		2. Proposed Internal Web Site Answer these questions: • What are your plans to upgrade or implement an intranet? • How will it be used that is different from current use? • Who will use it who is different from the people who use it now? • From where will it be used? • How will it be maintained and updated? • Which business process improvements do the changes support? • What will this cost? (Add to budget reminder sheet.) • By when do you need these changes? (Add to timeline reminder sheet.)
	C. Shared Databases (contains two subsections)	1. Current Shared Databases Discuss actual databases here, not the software driving them. Answer these questions: • Does your organization have any shared databases? How many? • How is each one used? • What data are shared? • Who uses the data? • Can users get the information they need in a timely way? • From where is the data used? • What are the current shared database security measures? 2. Proposed Shared Databases Answer these questions: • What are the specific plans to upgrade or implement shared databases? • How will each one be used that is different from current use? • Who will use each one who is different from the people who use it now? • From where will each one be used? • Does the organization need to enhance database security? • Which business process improvements do the changes support? • What will this cost? (Add to budget reminder sheet.) • By when do you need these changes? (Add to timeline reminder sheet.)
	D. E-Mail Services (contains two subsections)	1. Current E-mail Services Answer these questions: • Does your organization have e-mail services? • How are they provided? For example, by an ISP or by the organization's own server? • How does your organization use e-mail (for general communication or for special purposes)? • Who uses the organization's e-mail services (employees, volunteers, clients)? • From where are the services used? 2. Proposed E-mail Services Answer these questions: • What are your plans to upgrade or implement e-mail services?

Main Section	Subsection	Content
		• How will e-mail be used that is different from current use? • Who will use it who is different from the people who use it now? • From where will the services be used? • Which business process improvements do the changes support? • What will this cost? (Add to budget reminder sheet.) • By when do you need these changes? (Add to timeline reminder sheet.)
	E. Other Current and Proposed Network Services	Include subsections as appropriate for any additional network services that your organization currently has or proposes to implement: • Be sure to include the current and proposed descriptions for each. • Using the other question lists in this section, develop similar questions to guide your descriptions.
V. Equipment Narrative and Table	A. Current Equipment Inventory and Narrative	Provide an inventory of your organization's current equipment, in table form. Annotate your inventory tables as necessary with narrative to explain oddities, history, or other information you wish to capture for your own and others' understanding later. Provide three tables, one each for: • Desktop computers and laptops. • Peripherals (printers, scanners, external modems, external media drives, and so forth). • Servers. TIPS for completing your inventory properly: For desktop computers and laptops include: • Item name and model. • Brand. • CPU (central processing unit) type and speed. • Current operating system (OS). • Amount of memory (RAM) in megabytes. • Size of hard disk (HD) in megabytes or gigabytes and % free (or used). • Internal modem or not. • Network card (NIC) installed or not. • Other internal peripherals (list them). • Monitor attached to the computer or built in. For peripherals include: • Item name and model. • Brand. • Network available or not. • If not networked, which computer is it attached to? • Other relevant technical specifications. For servers include: • Item name and model. • Brand. • CPU type and speed. • Current OS. • Amount of memory (RAM) in megabytes. • Size of hard disk (HD) in megabytes or gigabytes and % free (or used). • Internal peripherals (list them).

Main Section	Subsection	Content
		• UPS (uninterruptible power supply) attached or not. • Backup unit installed or attached. For each item in the table indicate "keep," "upgrade," or "replace." If upgrade: • What element of it do you want to upgrade (memory, processor, network cards, disk, and so forth)? • Which business process improvements does upgrading support? • At what cost? (Add to budget reminder sheet.) • By when do you need to upgrade? (Add to timeline reminder sheet.) If replace: • Replace with what? • Will the item become obsolete, or will it go to another user? • Which process improvements does replacing support? • At what cost? (Add to budget reminder sheet.) • By when do you need to replace? (Add to timeline reminder sheet.)
	B. Proposed Hardware Acquisitions	Describe what you want or need to acquire. Answer these questions: • What do you want or need to acquire that is *different* from your planned upgrades and replacements? That is, what equipment are you adding to your inventory? • Does the organization have any special equipment needs beyond the minimum configuration guidelines? • Which business process improvements do these acquisitions support? • At what cost? (Add to budget reminder sheet.) • By when do you need the items? (Add to timeline reminder sheet.) NOTE: Replacements and upgrades were discussed in the current equipment inventory section. Do not repeat that information here.
VI. Software Narrative and Table	A. Current Software Inventory	Provide an inventory of your organization's current software, in table form. Annotate the inventory tables as necessary with narrative to explain oddities, history, or other information you wish to capture for your own and others' understanding later. Include software in these three categories: • Operating systems (on desktop computers, laptops, and servers). • End-user software (all programs your users use, communications software, antivirus software, desktop security software). • Server software (security, backup, and Web hosting software as well as programs that provide network services for the items listed in that section). TIPS for completing your inventory properly: For each item include: • Title. • Type of software. • Software description. • Release or version number. • What computer(s) it is on.

Main Section	**Subsection**	**Content**
		• Number of licenses on file. • Licenses needed. TIPS for completing your inventory properly: For each item in the table indicate "keep," "upgrade," or "replace." If upgrade: • How do you plan to upgrade (new versions, patches, and so forth)? • Which process improvements does upgrading support? • At what cost? (Add to budget reminder sheet.) • By when do you need to upgrade? (Add to timeline reminder sheet.) If replace: • Replace with what? • Which process improvements does replacing support? • At what cost? (Add to budget reminder sheet.) • By when do you need to replace? (Add to timeline reminder sheet.)
	B. New Software Acquisitions	Describe what you want or need to acquire. Answer these questions: • For what specific reasons are you adding new titles, copies, or licenses? • Which business process improvements do these acquisitions support? • Do these acquisitions replace any software currently in use? • How many copies or licenses do you need? • At what cost? (Add to budget reminder sheet.) • By when do you need the items? (Add to timeline reminder sheet.) Consider these categories of software. For operating systems: • Desktop computers. • Laptops. • Servers. For end-user software: • Communications (for example, e-mail clients). • Internet access (for example, Web browsers). • Word processing. • Spreadsheet. • Presentation tools. • Desktop publishing. • Database engines and clients. • Project scheduling and tracking. • Security software (for example, antivirus, desktop security). • Graphic art and illustration. • Web site authoring. For server-related software: • Security. • Backup. • Web hosting. • Database engine. • E-mail services.

Main Section	Subsection	Content
	C. Software License and Tracking (contains two subsections)	1. Current License Tracking Procedures Answer these questions: • What are your organization's current software license tracking procedures? • Are they adequate? • If inadequate, why? 2. Proposed License Tracking Procedures Answer these questions: • What measures will you take to inventory your current licenses, if not already done? • How will you track new acquisitions? • Will any costs be incurred? (Add to budget reminder sheet.) • In what time frame will this be implemented? (Add to timeline reminder sheet.)

VII. Network: LAN/WAN Narrative, Invento-ries, and Diagrams	A. Description of Current LAN/WAN	Write a narrative description of your current LAN and WAN that includes:
		• Wiring standards (for example, CAT5, fiber optic, LocalTalk, coax).
		• Network speeds (for example, 10Mbps Ethernet, 100Mbps Ethernet).
		• Networking protocols (for example, TCP/IP, AppleTalk, IPX/SPX [Novell], NetBEUI [Microsoft]).
		• Type of Internet connection (for example, frame relay, T1, DSL, ISDN, modem) and speed.
		• Your ISP relationship:
		  • Name of your ISP.
		  • Number and type of connections.
		  • Protocols.
		  • IP addressing scheme (if you use NAT or DHCP, describe).
		• Firewall capabilities.
		• Remote access services (RAS) or virtual private network (VPN).

	B. Current LAN/WAN Equipment Inventory	Provide an inventory of your organization's current network equipment, in table form. Annotate the inventory table as necessary with narrative to explain oddities, history, or other information you wish to capture for your own and others' understanding later. Both LAN and WAN equipment may be included in a single table. Consider all of these items: • Routers. • Switches. • Hubs. • Remote access services. • Modems or modem pools. • Firewalls. • Other. TIPS for completing your inventory properly: For each item in the table indicate "keep," "upgrade," or "replace." If upgrade: • How do you want to upgrade (memory, additional ports, and so forth)?

Main Section	Subsection	Content
		• Which business process improvements does upgrading support? • At what cost? (Add to budget reminder sheet.) • By when do you need to upgrade? (Add to timeline reminder sheet.) If replace: • Replace with what? • Which process improvements does replacing support? • At what cost? (Add to budget reminder sheet.) • By when do you need to replace? (Add to timeline reminder sheet.)
	C. Current LAN/WAN Logical Diagrams NOTE: A multisite nonprofit may need to separate LAN and WAN diagrams and provide diagrams for each site.	Provide a diagram of your organization's current LAN/WAN showing where equipment is placed relative to other equipment and type of wire connecting the parts. Include: • Hubs and switches. • Routers. • Firewalls. • Remote access servers (RAS) or virtual private network (VPN). • Servers. • Desktop computers. • Networked peripherals. • How equipment connects to the "outside." • How remote sites are connected (for a multisite organization). NOTE: Include a key defining the symbols on each diagram.
	D. Current Site Plan Diagram(s)	Provide a site plan drawing that shows: • Location of buildings, rooms, and wiring drops within them. • Location of server room(s). • Location of main distribution frame (MDF) (where all the wires go). • Location of intermediate distribution frames (IDFs) (where other hubs and switches are located). • Location of MPOE (minimum point of entry) for phone company. • Distances from MDF to IDFs, other buildings, and rooms, or a legend with building scale. NOTE: Include a key and scale defining the symbols and distances on each diagram.

	E. Description of Proposed LAN/WAN	Write a narrative description of your organization's proposed LAN and WAN that includes:
		• Wiring standards (for example, CAT5, fiber optic, LocalTalk, coax).
		• Network speeds (for example, 10Mbps Ethernet, 100Mpbs Ethernet).
		• Networking protocols (for example, TCP/IP, AppleTalk, IPX/SPX [Novell], NetBEUI [Microsoft]).
		• Type of Internet connection (for example, frame relay, T1, DSL, ISDN, modem) and speed.
		• Your ISP relationship:
		  • Name of your ISP.
		  • Number and type of connections.

Main Section	Subsection	Content
		• Protocols. • IP addressing scheme (if you use NAT or DHCP, describe). • Firewall capabilities. • Remote access services (RAS) or virtual private network (VPN). Answer these questions: • Which business process improvements do these acquisitions support? • At what cost? (Add to budget reminder sheet.) • By when do you need the items? (Add to timeline reminder sheet.)
	F. Proposed LAN/WAN Equipment Acquisitions	Describe what you want or need to acquire. Answer these questions: • What do you want or need to acquire that is different from your planned upgrades and replacements? That is, what equipment are you adding to your inventory? Be general (say "switch," rather than a specific model and configuration, unless you already know what you need). • Which business process improvements do these acquisitions support? • At what cost? (Add to budget reminder sheet.) • By when do you need the items? (Add to timeline reminder sheet.) Consider all of these items: • Routers. • Switches. • Hubs. • Remote access services. • Modems or modem pools. • Firewalls. • Other. NOTE: Replacements and upgrades were discussed in the current LAN/WAN equipment section. Do not repeat that information here.
	G. Proposed LAN/WAN Logical Diagrams	Provide a diagram of your organization's proposed LAN and WAN, showing where equipment will be placed relative to other equipment and type of wire connecting the parts. Include: • Hubs and switches. • Routers. • Firewalls. • Remote access servers (RAS) or virtual private network (VPN). • Servers. • Desktop computers. • Networked peripherals. • How equipment connects to the "outside." • How remote sites are connected (for a multisite organization) NOTE: Include a key defining the symbols on each diagram.
	H. Proposed Site Plan	Provide a site plan drawing that shows: • Location of buildings, rooms, and wiring drops within them. • Location of server room(s).

Main Section	Subsection	Content
		• Location of main distribution frame (MDF) (where all the wires go). • Location of intermediate distribution frames (IDFs) (where other hubs and switches are located). • Location of MPOE (minimum point of entry) for phone company. • Distances from MDF to IDFs, other buildings, and rooms, or a legend with building scale NOTE: Include a key and scale defining the symbols and distances on each diagram. If your current and proposed site plans are basically the same, state that and refer the reader to the current site plan section.
VIII. Other Technologies	A. Assistive Technologies (contains two subsections)	Describe any equipment needed or anticipated to accommodate people with special needs: 1. Current Assistive Technologies Answer this question: • What are your current strategies for providing assistive technologies? 2. Proposed Assistive Technologies Answer these questions: • What are your future strategies for providing assistive technologies? • How will you train your employees to use these technologies? Note: Add this to your training plan section. • At what cost? (Add to budget reminder sheet.) • By when do you need the items? (Add to timeline reminder sheet.)
	B. Business Technologies (contains two subsections)	1. Current Business Technologies Provide an inventory of any other business technologies necessary to achieving its mission that your agency pays for and supports, such as the local phone system, cell phones, pagers, PDAs, and copiers (not attached to the LAN). Answer this question: • How do these technologies relate to your business strategies? 2. Proposed Business Technologies Answer these questions: • Which business process improvements do these acquisitions support? • At what cost? (Add to budget reminder sheet.) • By when do you need the items? (Add to timeline reminder sheet.)

IX. Facilities Plan	A. Upgrades Required	Describe upgrades required to meet your projected needs in these areas:
		 • Electricity.
		 • Air conditioning.
		 • Implications of new wiring.
		   • Punching holes in walls.
		   • False ceiling access.
		   • Outdoor wire runs.
		   • Conduit.
		   • Fire code issues (for example, plenum air space).

Main Section	Subsection	Content
		• Physical security of servers, network. and other sensitive equipment.
	B. Impact of Upgrades	Consider the impact of your planned upgrades. Answer these questions: • Who does the work, you or your landlord? • Which business process improvements do these upgrades support? • At what cost? (Add to budget reminder sheet.) • By when do you need the items? (Add to timeline reminder sheet.)
X. Security Plan	A. Current Security Arrangements	For server security consider: • Physical location. • Data access. • Account access (both e-mail accounts and messages and server accounts and privilege definitions). • Antivirus, including definition updates. • Backup procedures. • Software updates (for example, service packs, patches, bug fixes). • Disaster recovery plan. For desktop and laptop security consider: • Desktop password protection. • Startup password protection. • Antivirus, including definition updates. • Backup procedures. • Software updates (for example, service packs, patches, bug fixes). • Physical security (both for computers that are locked down and for those that are not). • Disaster recovery plan. For network equipment security consider: • Physical location. • Firewall. For Web site security consider: • Physical security. • Web hosting service security. • Data access. • Firewall. • Disaster recovery plan.
	B. Proposed Security Plan	Describe where improvements could be or should be made. Answer these questions: • Which business process improvements do these changes support? • Does your disaster recovery plan need improvement? If so, why and how? If not, why not? • Is training needed? • At what cost? (Add to budget reminder sheet.) • By when do you need the items? (Add to timeline reminder sheet.)

Main Section	Subsection	Content
XI. Technology Support Plan	A. Current End-User Support	Describe procedures for reporting a software or hardware problem. Include an escalation path description for: • Local users. • Remote users.
	B. Proposed End-User Support	Describe changes or improvements to your end-user support. Answer these questions: • What are the procedural improvements? • What are the escalation path improvements, including accommodating remote sites? • Which business process improvements do these changes or improvements support? • At what cost? (Add to budget reminder sheet.) • By when do you need the items? (Add to timeline reminder sheet.)
	C. Current Periodic Maintenance	Describe current periodic maintenance. Include: • Virus updates. • Software patches. • Version upgrades. • Scheduled printer maintenance. • Disk defragmentation. For each item include: • A brief description. • Who does it? • When does the person do it? • On what equipment are the maintenance procedures performed? • How is maintenance performed at remote sites?
	D. Proposed Periodic Maintenance	Describe proposed periodic maintenance. Include: • Virus updates. • Software patches. • Version upgrades. • Scheduled printer maintenance. • Disk defragmentation. For each item include: • A brief description. • Who does it? • When does the person do it? • Which business process improvements do these activities support? • At what cost? (Add to budget reminder sheet.) • By when do you need the items? (Add to timeline reminder sheet.)
XII. Training Plan	A. Current Training Methods and Practices	Describe how you determine who needs what type of training. Cover these training issues: • New hire orientation. • Continuing employee training. • Tech support staff training. Cover these training topics: • Basic troubleshooting. • Common software used. • Common hardware used. • Special software or databases used.

Main Section	Subsection	Content
	B. Proposed Training Methods and Practices	Describe where training improvements could or should be made. Answer these questions: • What modifications can be made to current procedures, methods, or topics? • What improvements are needed in determining who needs what type of training? • Which business process improvements do these acquisitions support? • At what cost? (Add to budget reminder sheet.) • By when do you need the items? (Add to timeline reminder sheet.)
XIII. Evaluation and Continuous Improvement Strategy	A. Process Improvement Review	Determine the manner and timing of reviews of your business process improvement progress. Answer these questions: • With what frequency will you evaluate business process improvements? (Add to timeline reminder sheet.) • What will your review vehicle be (for example, board meetings, project team meetings, manager reviews)? • What will your review parameters be? Ask: Have we done what we said we would in the time frame, within budget, and meeting our measures of success? • Will you need to give progress reports?
	B. Technology Plan Review	Determine the manner and timing of reviews of progress on the technology plan. Answer these questions: • With what frequency will you evaluate business process improvements? (Add to timeline reminder sheet.) • What will your review vehicle be (for example, board meetings, project team meetings, manager reviews)? • What will your review parameters be (for example, acquisition, deployment, budget, timeline)? • Will you need to give progress reports?
	C. Technology Plan Update	Determine how and when you will update your technology plan to reflect: • Changing organizational needs. • Changing technologies. Answer these questions: • Who will be responsible for updates? • When will formal technology plan updates occur?
XIV. Acceptable Use Policy	A. Rules for Technology Use	Describe the rules that will govern technology use in your organization by employees, volunteers, and clients.
	B. Consequences for Abuse	Describe what consequences will result and what actions will be taken if the rules are abused.
XV. Budget	A. Remainder of Current FY B. Next Full FY C. Additional FYs as Appropriate	Differentiate capital and expense items, if appropriate for your organization. • Capital items: usually high purchase price, long life. • Expense items: usually small items, low-end equipment, monthly fees, consulting and outsourcing fees. Include in your budgets: • All expenses mentioned in all sections of your technology plan. • Start and end of your organization's fiscal year (FY). • Consumables. • Salaries (current and proposed).

Main Section	Subsection	Content

XVI. Implementation Timeline		A Gantt chart organized by date is very useful in seeing the big picture, including the ways tasks relate to each other in time. Include start and end dates, and milestone completion dates for:
		• All timeline items mentioned in all sections of your technology plan.
		• Action items assigned to people for documenting, researching, writing procedures.
		• Major purchases. Things it is wise to include:
		  • Purchase decision "drop dead" dates.
		  • Vendor selection.
		  • Cut PO.
		  • Purchases received.
		  • Purchases implemented or deployed.
		  • User training preparation.
		  • User training delivery.
		• Grant applications. Things it is wise to include:
		  • Preparation.
		  • Filing date.
		  • Waiting period.
		  • Funds or in-kind received.
		  • Funds or in-kind deployed.
		  • Contingencies should your proposal be rejected.
		  • User training preparation
		  • User training delivery.
		• Process Review. Include:
		  • Review dates.
		  • Status reports to board or other groups.
		  • Checkpoints for reviewing implementation progress and evaluating process improvements.
		• Tech Plan updates. Include:
		  • Review dates.
		  • Revision dates.
		  • Status reports on progress to board and others.

XVII. Appendixes NOTE: All appendixes are optional and need to be included only if they are applicable.	A. Glossary of Terms	Provide brief definitions for terms and acronyms specific to your *industry* and that "outsiders" may not know. Provide brief definitions for terms and acronyms specific to your *organization* that "outsiders" may not know.
	B. Consulting Contracts	Provide copies of any consulting contracts your organization currently has.
	C. Support and Maintenance Contracts	Provide copies of any contracts for equipment or software maintenance.
	D. Technology Job Descriptions	Provide job descriptions for any technology jobs your organization has or plans to hire for. Consider: • Help desk technician. • Network manager. • IT director. • Support technician. • Others, as applicable to your organization.
	E. Other Appendixes as Appropriate	

Resource B

Flowchart Symbols

Start or End

Activity,
procedure, step,
or process

Report or
document

Data input

Decision?

Those points in the process
where a yes or no question is being
asked or a decision is required.

A | Continued. Look
for matching symbol
on another page.

Connector
between boxes.

Loop.
Go back and repeat.
Usually with a decision.

Resource C

Technology Plan Checklist

1. Are all sections and subsections included?

2. Do sections and subsections follow the outline provided in Resource A?

3. Does the cover page fully identify your organization and the document and the document's date and revision number?

4. Does the table of contents contain all sections, including appendixes, and page numbers for each? (Note: Number continuously; do not restart each section with page one.)

5. Are all subsections of the plan introduction (Section II) included?

6. Are the strategic goals clearly articulated and to the point?

7. Are the business processes, business process improvements, role of technology in process improvements, and technology strategies clearly articulated?

8. Are the measures of success quantifiable—measurable in some concrete way?

9. Do all sections from Section III through Section XII have *both* current and proposed scenarios?

10. Do inventories include designations of "Keep," "Upgrade," or "Replace" for all items counted?

11. Are inventories included for

    a. Hardware?

    b. Software?

    c. Network equipment?

    d. Office equipment?

12. Is each inventory preceded by a narrative or other explanatory text describing what is to follow?

13. Do the network diagrams
    a. Have a key?
    b. Have a scale?
    c. Identify elements critical to understanding the network (for example, MDF, IDFs, MPOE, server locations, and so forth)?
    d. Provide both physical and logical information?

14. Is the plan budget internally and externally consistent?
    a. Is the time frame covered by the budget clearly identified?
    b. Is the fiscal year clearly identified?
    c. Do quantities in narratives, tables, and budget match?
    d. Are budget items annotated?
    e. Do budget purchases agree with timeline milestone dates?
    f. Is the arithmetic correct?
    g. Have multiple budgets been prepared for phased or multiyear projects?
    h. Is there a narrative describing the budget parameters, process, and other salient information needed by a naive reader?

15. Is the timeline internally and externally consistent? Does it
    a. Include every date mentioned for proposed plans?
    b. Begin with the present and go through the end of the projects, even if they are multiyear?
    c. Include both milestone dates and beginning and end dates for tasks?
    d. Include business process improvement dates?
    e. Include a technology plan review date?
    f. Include a technology plan update date?

16. If the plan uses industry or organizational jargon, do the appendixes include a glossary?

17. Do the appendixes include copies of any consulting contracts for technology consulting?

18. Do the appendixes include copies of any maintenance contracts for equipment?

19. Do the appendixes include technology job descriptions for current and anticipated technology jobs?

20. Has someone run a spell and grammar check?

21. Has someone proofread for style and grammatical consistency (to solve the problem of multiple authors producing multiple styles)?

22. Do all pages have a page number, even if it is handwritten?

Resource D

Glossary of Terms

The purpose of this glossary is to provide definitions for terms used throughout this book and terms that you might run across when developing your technology plan or talking with vendors and consultants. It includes business and budgeting terms along with technical terms. **Boldface** indicates a term that is defined in this glossary.

Additional networking and computer glossaries can be found at these Web sites:

"Glossary of Internet Terms": www.matisse.net/files/glossary.html

"Technical Term Glossary" (general technology terms): www.techsoup.org/glossary.cfm

"Computer, Telephony & Electronics Industry Glossary" (comprehensive and highly technical): www.csgnetwork.com/glossary.html

"Internet for Beginners Glossary": http://netforbeginners.about.com /library/glossary/blglossary.htm

Numeric Terms

10BaseT An **Ethernet** implementation in which data are carried over standard CAT5 wire, basically standard telephone wire, with a data throughput of 10 megabits per second (10Mbps).

100BaseT An **Ethernet** implementation in which data throughput is 100Mbps, 10 times faster than 10BaseT.

802.11b The current standard for wireless **LAN** networking. 802.11b is also referred to as *Wi-Fi*.

A

Accessibility The degree to which a computer system and software are usable by people with various physical challenges: for example, limited limb motion or vision impairment.

All-in-one A computer that combines all its hardware components, including the monitor, in a single package that sits on a desk.

AppleTalk The **protocol** used by Macintosh computers to communicate with each other.

Application or **application program** Software that performs a specified set of features. For example, Microsoft Word is a word processing application. Application programs make use of **operating system** features for such things as saving files to a hard disk or providing user interface features.

ASP (application service provider) ASPs are companies that set up, administer, and maintain **applications** for other organizations, usually away from the other organizations' sites (off-site) on the ASP's equipment. Access is via the **Internet**.

Assistive technology A technology that renders a computer system or software accessible, or more accessible. See also **accessibility.**

ATM (asynchronous transfer mode) Telecommunications technology for transferring voice, data, and video signals at high speeds. It is high cost for individual companies, and is more commonly used as a **backbone** technology.

AUP (acceptable use policy) A written policy that outlines rules for computer and network use in an organization and the consequences of violating or abusing those rules.

B

Backbone (1) A central network connecting other networks together. Companies such as MCI, Sprint, UUNet, and AT&T all run central backbones. (2) In a large **LAN,** the segment between the **IDFs** and **MDF.**

Bandwidth Determines the amount of data (capacity) that can travel in a given time period (speed) through a circuit.

BIOS (basic input output system) Low-level software that comes with computer **hardware** and that is used during starting up the computer and may be used by the **operating system** for low-level hardware access.

Bleeding-edge technology Technology that is so new as to be unproven in the marketplace.

Bridge A specialized, dedicated device that connects segments of a large **LAN** together, similar to a switch, or separate LANs together into an **internet.** See also **hub, switch, router, MDF, IDF.**

C

Cable modem A device that provides high-speed Internet access over television cable.

Capital item In budgeting, a high-priced item that is usually either insured or depreciated or both. In many organizations, capital items are things that cost $500 or more each.

CAT5, CAT3, CAT5e, and **CAT6** A specification for twisted pair wiring (two wires twisted together) that supports high-speed networking, commonly used for **Ethernet** up to **100BaseT.** CAT3 is a twisted pair standard that is commonly used for voice communications and can be used for Ethernet up to **10BaseT.** CAT5e and CAT6 are similar to CAT5 but can be used at speeds higher than 100 Mbps.

Client Any computer on a network that uses resources from a **server.** A single computer can be both a client and a server.

Client-server computing Computing that is done on the server while the user's desktop computer runs a client that merely fetches and stores data.

Client-server database A database implementation in which the database engine and all data reside on a server, and users access that data through client software that runs on their desktop computers.

Client-server network A network in which one or more separate, larger computers provide services to all devices on the network. The **server** is centrally administered by a knowledgeable person, and it typically enforces use policies on the users.

Co-location The housing of an organization's server resources, usually Web site services, at a third-party facility that handles periodic maintenance, data backup, and security. Access is via the **Internet.**

Configuration Software settings that determine the behavior of either hardware or software according to a user's needs and preferences. For computers, **hardware** and **operating system** configuration is set through a control panel program. In many **application programs,** configuration is set through a "preferences" command on one of the menus.

Consumables Materials that are used up and must be replenished, such as printer toner, ink cartridges, paper, and **removable media.**

CPU (central processing unit) The brain of the computer—a computer chip that performs most of the processing.

D

Database A file or set of files of data that, when combined with associated data entry functions, report appearance specifications, and reporting functions, performs specific tasks and provides specified functionality to the user. A database has two parts: (1) the database engine, or software, that drives the functionality available to users and (2) the actual data, report layouts, and scripts that permit users to access data in ways useful to them. A database may be single-user or multiuser. A single-user database resides on one person's computer and is not shared with any other user. A multiuser database is used by many people and is accessed either through **file sharing** or **client-server** design. A **file sharing** arrangement permits one person to write data into the database at a time, during which time other users can only read the data. **Client-server** implementations permit multiple people to both read and write data into the database at the same time.

Data communications network The equipment and wiring needed to connect computers in a organization together so they can communicate, share information, and access the Internet.

Device A piece of equipment. In the context of networks, *device* refers to equipment that is connected to the network. In the context of computers, *device* refers to a **peripheral.**

DHCP (dynamic host configuration protocol) Allows **TCP/IP** configuration to be managed from a **server,** rather than requiring each computer to be individually configured.

DNS (1) **Domain name system:** the ICANN (Internet Corporation for Assigned Names and Numbers) sanctioned system for allocating **Internet domain names.** (2) **Domain name server:** software running on a network that permits computers on that network to communicate with other computers on the Internet.

Domain A group of related computers. In the context of the Internet, it refers to computers within the domain name system (see **DNS**). In the context of Microsoft Windows operating systems, it refers to a system for validating users and assigning privileges.

Domain name The unique name given to each computer on the Internet. Domain names are hierarchically structured, ending in commonly recognized abbreviations, such as, in the United States, .org, .com, .gov, and .edu. For computers located outside the United States, domain names end in a two-letter country abbreviation: for example, .ca for Canada. The parts of a domain name are separated by dots. For example, the full domain name for the Center for Excellence in Nonprofits is www.cen.org. See also **DNS.**

Dot The period character (.) in a **URL, e-mail address,** or **IP address;** pronounced "dot." For example, www.wfg.org is pronounced "w-w-w dot w-f-g dot org."

DSL (digital subscriber line) A last-mile transport system, which can carry about 1 to 6 megabits per second (Mbps) over an existing copper line.

E

E-mail (electronic mail) Messages and information sent and received via an e-mail **client** on a computer. To send and receive e-mail, the user needs a valid **e-mail address,** acquired from either an **ISP** or a **network administrator.**

E-mail address A series of numbers and/or letters that uniquely identifies an entity (an individual, an organization, a group, and so forth) out of all the entities in the world that are using the Internet for sending and receiving e-mail. An e-mail address takes the form YourName@YourDomainName. For you as an individual employee of your organization, for example, the "YourName" part is assigned to you by your **network administrator** or **ISP.** The "YourDomainName" part is determined by your organization's domain name. The two parts *must* be connected by the "at sign," @. An e-mail address may *not* contain any spaces.

Encrypt To encode data sent over a network so that it cannot be read by users, computers, or devices other than the intended recipients. Encryption is performed with the aid of complex mathematical formulas.

Escalation path The sequence of steps to be followed by an end-user or technical support person in order to successfully resolve the user's problem. The escalation path begins with the simplest things to try and moves on to increasingly more complicated things to try and progressively more expert people to contact until the problem is resolved. Escalation paths are most commonly represented as a list of steps or a flowchart of contacts and activities at each major step of the way to resolution.

Ethernet A local area network (LAN) standard defining a physical medium and its method of placing data on a wire.

Expense item In budgeting, a low-cost item that is neither depreciated nor insured. Note that some high-cost items may also be expenses: for example, a consulting fee or a maintenance contract. In many organizations, items that cost less than $500 are expensed.

Extranet A network based on Internet technologies that can be accessed only by people inside an organization and possibly some selected outsiders such as clients or suppliers. An extranet provides services in a Web site format, accessible with a standard Web browser and communicating via TCP/IP.

F

Fault tolerance The ability to keep a network or equipment running in the face of a fault.

Fiber optic A glass filament sheathed in a protective covering used for high-speed data network communications.

File sharing The shared use by designated users of files residing on a server that allows general access. The server simply provides file storage; all processing on the file is done on the user's desktop computer.

Firewall Hardware and software that provide a defense against unauthorized access to a **network.** A firewall often provides differing levels of defense for different parts of the network. It does not protect against viruses or other damage that might be imported by people with authorized access to secure locations.

Flame mail E-mail that is deliberately inflammatory, derogatory, and insulting and is sent with the intent to incite the recipient. **Flaming** is the act of sending flame mail. A **flame war** is two or more people engaging in the mutual exchange of flame mail.

Frame relay A fast-packet switching technology that offers the benefits of private lines and shared network products. For smaller organizations with expanding networks, frame relay offers cost-effective advantages in the areas of **LAN** interconnection, **Internet** access, and SNA network transport.

FTP (file transfer protocol) The **protocol** used for transferring one or more files from one computer to another over the Internet.

FTP server A computer on the Internet that stores files for transmission by FTP.

G

Gantt chart A project management tool in the form of a timeline that shows (1) tasks to be completed, (2) milestones to achieve, (3) duration of each task, and often (4) manpower allocation to tasks.

H

Hard disk High-volume, semipermanent storage for data on a computer. When the computer's power is turned off, the data remain intact and can be accessed again when power is turned back on. Users can write data to and erase data from hard disks. Hard disks are typically magnetic media.

Hardware The tangible portions of a computer system or **peripheral**—the parts you can see and touch. Hardware needs companion software in order to make up a complete and useful system.

Hardware inventory A detailed listing of every computer, **peripheral,** and network device (see **device**) in an organization, giving **OS** name and version, processor type, amount of RAM, and size of hard disk.

HIPPA The federal Health Insurance Portability and Privacy Act. Any organization working with individually identifiable health information must be prepared to handle the security and privacy requirements of HIPPA.

Home page The page of a Web site that is designated by the Web site's author as its "first page." The home page is what people will see first when going to a Web site's designated **URL.**

Hot swap A process that allows a user to replace failed hardware, such as a disk drive or memory card, or to upgrade it without either turning the equipment off or taking it off of the network.

http (hypertext transfer protocol) The main **protocol** used to access **Web pages** on the **World Wide Web. Web browsers** are programmed to recognize the http designation at the beginning of a URL and to respond appropriately.

Hub An active network hardware device (see **device**) into which several other devices plug, enabling them to talk to each other. The available network bandwidth is *shared by* the devices connected to the hub, somewhat like an old-fashioned party line. For example, if two devices on the hub are active simultaneously, then each gets half the bandwidth, but if four are active then each gets one-quarter. Traditionally used with star **topology** networks. See also **switch, router, bridge.**

Hyperlink An embedded command on a Web page or in text or images, that, when an **icon** or other element is clicked, causes another Web page to be loaded.

I

Icon A small graphic symbol on a computer screen (monitor) that represents something available to the computer's user, such as application programs, documents, or printers.

IDF (intermediate distribution frame) The equipment that makes up an intermediate connection point for devices on segments of a large **LAN.** IDF is sometimes referred to as a *wiring closet.* See also **MDF.**

Information technology (IT) IT is any form of hardware or software (such as computers, software applications, telephones, modems, or servers) that supports the management of information for an organization's functions.

internet (not capitalized) A network of networks. Two or more networks connected together. See also **Internet.**

Internet or **the Internet** (capitalized) The worldwide collections of networks running **TCP/IP.** The Internet is completely public, and has no one arbiter or owner. Each person or organization is responsible for the operation of its own piece of the Internet. The Internet is *more* than the **World Wide Web.** It also includes such functions as **e-mail, FTP, Telnet,** and newsgroups.

Internet appliance An Internet server that provides all the services needed for an organization to access the Internet without requiring extensive in-house configuration and administration. The organization simply connects the Internet appliance to the **LAN.** This ready-to-go consumer device permits end-users to plug easily into home or office Internet access in order to browse Web sites and send and receive e-mail without the need to install software and do complex configuration.

Intranet A network based on Internet technologies that is limited to people within an organization and accessed via a **LAN** or **WAN.** An intranet provides in-house services in a Web site format, accessible with a standard Web browser and communicating via **TCP/IP.**

IP address A unique number used to identify each computer that is connected to the Internet. IP addresses have four numeric parts, each three digits long, separated by periods: for example, 123.456.789.012

IPX/SPX Novell proprietary network **protocols.**

ISDN (integrated services digital network) A fast, digital data communications line that can be provided by most telephone companies. To reap the benefits, you need to add a special card to your PC or attach an external device, and your Internet service provider must be able to provide an ISDN connection.

ISP (Internet service provider) A company that provides a connection to the Internet. ISPs may also offer domain name registration, IP address, disk space, Web hosting, data transmission, and site management services.

J

Jack The wall outlet into which a connecting cable for a device (telephone, **Ethernet,** and so forth) is plugged to make a network connection.

L

LAN (local area network) All of the wiring and equipment connecting devices within buildings and between buildings on a single campus. A LAN's connections all ultimately terminate at an **MDF.** A very large LAN may be divided up into segments whose connections terminate at intermediate points, called **IDFs.**

Launch Start up an **application program,** either by double-clicking its icon or shortcut icon with the mouse pointer or double-clicking on a document created by that application program.

Leading-edge technology Technology that is at the forefront of technology development and advancement but that is tried in the marketplace.

Legacy system An older computer and its older software.

Link See **hyperlink.**

Listserv or **listserve** A managed list of **e-mail addresses,** all of which can receive each e-mail message sent by the list manager and by members of the list. Some listserves are moderated, meaning that the list manager reads all messages and judges them for appropriateness before passing them on to list members. Some are not moderated, meaning that all messages are sent out to all members without a preview for appropriateness.

M

Magnetic media Computer storage media on which data are read and written as variations in a magnetic field. A moderately strong magnet held near magnetic media will erase data, so it is wise to keep magnets away from computer areas. Magnetic media are hard disks, floppy disks, Zip disks, and data storage tapes.

Mail server A **server** that receives and stores incoming and outgoing **e-mail.**

Mailing list A type of e-mail address that forwards all incoming mail to a list of subscribers interested in a specific topic.

Maintenance Technical support tasks that include activities to maintain hardware and software in good working condition. See also **periodic maintenance.**

MDF (main distribution frame) A piece of equipment that is the main connection point for all devices on a **LAN** or for all segments of a large LAN. See also **IDF.**

Measures of success Numerically quantifiable parameters that can be taken at specified points in time and compared to a set of baseline values to determine progress in implementing network and technology plans.

Media Forms of storage onto which computer data are written, including disks, CD-ROMs, and even paper, though the latter is not typically referred to as a medium.

Memory Temporary storage of computer data and programs. When the computer's power is turned off, data in memory are erased. This information will not be there when the computer is turned back on. Memory is sometimes called RAM.

Migration plan A plan for the future growth of a technology network.

Modem A hardware device, located either inside the computer or in a separate box that plugs into the computer, that permits users to transmit data via an ordinary telephone line. See also **remote access, RAS.**

MPOE (minimum point of entry) Point at which the telephone company lines terminate on a site. The MPOE designates where site occupant responsibility begins.

Multimedia Made up of a variety of media. Web pages are multimedia when they combine text, photos, animations, and movie clips to convey the site's message.

N

NAT (network address translation) A mechanism for automatically translating IP addresses, typically used to allow a number of computers with private IP addresses to share one public IP address. Public IP addresses are visible on the Internet. Private IP addresses are not visible on the Internet, and must be specifically in these ranges

10.0.0.0 to 10.255.255.255

172.16.0.0 to 172.31.255.255

192.168.0.0 to 192.168.255.255.

IP addresses in the private range are *not* routable on the Internet under any circumstances.

Net, the The **Internet.**

NetBEUI A **protocol** used by computers running the Windows operating system to communicate with each other.

NetBIOS A **protocol** used by computers running the Windows operating system to communicate with each other.

Network The unit formed by computers and related equipment, such as printers, when they are connected to one another.

Network administrator A person whose job is **network management.**

Network computer A computer with no hard disk that gets its application programs and data from a **server** over a network.

Network interface card See **NIC**.

Network management The practice of network oversight, from troubleshooting network problems to planning additions. It includes tasks such as documenting network topology; setting up routers, hubs, and communication services; and managing the operation of all devices on the network. These tasks are usually performed by a network manager, but may be performed by tech support personnel.

Network protocol A protocol used by computers on a network to talk to each other. When you configure your computer to connect to a network, you must add the appropriate protocol(s). Examples of protocols are **TCP/IP, IPX,** and **AppleTalk.**

Network services Shared services that are provided by a server on a **WAN** or **LAN** to computers connected to the network. Common network services include shared printers; incoming and outgoing e-mail management, storage, and retrieval; **domain name service** and Web site hosting; **remote access;** fax services; **file sharing;** CD-ROM sharing; and **database** hosting.

NIC (network interface card) A printed circuit card installed in a computer that enables the computer to communicate with other equipment on the **LAN.** This is the part of the computer a network cable plugs into when it connects the computer to a LAN outlet in the wall.

Node Any device that is connected to a network. For example, a **LAN** with ten nodes has ten devices connected on it.

O

Online or **on-line** Using the Internet or having access to the Internet. Often people will say they are on-line meaning that they have access to the Internet and have an e-mail address, but they may not necessarily be connected to the Internet at that moment.

Operating system Essential software that manages all of a computer's basic functions, including the operation of **application programs** and system-level functions such as tracking date and time, saving files, and retrieving data. It is the operating system that lets you run several **applications** at the same time, for example. Some commonly known operating systems are Windows NT, Windows XP, Linux, and MacOS.

Optical media Storage media that are read and written to optically, by means of a laser beam. Although optical media cannot be damaged by magnets, they can be damaged by scratching the surface deeply enough to affect the data, which are written just under the clear, protective surface coating. Examples of optical media are CD-ROMs, CDR/Ws (user erasable and writable CDs), and DVDs.

OS See **operating system.**

P

Patch (software) A "fix" for a software bug, or problem, often downloaded from a Web site and installed on a desktop computer or server.

Patch cord or **patch cable** A length of wire that connects a piece of equipment, such as a computer or a printer, to a **LAN.** One end of the patch cord plugs into an **NIC** and the other end plugs into a LAN **jack** on the wall or into a **patch panel.**

Patch panel A device that connects permanent wiring in a building (at the point where it terminates) to a **switch** or **hub**. Patch panels reside in **MDFs** and **IDFs.**

PDA (personal digital assistant) A compact, handheld device used for organizing a calendar, contacts, memos, notes, and reminders.

Peer-to-peer network or **peer network** A direct connection between one desktop computer and another to transfer files, access a **database,** or share other resources, such as a printer, without the need for a **server.** There is no central administration for this type of network; each user decides what to make available to others on an ad hoc basis. The computers must share a common operating system. Peer-to-peer networking is built into the Windows 95 and 98 operating systems and Windows NT 4.0 Workstations.

Periodic maintenance Regularly scheduled maintenance activities on hardware and software. Periodic maintenance includes such tasks as cleaning, running diagnostics, and installing software updates.

Peripheral An input/output device connected to a computer, such as a hard disk, floppy disk drive, printer, or modem.

PERT chart A project management tool in the form of a timeline that shows (1) tasks to be completed, (2) duration of tasks, and (3) *dependencies* between tasks in order to highlight time-critical elements of the project plan.

Pizza box A computer with all its hardware components packaged in a flat, horizontal box resembling a large pizza box. A separate monitor sits on top of the box and plugs into it in the back.

Platform The **hardware** and **operating system** of a computer considered together.

Plenum, plenum rated cable **Plenum** is the air space between a suspended ceiling and the real ceiling. **Plenum rated cable** is cable that will not give off noxious fumes if it burns in a fire. It is used in the plenum when heating and air conditioning systems use the plenum for air return without ducting.

POTS (plain old telephone service) Basic telephone voice service.

Process A sequence of repeatable steps that leads to some desired end or output.

Processor See **CPU**.

Productivity software Software that provides general tools that support doing business. Word processing, spreadsheet, e-mail, and desktop presentation **programs** are all productivity software.

Program See **application**.

Protocol A set of rules by which computers and other equipment communicate on a network. Different protocols are in use for different purposes: for example, communication between computers on a **LAN** or accessing the Internet. Some LAN protocols are **NetBEUI, IPX/SPX,** and **AppleTalk.** Internet protocols include **TCP/IP, http, Telnet, SMTP,** and **FTP.**

Q

Qwerty Refers to the standard keyboard layout, with the letters QWERTY making up the top left alphabetical row.

R

RAM See **memory**.

RAS (remote access server) A bank of **modems** on a **LAN** that provides LAN access to users at remote locations. See also **remote access.**

Remote access Entry to a network from an off-site location. Users who connect to their organization's **LAN** from a home office (typically by modem) are using remote access. See also **RAS.**

Removable storage media Storage media that the user can remove from the computer, typically with a much smaller capacity than a hard disk. Removable storage media may be either magnetic (floppy disk, Zip disk, data storage tape), or optical (CD-ROM, DVD).

RJ11 The type of connector on the cord that connects a telephone to a telephone jack in the wall.

RJ45 The type of connector on both ends of the patch cord that is required to connect a computer's **NIC** to a **LAN.**

Router A specialized, dedicated computer that connects either segments of a large LAN or separate LANs together into **internets**. For example, a router connects a **LAN** to an organization's **WAN**. See also **hub, switch, bridge, MDF, IDF.**

S

Scalability A network design factor that accommodates expanding network capabilities as users' needs increase.

Server A computer and its software that provide a service to other computers on a network. The computer stores information centrally and the software determines how to respond to requests from the other computers on the network for access to the information.

Site plan A diagram showing the physical features of the network site, with dimensions and the locations of **MPOE, MDF, IDFs**, and **servers** and possibly other network information, depending on the level of detail desired.

SMTP (simple mail transfer protocol) The protocol used to send mail between servers and to send mail from a client to a mail server.

Software Computer programs, including both operating system and application programs, without which the computer hardware would be just so much sheet metal, plastic, and screws. The software is the intangible part of a complete computer system—you can't see it or touch it, but you need it for the computer to do useful work.

Software inventory A detailed listing of every application program at a site, providing version number, the computer on which program is installed, and license or serial number, if applicable.

Switch An active network hardware device into which several other devices plug, enabling them to talk to each other. The *entire* network **bandwidth** is available to all devices connected. See also **hub, router, bridge.**

Systems administration The performance of tasks such as setting up new mail accounts, user accounts, and new servers; updating software; and enforcing standard protocols, policies, and procedures. This set of tasks may be performed by **tech support** personnel.

Systems administrator Someone who performs system administration.

T

T1 A T1 is a leased line provided by a data communications company. It transmits data at 1.544 megabits per second. A line is made up of twenty-four separate channels of 64Kbps each, plus one 8Kbps channel for signaling and control. T1 is used mainly for bulk connections, typically among ISPs or private corporate networks.

T3 A T3 is a leased line provided by a data communications company. It transmits data at 45 megabits per second (equivalent to 30 T-1 lines). T3s are used for Internet **backbones** and large corporate networks. These lines are fiber optic or coaxial based and make up the majority of links in public switched networks deployed by telephone companies.

TCO (total cost of ownership) The total cost of owning technology, including such factors as user training, ongoing support, **maintenance,** and **consumables.**

TCP/IP (transmission control protocol/Internet protocol) The protocol used for all Internet traffic.

Technical support or **tech support** (1) Tasks performed in support of the general computer user community in an organization, to both respond to user problems on a daily and ongoing basis and maintain hardware and software in good working order. Tasks involving help desk staffing, equipment repairs, software installations, and configuration problems with both servers and desktop computers are often carried out by tech support. See also **maintenance** and **periodic maintenance.** (2) The personnel who carry out tech support tasks.

Telnet A method of connecting to another computer over the Internet.

Thin client A **client** designed to be especially small, so that the bulk of the data processing occurs on the server. A thin client is a network computer without a hard disk drive, whereas a *fat client* includes a disk drive. See also **client.**

Thin server A single-function server that does one thing well, such as providing Internet service, CD-ROM service, or file service.

Topology The "shape" of a network—how it would look if you drew it out on paper. Topology is determined by the way the cables physically connect network components, and may be described as, for example, a star, a ring, or a bus (a straight line).

Tower A computer with its hardware components arranged in a vertical, towerlike case, with a separate monitor that plugs into the tower. Towers are often floor standing, although some computers have a **mini-tower** configuration and can be placed on a desk.

Trojan horse A type of virus that neither replicates itself nor copies itself but does damage to the computer on which it runs or compromises the security of the computer.

U

UPS (uninterruptible power supply) A device that provides battery backup power to equipment in case of a main power supply failure.

URL (uniform resource locator) A **Web site** address, usually starting with the characters http://

V

Virus A computer program that is designed to cause damage to a computer's hard disk and to copy itself to other computers. The most common ways viruses are transmitted are via removable media and via infected files downloaded from the Internet.

VPN (virtual private network) A network in which some of the parts are connected through the public Internet, but the data sent across the Internet are **encrypted,** so the entire network is "virtually" private. A typical example is a VPN connecting two offices in different cities. Using the Internet, the two offices merge their networks into one but encrypt traffic that uses the Internet link.

W

WAN (wide area network) A network configuration in which the parts of the network are geographically dispersed, each part consisting of a **LAN.** A LAN connects to the **Internet** by means of a WAN. See also **router.**

Web, the Short for **World Wide Web.**

Web browser An application program used to access and peruse **Web sites.** Examples of Web browsers are Netscape Navigator and Internet Explorer.

Web page One "page" of information on the World Wide Web, accessed by typing a **URL** into a **Web browser.**

Web site or **Website** One or more **Web pages** (with one page designated as the main page, or **home page**); the pages you see when you type a **URL** into a **Web browser.**

WINS A **protocol** that allows Windows computers using **TCP/IP** to find each other, typically on a **LAN,** and communicate. It is administered by the server, not the individual computer.

Wire drop The place at which a **wire run** for a user to connect to the network terminates: for example, in an office or conference room.

Wire run The total length of a wire connecting a device to the **MDF** or **IDF** in a LAN. For **10BaseT** and **100BaseT** a wire run is limited to 100 meters.

Workstation See **client.**

World Wide Web See **WWW.**

Worm A type of virus that copies itself over a network and is designed to harm the network rather than individual computer hard disks.

WWW (World Wide Web) The total collection of Web pages available globally to computers running **TCP/IP.** Pages are accessed via a **URL** and connected by and navigated with **hyperlinks.** WWW is the fastest growing and most commonly recognized portion of the Internet. Each person or organization making Web pages available on the WWW is responsible for the content and integrity of those pages.

Zip disk A removable disk that stores 100 megabytes of memory. A zip disk can be read only by a zip drive built into or attached to a computer. Zip disks can be used to back up files or transport large amounts of data.

Zip drive A disk drive that accommodates 100 megabyte hard disks (zip disks). Both internal and external drives are available, making the drive suitable for backup, mass storage, or moving files between computers.

Resource E

Where to Go for More Information

The purpose of this list is to provide leads to places to go for more information about the topics covered in this book. It is a selected rather than an exhaustive list. Note that because Web sources are sometimes transient, the Web sites listed here may change their addresses or become inactive at any time.

Nonprofit Technology and Technology Planning

- Arts Wire Spider School. www.nyfa.org/nyfa/artswire/spiderschool

- The Benton Foundation. www.benton.org

- Coyote Communications. www.coyotecom.com

- Hecht, B., and Ramsey, R. *ManagingNonprofits.Org: Dynamic Management for the Digital Age.* New York: Wiley, 2002.

- The Npower National Network. www.npower.org

- Summit Collaborative. www.summitcollaborative.com/links.html

- Tech Soup. www.techsoup.org

Assistive Technology

- The Alliance for Technology Access. www.ataccess.org

- *Americans with Disabilities Act.* www.usdoj.gov/crt/ada/adahom1.htm

- CAST (Center for Applied Special Technology). www.cast.org

- EASI (Equal Access to Software and Information). www.rit.edu/%7Eeasi/index.htm

- NCAM (National Center for Accessible Media). ncam.wgbh.org

Funding

- *Chronicle of Philanthropy.* www.philanthropy.com

- *Federal Register.* (This government publication lists all federal notices of availability of funding.) www.access.gpo.gov/nara

- Foundation Center. (This site includes a state-by-state foundation directory.) www.fdncenter.org

- Network for Good. www.networkforgood.org

Change Management

- Beckhard, R., and Pritchard, W. *Changing the Essence: The Art of Creating and Leading Fundamental Change in Organizations.* San Francisco: Jossey-Bass, 1992.

- Bridges, W. *Surviving Corporate Transition: Rational Management in a World of Mergers, Layoffs, Start-Ups, Takeovers, Divestitures, Deregulation, and New Technology.* New York: Doubleday, 1988.

- Bridges, W. *Managing Transitions: Making the Most of Change.* Cambridge, Mass.: Perseus Books, 1991.

- Conner, D. R. *Managing at the Speed of Change: How Resilient Managers Succeed Where Others Fail.* New York: Villard Books, 1993.

- Johnson, S. *Who Moved My Cheese?* New York: Putnam, 1998.

Index

A

Abuse of technology, consequences for, 193, 196, 256
Acceptable use policy (AUP), 99, 191–196, 256, 264
Accessibility (to people with disabilities), 264
Accidental techies, 170, 173, 176
"Act" stage of plan, 9, 10, 186, 238
ADA (Americans with Disabilities Act) compliance, 150–151, 151n.1, 154
Addressing resistance, 18–23, 230
Administrative assistant, 41, 46
Agendas, planning meeting, 29–30
AIDS Community Research Consortium, 11, 23, 55, 234
Air conditioning, 157–158, 160, 161
American Red Cross, Santa Clara Valley Chapter, 39–40, 123–124, 153, 154
Analysis, business. *See* Business analysis
Andover Newton Theological School, 198
Antivirus software, 164, 165–166, 167, 168, 172, 177, 278
Appendixes, technology plan, 217–221, 257; checklist for, 262; examples, 218–221; types of, 75, 77, 217–218
Application program, 264
Approvals, tech plan component, 34
Assessment, organizational readiness, 14–17, 227–228
Assistive technologies, 264; current, 150–151, 154; proposed, 151–152; resources, 281
At sign (@), 267
ATM (asynchronous transfer mode), 264
Attitudes of resistance, 20–22, 230
AUP. *See* Acceptable use policy

B

Backbone network, 264
Backup procedures, data, 166, 167, 168, 194; and file retention, 196
Bandwidth, 264
Baseline measurements, 81, 82, 187
Beckh, P., 19
Binding, tech plan document, 224
BIOS (basic input output system), 264

Bleeding-edge technology, 109, 239, 264
Blueprints, building, 138
Board, governing, 29; support from, 14, 49–50
"Bobby Approved" Web site, 154
Brandin, P., 36–37, 39, 78, 233
Bridges, W., 227n.1
Budget, tech plan, 188, 197–209; capital and expense items, 197–198, 256; changing the, 237; checklist, 262; developing the, 34–35, 69, 70; examples, 101, 201–203, 204; fiscal years in, 61, 198–199, 201, 204; line items, 199; multiyear, 201–203; worksheet forms, 69, 70, 205–209
Buildings: facilities plan, 157–161, 253–254; moving to new, 16, 141, 190, 235; multiple, 144, 148, 160; site plans, 137–138, 147, 148
Business analysis, 20–21; business processes charts, 35, 36, 87, 219–220; current business processes, 5, 73–76, 83, 88–89, 218–219, 244, 256; discoveries and documentation, 6, 57–58, 67, 188, 239; examples, 84, 85–86; five-step process of, 67–69, 72–82, 238; measures of success, 80–83, 85–86, 87, 89, 245, 271; process improvement goals, 67–69, 76–79, 78–79, 82, 85–86, 89, 164–165, 181, 244–245, 256; process improvement reviews, 186–187, 189, 190, 256; reviewing the, 238; strategic goals, 72–73, 82–83, 87, 244; technology impacts chart, 219–220; technology strategies, 77–80, 82, 245
Business technologies, 150, 156, 202; proposed (types of), 152–153, 155, 253

C

Cable and locks, desktop computer, 168
Cable modem, 265
Camara, C., 19, 41
Cambridge Forum, 29, 47
Capital campaigns, nonprofit, 42, 234–235
Capital expense items (budgeting), 202, 265; expense versus, 197–198, 256
Cascading equipment, 109, 112

Case studies. *See names of specific organizations; numbered Examples*

CD-ROM (compact disk) sharing, 92

Change management: and addressing resistance, 18–23, 230; fifteen tips on, 230–231; organizational, 227–230; resources, 282; and transition, 225, 227, 229; and updating the technology plan, 188, 189, 190, 237–239, 256

Charts: business processes, 219–220; computer skill levels, 181, 183; Gantt, 34, 210–211, 213, 257, 268; organization, 63, 64, 65; tech plan wall, 35, 36. *See also* Business analysis; Flowcharts

Checklist: budget, 262; inventories, 261; network diagrams, 262; tech plan document, 223, 261–262; tech plan outline, 243–257; timeline, 262. *See also* Comprehensive Technology Plan Outline

Child Care Coordinating Council of San Mateo County, Inc., 102, 103, 144, 146, 214, 215

Circuit riders, 53

Clara Mateo Alliance, Inc., 112, 116, 161

Client (server), 265; thin or fat, 277

Clients, agency: assistive technologies for, 151–152; benefits of technology for, 19, 23, 87, 230; and human interaction, 22, 39–40, 229; program grants for, 233

Client-server implementations, 266

Client-server network, 265; workstation requirements, 116

Color printing, avoiding, 137, 153, 224

Committee, technology. *See* Team, technology planning

Communication: business equipment for, 152–153, 155, 253; and file sharing, 78–79, 91, 266, 268, 273; frequency and efficiency, 35–37, 39–40; new software for end-user, 125, 130, 249; of plan changes, 237; strategy for change, 228–229. *See also* Network services

Community Association for Rehabilitation, 19

Community Technology Consortium, Lowell, 234

Comprehensive Technology Plan Outline, 243–257

Computers, 117; acceptable use of, 194; CPU, 266; desktop, 114–115, 163, 167, 168, 247–248; donations of older, 234; employee-owned personal, 195; equipment narrative and table, 247–248; laptop, 114–115, 163, 166, 167, 247–248; legacy system, 271; personal use of, 192; security, 163, 166, 167, 168, 254; software information for all, 121; tower, 277

Configuration guidelines, equipment, 111

Configurations and "preferences," 265

Connectivity, TCO and levels of, 13

Consequences for abuse of technology, 193, 196, 256

Consortium for School Network (CoSN), 12–13

Constraints, the Triangle of, 17, 32

Consultants, 40, 51–54, 58, 79; ASPs, 264; characteristics of good, 51–52; contracts with, 199, 217, 257; fees, 54, 199; hiring, 42, 49; interview questions for, 52; tech support, 173, 176; and trainers, 180

Consumables, 197, 199, 265

Contingency planning: disaster recovery plan, 158, 163, 164, 165, 254; and timeline update, 212; "What if . . ." security issues, 164–165

Continuous improvement. *See* Evaluation and continuous improvement strategy

Contractors, hiring, 159, 161

Contracts: consulting, 199, 217, 257; support and maintenance, 257

Copier machines, 153, 155

Copyright, software, 126

Corporations, donations and help from, 55, 234, 236

Cost of the tech plan, 34–35

Cover page, tech plan, 59, 223, 243

CPU (central processing unit), 266

Critical path items, 34

Cross referencing plan sections, 200, 211

Culture, organizational: and acceptance of technology, 19–20, 23; and benefits of teamwork, 38, 43; and fears of technology, 20–22, 23; and information flow, 35–37

Cupertino Community Services, 16, 19–20, 42, 60–61, 82, 83, 127, 129, 130, 131, 153, 155, 176

Cycle, the implementation. *See* Technology implementation cycle

D

Data: backup procedures, 166, 167, 168, 194; security and vulnerability of, 162, 164

Data communications network, 266. *See also* Network services

Database, 92, 266

Databases, shared electronic, 96–98, 179; developing, 10, 213, 228, 229, 231; issues, 228; proposed, 97–98, 104, 246; total cost of ownership of, 190; types of, 105

DBTACs (Disability Business Technical Assistance Centers), 151n.1

Deadlines. *See* Timeline, tech plan

Decision log, 30, 31

Decision making: advocacy and involvement in, 228; documenting plan changes, 188, 239; planning benefits, 6; technology team, 3, 29–30, 228

Defragmentation, disk, 172, 177

Deming, W. E., 9

Description of the nonprofit, 62–63, 64, 243; detail of, 74–75, 76

Descriptions, narrative. *See names of specific tech components*

Desktop computers. *See* Computers

Diabetes Society of Santa Clara Valley, 64, 66, 82, 83–84, 88–89

Diagrams, LAN/WAN, 144, 223; checklist, 262; logical, 136–137, 146, 251; proposed logical, 140–141, 145, 252; proposed site plan, 141, 252–253; site plan, 137–138, 147, 148, 251

Digital divide, 232

Disabilities, equipment for people with, 150–151, 151n.1, 154

Disaster recovery plan, 158, 163, 164, 165, 254

"Do" stage, project, 8–9, 238

Dobbs, D., 47n.1

Document, the tech plan. *See* Technology plan (document)

Domain name service (DNS), 91, 273

Donations, 110; budget including anticipated, 200; in-kind, 50, 232–236; of IT staff time, 55; TCO and, 11, 13, 236; using technology plans to leverage, 233–234

Donors database, 228, 229, 231

Dot (URL period character), 267

Drawings. *See* Diagrams, LAN/WAN; Site plan, LAN/WAN

Dunham, A., 42

E

Edell, M., 11, 23, 55, 234

Efficiency, improving work, 19–20, 67–69

Electricity systems, 157–158, 160, 161, 253; jack wall outlet, 270; LAN timeline, 216

E-mail address: the author's, xxiii; dot (.), 267; mailing list, 271

E-mail (electronic mail), 91, 213; acceptable use of, 195–196; at sign (@), 267; current and proposed centralized, 98–99, 106, 246–247; employee use of, 192, 195–196; flaming, 268; personal, 192. *See also* Network services

EMQ Children and Family Services, 144, 148

End-user software: inventories, 127, 128, 248–249; proposed new, 125, 130, 249

End-users: current tech support for, 105, 169, 170–171, 174, 176, 255; current training of, 178–179, 182, 255; local and remote, 170, 171; proposed tech support for, 171–172, 175, 176, 255; proposed training of, 179–181, 182, 184, 256; software inventory by names of, 127, 128; workstation, 116

Enterprise license, software, 126

Environmental League of Massachusetts, 29, 78

Equipment (hardware), 107–119; assistive technologies, 150–152, 253; business technologies, 152–153, 155, 253; configuration guidelines, 111; donated or discounted, 11, 236; guiding principles for acquiring, 112, 116; implementation timeline, 211, 257; inventory, defined, 269; inventory of current, 107–110, 247–248; inventory worksheets, 107, 117–119, 156; minimum specifications for, 110, 112, 140; narrative descriptions of, 116; not yet needed, 142, 153, 154; older or legacy, 234, 271; peripherals, 248; proposed acquisitions, 111–112, 195, 248; purchasing, 6, 211, 257; recommendations, 29; special needs, 150–152, 153, 253; tables of, 107, 113–115, 117–119; training on, 179; types of information on, 108–109; upgrade questions, 109. *See also* Servers, web

Ergonomic needs, 150–151, 151n.1, 154, 264

Escalation paths, 170–171, 267; flowcharts, 174–175

Evaluation and continuous improvement strategy, 186–196; narrative, 190; process improvement goals, 76–77; process improvement review, 67–69, 186–187, 237–239, 256, 257; table, 189. *See also* Measures of success; Technology strategies

Examples, nonprofit. *See numbered Examples*

Executive director, the, 14, 29, 46–48; nine key roles and responsibilities of, 48

Executive summary, 60–61, 243; budget, 201, 204

Expense items (budgeting), 197–198, 256, 267; consumables, 197, 199, 265; of the technology planning project, 7, 34–35

Expertise: of nonprofit staff, 7, 21, 40–41, 181, 183; of team members, 29, 38–40, 66; tech plan writing and, 7, 58

Extranet (web server partners), 91, 106, 268

F

Fabre, J. P., 16, 19–20, 42

Facilitators, meeting, 34, 38

Facilities plan, 253–254; physical security, 157–161, 162; table, 160; upgrades impact, 158–159, 160, 161, 254; upgrades required, 157–158, 161

Fat client, 277

Fault tolerance, 268

Fax machine, 92, 155

Fears about technology, addressing, 18–23

Ferrari, C., 55

Fiber optic, 268

Figures and drawings, tech plan, 223

File sharing, 78–79, 91, 266, 268, 273

Fire code issues, 159, 160

Firewalls, 134, 140, 164, 268; building, 159; proposed, 167; unnecessary, 166

Fiscal years (FYs). *See* Budget, tech plan

Flowcharts: business process, 74–75, 76; product inventory, 89; symbols, 259; technology support plan escalation, 174–175; tracking progress on, 35, 36. *See also* Charts

Fonts, tech plan document, 224

Forms: computerizing, 19–20, 103; timeline reminder, 212; word processing template, 179

Free or discounted work, 54

Frequency of progress measurement, 81, 189

Front matter, tech plan, 59–61, 243

FTP (file transfer protocol), 268

"Fudge factor," time estimates, 212

Funding: and in-kind support or donations, 50, 232–236; resources, 15, 282; and technology planning expenses, 7, 34–35

Fundraising, planning as a tool for, 6–7, 232–235

G

Gantt chart, 34, 210–211, 213, 257, 268

"Gee whiz!" factor, 28

Getting started, 1–23; and addressing resistance, 18–23; and organizational readiness, 14–17; and the technology implementation cycle, 8–13; understanding technology planning, 3–7

Girl Scouts of Santa Clara County, 82–83, 87, 102, 105, 106, 218, 219–220

Glossaries: tech plan, 217, 218, 257; Web networking and computer, 263

Glossary of Terms (A-Z), 263–279

Goals: alignment of technology with, 233; business process improvement, 5, 67–69, 76–77, 82, 85–86, 89, 244–245; measurement of, 80–81; strategic, 5, 72–73, 82–83, 87, 244. *See also* Measures of success

Gomes, J., 29, 78

Grammar, checklist for tech plan, 262

Grants: applications for, 211–212, 257; for infrastructure, 232–233

Graveyard edge technology, 109

Guiding principles for technology acquisitions, 112, 116, 131, 195

H

Hard disk, 268–269

Hardware, definition of, 269. *See also* Equipment (hardware)

Health care. *See names of specific organizations*

HIPPA (Health Insurance Portability and Privacy Act), 97n.1, 269

Hiring: consultants, 51–54; volunteers, 42, 49, 54–55

Historical record, planning documents the, 6, 57–58, 67, 239

Home page, 269

Hope Rehabilitation Services, 102, 104, 142–144, 145, 159–160, 214, 216

http (hypertext transfer protocol), 269

Human interaction: people skills, 39–40, 229; and technology, 22

I

Icons: network equipment, 137, 138, 145, 146, 147, 269; skill level, 183; timeline, 214, 216

IDFs (intermediate distribution frames), 137, 161, 269, 271; patch panels in, 274. *See also* MDF (main distribution frame)

Implementation, technology *See* Technology implementation cycle

Improvement. *See* Evaluation and continuous improvement strategy

Inefficiencies, organizational, 5, 22

Information: individual team member, 63, 64, 66, 244; organization background, 62–66, 218, 219–220; privacy of, 194, 196; resources and Web sites, 281–282. *See also* Communication

Information security. *See* Security plan

Information technology (IT), 270

Infrastructure, network. *See* Network inventories and descriptions

Infrastructure, organization, 3–4, 232–233

Intellectual property. *See* Software licenses and tracking

Intelligent network devices, 140

Internal web site, 94, 104, 245–246; proposed, 95, 103, 246. *See also* network services

internet (not Internet), 134, 270

Internet or The Internet, and the World Wide Web, 270

Intranet, 91, 103, 270

Introduction, tech plan, 62–66, 243–244

Inventories: business technology, 156; checklist, 261; flowchart, 89; nonprofit agency product, 88–89; software, 276. *See also* Equipment (hardware)

Invoicing, consultant, 54, 199

IP address, 270; dot (.), 267

IS (information system). *See* Technology plan (document)

ISP (Internet service provider), 134, 166, 203, 270

IT (information technology) director: job description, 221; roles, 15, 18–23, 39–40, 230, 237

J

Job descriptions, technology: adjusting, 41; consultant, 52; desired skills by names of, 183; example of, 221; IT director, 221; types of, 217, 257

Junior Achievement of the Bay Area, Inc., 112, 116, 130, 131, 166, 167, 193

K

Key, chart or diagram, 137, 148, 183

Key contributors, 40–41, 42–43, 44–45; business process, 73

L

LAN (local area network), 78, 116; definitions of, 133, 271; diagram, 136–137, 144, 146; proposed, 143; site implementation timeline, 216

Language: key search words, 235; of technology, 18, 233, 235; used by consultants, 51–52, 53

LAN/WAN: current inventory, 134–135, 143, 149, 250; proposed, 138–139, 140–141, 143, 144–145. *See also* Network inventories and descriptions

LAN/WAN diagrams. *See* Diagrams, LAN/WAN

Laptops. *See* Computers

Leadership roles and responsibilities: and accidental techies, 170, 173, 176; key, 40–42; planning team, 39–40; project manager, 15, 40; for staff support, 19–20, 23; tech plan, 34, 46–50. *See also* Project management; Team, technology planning

Leading-edge technology, 29, 271

Learning, organizational, 5, 38, 43, 230

Learning styles, staff, 180

Legacy system, 271

Legend: site plan, 147; timeline, 215

Lending out laptops, 167

Liability, organization, 159, 195

Libraries, 96

Licenses. *See* Software licenses and tracking

Listserv or listserve, 271

Log: actions required, 32, 33; decision, 30, 31; problem report tracking, 170, 172, 176

Logical diagrams. *See* Diagrams, LAN/WAN

Lowell Community Technology Consortium, 234

M

Madden, J., 198

Magnetic media, types of, 271

Mailing list, e-mail address, 271

Maintenance: budget, 202; contracts and fees, 173, 257; periodic, 169, 172, 177, 255, 274; technical support, 255, 271. *See also* Technology support plan

Manager (MIS), 15, 40. *See also* Staff, IT

Mapping roles and responsibilities, 42–45

Marketing responsibilities, 221; wish list, 7, 236

Materials management responsibilities, 221; consumables budget, 197, 199, 265

Matrix: process-responsibility, 42–45; training plan, 181, 185

MDF (main distribution frame), 137, 213, 271; patch panels, 274. *See also* IDFs (intermediate distribution frames)

Measures of success, 80–83, 85–86, 245, 271; definition of, 80; examples, 86, 87, 89; in grant applications, 236; and process improvement, 187, 189, 239; subjective input and objective, 187; things which are not, 80–81

Media, storage, 272; hard disk, 268–269; off-site, 166; types of magnetic, 271. *See also* Backup procedures, data

Meetings: facilitation of, 34, 38; plan progress evaluation, 187, 188; planning, 28–30; Wired for Good program, 42

Memory (RAM), 213, 272

Mentors, 49, 179

Milestones, 80–81; identifying key, 32

Mini-case studies. *See names of specific organizations*

Minimum system requirements (narrative), 116

Mission: distraction from the, 21, 193; focus on organizational, 3–4, 5, 29, 57. *See also names of specific organizations*

Mission Hospice, Inc., 189

Mission statement information, 14, 62, 63, 64, 72, 243

Modem, 272

MPOE (minimum point of entry), 138, 272

Mulpeters, P. M., 23, 79, 233–234

Multisite network, 140, 144, 148, 160

Multiyear budget, 201–203

Myths of technology planning: five, 7; and resistance worries, 20–22

N

Nanus, B., 47n.1

Net, The. *See* Internet or The Internet

Network administrator, 272

Network diagrams checklist, 262

Network inventories and descriptions, 133–149, 250–253; current diagram, 136–137, 146, 251; current overview, 134–135, 143, 250; donor interest in, 233–234; equipment inventory, 135–136, 149, 250–251; logical diagrams, 136–137, 140–141, 145, 146, 251, 252; narrative, 134–135, 138–139, 143, 250, 251–252; plan subsection names, 133–134; proposed equipment, 139–140, 142, 252; proposed LAN/WAN, 138–139, 143, 144–145, 251–252; replacements, 135–136, 149, 251; site plan diagrams, 137–138, 141, 147, 148, 251, 252–253; tables, 135–136, 149, 250–251; upgrade, 135, 158–159, 160, 161, 250–251, 254; worksheet, 149

Network management, 272

Network protocol examples, 134, 251, 273

Network services, 90–106, 245–247, 273; common types of, 91–92; current and not planned, 92; current and proposed, 93; definition of, 90–91; eight common questions about, 93; e-mail, 98–99, 106, 246–247; impact of upgrades to, 158–159, 160, 161, 254; internal web site, 94, 104, 245–246; other current and proposed, 99, 247; public Web site, 94–95, 100–101, 247; shared databases, 96–98, 105, 246; system security, 162, 163–164, 167, 168, 194–196, 254

Nonprofit organizations: background information, 62–66, 218, 219–220; describing, 62–63, 64, 243; executive director roles, 46–48; funding and in-kind donations to, 232–236; human interaction focus of, 22; mission statement information, 14, 62, 63, 64, 72, 243; readiness assessment, 14–17; task versus department descriptions, 75; in transition, 16, 227, 229. *See also* Business analysis

Nonprofit technology: assistance providers (consultants), 51–54; resources, 15–16, 281; TCO and levels of, 4, 12–13

Norton AntiVirus, 167, 177

Numbering, tech plan: of business processes, 75, 245; of table rows, 110, 122

Numeric terms: IP address, 270; private IP address range, 272; wiring specification standards, 263, 265, 278

O

Office equipment. *See* Business technologies

Office rooms diagram, tech equipment, 147

Online or on-line, 273

Operating systems (OSs), 10, 130, 248, 249; commonly known, 273

Operational level, technology, 4

Optical media, 273–274

Organizational readiness assessment, 14–17

Other technologies, 150–156

Outline, Comprehensive Technology Plan, 243–257

Owners: business process, 73; technology planning process, 42, 44, 45

Ownership costs. *See* TCO (total cost of ownership)

P

Page headers and footers, document, 223–224

Pagers, 152, 155

Parents Helping Parents, Inc., 99–101, 153, 154, 168, 218, 221

Password protection, 163, 165

Patch panel, 216, 274

Patch (software), 168, 177, 274

Paying bills process, 74

PDAs, 152–153, 253, 274

Peer mentoring, 49, 179

Peer-to-peer network (peer network), 274

Peninsula Center for the Blind and Visually Impaired, 36–37, 39, 78–79, 233

Periodic maintenance: current, 172, 177, 255; proposed, 172–173, 176, 177, 255; types of, 172–173, 274. *See also* Technology support plan

Peripherals, 274; internal, 108; inventory of, 108, 118, 248

Personal e-mail, 192

Personal technological property, 195

Pizza box computer, 274

"Plan" stage, project, 8–9, 238

Planning the technology plan, 25–58; and building the team, 7, 38–45; with consultants and volunteers, 51–58; and the implementation cycle, 8–13, 238; and the implementation timeline, 210–216, 257; leadership for, 46–50; managing the process of, 27–37. *See also* Technology plan (document)

Plenum, ceiling, 158, 159, 275

Policy development: acceptable use, 99, 191–196, 256, 264; and TCO, 13. *See also* Evaluation and continuous improvement strategy; Strategic goals

Presentation Center, 23, 55, 79, 141–142, 181, 182–184, 200, 204, 233–234

Printers, 91, 153, 177, 199

Printing, tech plan document, 224; avoiding color, 137, 153

Privacy: and HIPPA requirements, 97n.1, 269; and office information, 194, 196

Pro bono labor. *See* Donations; Volunteers

Problem solving. *See* Technology support plan

Process, definitions of, 5, 275

Process improvement goals and reviews. *See* Business analysis

Processor (CPU), 266

Process-Responsibility Matrix, 42–45

Productivity software, 275

Professional development: computer skill levels, 181, 183; skills and expertise, 29, 38–40, 183; TCO and levels of, 12. *See also* Training

Programs. *See* Application program; Software

Progress reviews. *See* Evaluation and continuous improvement strategy; Technology plan (document)

Project management: and priorities, 15, 34, 80, 210–211; the process of, 27–37; PSDA cycle, 8–9, 238; software, 214–216; Technology Implementation Cycle, 8–10, 238; tools, 30, 34; Triangle of Constraints, 16–17, 32. *See also* Leadership roles and responsibilities

Project manager or team leader, 15, 40

Proofreading, tech plan document, 55, 222–223; checklist, 261–262

Protocols, types of network, 134, 275

PSDA cycle, 8–9, 238

Public Web site, 91, 247; proposed, 94–95, 100–101. *See also* Network services

Publication components, tech plan, 223–224; checklist details, 261–262; outline chart of, 243–257

Purchases, implementation timeline, 211, 257

Pyramid, Technology Plan, 3–4, 57–58

Q

Quantification of improvements. *See* Measures of success

Questions asked: about consultants, 52–53; about network services, 93

QuickBooks, 88

R

RAM (memory), 213, 272

Readiness, organizational, 14–17, 227–228

Reasons for technology planning: and benefits, 3–4, 19–20; eight essential, 5–7; practical and useful, 19–20; reasons against and, 20–22; ROI, 18, 20. *See also* Mission

Record-keeping: business analysis documentation, 6, 57–58, 67, 188, 239; improved, 19

References, questions for consultant, 52–53

Remote access, 116, 134, 170, 171, 273; definitions of, 91–92, 275

Removable storage media, 275

Render, S., 123–124

Replacement costs and TCO, 13

Replacing equipment, 135–136, 247

Reporting, team member, 36–37, 187

Resistance to technology planning, 18–23, 230; myths and, 7

Resources: effectively targeting organizational, 6, 15–16; locating community, 49–50, 55; for more information, 281–282

Return on investment (ROI; the "why"), 18, 20

Reviewers, tech plan document, 222–223

Reviews, progress. *See* Technology plan (document)

RFP (request for proposal), 140

Rules for technology use, 192, 256; by equipment categories, 194–196

S

Salaries (current and proposed), 203, 256

San Jose Repertory Theatre, 64, 65, 82, 85–86, 112, 114, 174, 177, 193–194, 200, 201

Scheduling. *See* Timeline, tech plan

Scope, project, 16–17; and scalability, 276

Search terms, technology funding, 235

Section headings and subheadings, tech plan, 57, 59, 223; comprehensive outline of, 243–257

Security plan, 162–168; and acceptable use policy, 99, 191–196, 256; current, 163–164, 254; encryption, 267; narrative, 167; for physical facilities, 157–161, 162; proposed, 164–166, 167, 254–255; table, 166, 168; Web site, 95, 164, 166, 254

Security, three kinds of, 162–163

Serif fonts, 224

Servers, web: air conditioning for, 158; co-location, 265; definition of, 276; hardware inventory, 108–109, 119, 248; mail, 271; security, 161, 163, 167, 254; software, 121–122, 125, 248–249; types of, 91, 92. *See also* WWW (World Wide Web)

Service level agreements, vendor, 173

Services for Brain Injury, 19, 41, 64, 102, 106, 190, 213

Shared databases. *See* Databases, shared electronic

Site licenses. *See* Software licenses and tracking

Site plan, LAN/WAN, 137–138, 190, 223, 251; definition of, 276; distances information, 138, 141, 148; overview table, inset, 148; proposed, 141, 252–253; rooms diagram, 147. *See also* Diagrams, LAN/WAN

Skills: levels of computer, 181, 183; people, 39–40, 229

Software: antivirus, 164, 165–166, 167, 168, 172, 177, 196, 278; budget, 202; database, 97–98; definition of, 276; donated (received), 11; downloading issues, 192, 194, 196; employee-owned, 195; narrative, 130; personal use of, 192; program names, 127, 129, 182, 184, 215; programs training, 182–184, 185; project management, 214–216; proposed acquisitions of, 124–125, 130, 171, 195, 238–239, 249; resale or donation (given away), 123; server-related, 125, 130, 249; spreadsheet, 88, 199, 211, 213; standardizing, 10, 123; TCO, 12; upgrades or replacement, 123–124, 168, 177, 238–239, 249; Web-based auctions, 125

Software inventories, 120–132, 248–250; current, 120–124, 128, 129, 248–249; by names of users, 127, 128; narrative descriptions, 130, 131; by software titles, 127, 129; tables, 128, 129; types of information on, 121–122; worksheet form, 132. *See also* Equipment (hardware)

Software licenses and tracking, 123, 125, 126–127, 128, 129, 249, 250; proposed procedures for, 127, 131

Spelling and grammar checking, 222, 224

Staff, IT, 21; and accidental techies, 170, 173, 176; IT director, 18–23, 39–40, 221, 230, 237; network administrator, 272; project manager or team leader, 15, 40

Staff, nonprofit organization: addressing resistance by, 18–23, 230; AUP orientation for, 191–196; to be trained, 178, 183–185; blind or low-vision, 78–79; computer skill levels chart, 181, 183; empowerment through technology, 230; expertise of, 7, 21, 40–41, 181, 183; fears about technology, 20–22, 23; offices equipment diagram, 147; software inventory by names of, 127, 128; tech plan support by, 15, 23, 215, 230; tech support and maintenance, 173; time budgeting, 35, 48. *See also* Team, technology planning

Stakeholders, project, 14–15, 19–20, 41; meetings, 28–30. *See also* Support for technology planning

Standalone machines. *See* Business technologies

Standardizing: software, 10, 123; wiring, 134, 137, 140, 263

Strategic goals: examples of, 83, 84; technology goals as different from, 7, 72–73; technology plan documentation of, 57, 72–73, 82–83, 87, 237–239, 244

Strategies. *See* Technology strategies

Students, 173

"Study" stage, project, 9, 186, 238

Success. *See* Measures of success

Suhrcke, P., 29, 47

Sullivan, F., 234

Summary, executive, 60–61, 243

Support, technical. *See* Technology support plan

Support for technology planning, 58; by individual supporters, 43, 44–45; ongoing, 235; organizational, 14–15, 23, 47; resistance or, 18–23, 230

Surveys of improvement, 81, 82

Symbols, flowchart, 76, 89, 259

System requirements, minimum, 116

System security, 162, 194–196

Systems administration, 276

Systems administrator, 276

T

Table of Contents, tech plan, 59, 223, 243

Tables, tech plan, 223

Tape backup, 166, 167, 168

Tax exempt certificate, 198

TCO (total cost of ownership), 4, 6, 10–11, 109, 277; calculating, 198; of database solutions, 190; of donated tech equipment, 11, 13, 236; in relationship to actions chosen (table), 12–13

Team, the nonprofit. *See* Staff, nonprofit organization

Team sponsor. *See* Leadership roles and responsibilities

Team, technology planning, 27–28; administrative assistant, 41, 46; benefits, 38, 43, 228; building the, 7, 38–45; committee table, 64, 66; communications management, 35–36; individual member information, 63, 64, 66, 244; key roles and responsibilities, 40–42, 44–45, 215; meetings, 28–30; Process-Responsibility Matrix, 42–45; reporting by team members, 36–37, 187; size of, 38; skills and expertise, 29, 38–40, 183; time budgeting, 35; volunteers on the, 54–55. *See also* Staff, IT

Technical support (tech support), 277; contracts, 217, 257; TCO and levels of, 12. *See also* Staff, IT; Technology support plan

Technology: demonstrations, 230; "Gee whiz!" factor, 28; impacts on business processes, 218, 219–220, 229; using the word, 18

Technology committee. *See* Team, technology planning

Technology implementation cycle: diagram, 9; the ongoing, 188, 238; phases, 199, 210; planning and, 8–13; and timeline, 7, 210–216, 257

Technology plan (document): appendices, 217–221, 257; change ideas, documentation of, 188, 239; checklist, 223, 261–262; comprehensive outline for, 243–257; cover page, 59, 223, 243; overview, 57–58; page headers and footers, 223–224; preparation, 222–224; printing and binding, 224; proofreading and spell checking, 222–223, 224; publication components, 223–224, 261–262; reviews, 187–188, 189, 190, 256, 257; revisiting the, 6, 237–239; section headings, 57, 59, 223; table of contents, 59, 223, 243; tasks and timelines, 213, 215, 237; updating the, 188, 189, 190, 237–239, 256, 257. *See also* Planning the technology plan

Technology plan examples. *See* numbered *Examples*

Technology planning: addressing resistance to, 18–23, 230; assessing readiness for, 14–17; benefits of, 3–4, 19–20; budget and expenses of plan creation, 7, 34–35; checklist, 261–262; deadlines and milestones, 32, 34; and donations leveraging, 233–234; eight essential reasons for, 5–7; five myths of, 7; implementation timeline, 7, 210–216, 257; managing the process of, 27–37; and the organization's strategic plan, 5–6; outline, comprehensive, 243–257; practical reasons for, 19–20; and progress tracking, 35, 187–188; pyramid, 3–4, 57–58; resources, 15–16, 281; reviews, 187–188, 189, 190, 256; stakeholder meetings, 28–30; stakeholder support for, 14–15, 19–20, 41; task dependencies, 30, 34, 210, 214, 216; tasks lists, 30–32; and the technology implementation cycle, 8–13, 238; understanding, 3–7; variables and delays, 239; volunteer tasks, 54–55. *See also* Timeline, tech plan

Technology strategies, 77–80, 82, 86, 245; consideration questions, 79; evaluation and continuous improvement, 186–196, 237–239, 256

Technology support plan, 169–171; budget, 202; current end-user, 171–172, 175, 176, 255; flowchart, 174–175; narratives, 176, 177; proposed for end-users, 171–172, 175, 176, 255

Telephone lines, 253; terminal at MPOE, 138, 272

Telephone service: equipment, 152–153, 155; POTS, 275

Telephones: acceptable use of, 192, 196; cell, 152

Templates, word processing, 179

Theft prevention, 167, 168

Thin server, 277

Timeline, tech plan, 7, 210–216, 231; changing the, 237; checklist for, 262; contents, 211–212; delays, 239; developing the, 32, 34, 210–211; examples, 101, 213–216; and organizational readiness, 14–17; PERT chart, 274; prioritizing the, 34; process improvement review, 186–187; for progress measurements, 81, 189; and project priority, 15; reminder sheets, 69, 71; revisiting the, 237; tech plan writing during, 57–58; variables, 239

Topology, network, 277

Total Cost of Ownership (TCO) in Relationship to Actions Chosen, 11, 13. *See also* TCO (total cost of ownership)

Tower or mini-tower computer, 277

Tracking licenses. *See* Software licenses and tracking

Tracking procedures. *See* Flowcharts

Tracking progress. *See* Timeline, tech plan

Trainers, technology, 180, 181, 184

Training, 179; corporation-sponsored, 234; matrix, 181, 185; organization-sponsored, 19, 22, 151, 152, 230; TCO and levels of, 12

Training plan, 178–185; current methods and practices, 178–179, 182, 255–256; implementation, 212, 257; proposed methods and practices, 179–181, 182, 184, 256; topics, 182–185

Transition: and change, 225, 227, 229; times of organization, 15, 16, 155, 190

Triangle of Constraints, 16–17, 32

Trojan Horse, 277

U

Unlawful or unauthorized downloads, 192, 194, 196

Unnamed nonprofit LAN/WAN diagram, 144, 147

Updating the plan. *See* Technology plan (document)

Upgrading facilities. *See* Facilities plan

Upgrading technology: equipment, 135, 213, 247; impact of on LAN/WAN networks, 158–159, 160, 161, 254; planning for, 21; and software, 123–124, 238–239, 249. *See also* Equipment (hardware)

UPS (uninterruptible power supply), 278

URL (uniform resource locator), 278; dot (.) in address of, 267

V

Values statement, organization, 64

Vendor support, 173, 176, 177, 236

Virus definition program, 164, 165–166, 167, 168, 172, 177, 196, 278

Vision statement, organization, 64

Voice mail, 155

Volunteers: and accountability, 173; hiring, 42, 49, 54–55; and liability, 159; management and scheduling, 85–86; planning with, 51–58; prospective donor's employees as, 236

VPN (virtual private network), 92, 134, 278

W

Wall charts, tech plan, 35, 36

WAN (wide area network), 133, 278

Web browser, 278

Web page, 278

web site (intranet site), 91, 103, 270

Web site or Website (Internet site): "Bobby Approved" accessibility of, 154; definition of, 278; necessity of, 29; posting technology needs on, 236; proposed, 103; security, 95, 164, 166, 167, 254; types of, 91; URL address, 278

Web sites for information and resources, 281–282

Web, The. *See* WWW (World Wide Web)

"What if . . ." security issues, 164–165

Wire drops, 139, 278

Wire runs, 158–159, 278

Wired for Good program, 42

Wiring: new or additional, 158–159, 160, 161; standards, 134, 137, 140, 263, 265, 278; timeline, 216; types of twisted pair, 265

Wish lists, nonprofit agency, 7, 236

Work and time: budgeting the project, 35, 48; business process key questions, 73, 74; business processes chart, 219–220; free or discounted, 54; and process improvement, 76–77; too much, 20–21; volunteer, 54–55

Workstations, 113, 116

World Wide Web. *See* WWW (World Wide Web)

Writing: an AUP, 191; the tech plan, 7, 189, 222, 223; thank-you notes, 22. *See also* narrative descriptions (for tech components); numbered Examples

WWW (World Wide Web), 279; relationship to The Internet, 270; resources, 281–282

Y

Youth Science Institute, 42, 112, 113, 127, 128

Z

Zip drive, 167, 168, 279

In Chapter Two the source of the "Total Cost of Ownership of Donations" Planning in Practice case is Michael Edell, former executive director, AIDS Community Research Consortium.

In Chapter Three the source of the "Using Times of Transition to Your Advantage" Planning in Practice case is Jaclyn Phuong Fabre, executive director, Cupertino Community Services.

In Chapter Four the sources of the "Getting Everyone on Board" Planning in Practice case are Christine Camara, executive director, Services for Brain Injury; Peter Beckh, associate director, Community Association for Rehabilitation; and Jaclyn Phuong Fabre, executive director, Cupertino Community Services.

The sources of the "Role of a Supportive Organizational Culture" Planning in Practice case are Patricia Marie Mulpeters, executive director, Presentation Center, and Michael Edell, former executive director, AIDS Community Research Consortium.

In Chapter Five the sources of the "Don't Let the 'Cool' Factor Get You Off-Track" Planning in Practice case are Jim Gomes, president, Environmental League of Massachusetts, and Patricia Suhrcke, executive director, Cambridge Forum.

The source of the "Keeping Technology Planning a Priority" Planning in Practice case is Pam Brandin, executive director, Peninsula Center for the Blind and Visually Impaired.

In Chapter Six the sources of the "Get the Big-Picture People on the Planning Team" Planning in Practice case are Pam Brandin, executive director, Peninsula Center for the Blind and Visually Impaired, and Scott Render, chief executive officer, Santa Clara Valley Chapter, American Red Cross.

The sources of the "Ask For Help When You Need It" Planning in Practice case are Christine Camara, executive director, Services for Brain Injury; Jaclyn Phuong Fabre, executive director, Cupertino Community Services; and Anne Dunham, executive director, Youth Science Institute.

In Chapter Seven the source of the "Role of the Executive Director in Technology Planning" Planning in Practice case is Patricia Suhrcke, executive director, Cambridge Forum.

In Chapter Eight the sources of the "Blessed with Volunteers" Planning in Practice case are Cathy Ferrari, volunteer, Presentation Center; Patricia Marie Mulpeters, executive director, Presentation Center; and Michael Edell, former executive director, AIDS Community Research Consortium.

In Chapter Nine the source of the "Cupertino Community Services: Front Matter" example is Cupertino Community Services.

In Chapter Ten the source of the "Services for Brain Injury: Background Information" example is Christine Camara, executive director of Services for Brain Injury.

The source of the "San Jose Repertory Theatre: Background Information" example is the San Jose Repertory Theatre technology plan.

The source of the "Diabetes Society of Santa Clara Valley: Background Information" example is the Diabetes Society of Santa Clara Valley.

In Chapter Eleven the sources of the "Process Improvements" Planning in Practice case are Jim Gomes, president, Environmental League of Massachusetts; Pam Brandin, executive director, Peninsula Center for the Blind and Visually Impaired; and Patricia Marie Mulpeters, executive director, Presentation Center.

The source of the "Cupertino Community Services: Business Analysis" example is Cupertino Community Services.

The source of the first "Diabetes Society of Santa Clara Valley: Business Analysis" example is the Diabetes Society of Santa Clara Valley.

The source of the "San Jose Repertory Theatre: Business Analysis" example is San Jose Repertory Theatre technology plan.

The source of the "Girl Scouts of Santa Clara County: Business Analysis" example is the Girl Scouts of Santa Clara County.

The source of the second "Diabetes Society of Santa Clara Valley: Business Analysis" example is the Diabetes Society of Santa Clara Valley.

In Chapter Twelve the source of the "Parents Helping Parents, Inc.: Network Services" example is Parents Helping Parents, Inc., of Santa Clara County.

The source of the "Child Care Coordinating Council of San Mateo County, Inc.: Network Services" example is the Child Care Coordinating Council of San Mateo County, Inc.

The source of the "Hope Rehabilitation Services: Network Services" example is Hope Rehabilitation Services.

The source of the first "Girl Scouts of Santa Clara County: Network Services" example is the Girl Scouts of Santa Clara County.

The source of the "Services for Brain Injury: Network Services" example is Christine Camara, executive director of Services for Brain Injury. Credit for the material belongs to Greg Marlan, who made SBI's tech plan a reality.

The source of the second "Girl Scouts of Santa Clara County: Network Services" example is Girl Scouts of Santa Clara County.

In Chapter Thirteen the source of the "Youth Science Institute: Equipment Table" example is the staff of the Youth Science Institute.

The source of the "San Jose Repertory Theatre: Equipment Table" example is the San Jose Repertory Theatre technology plan.

The source of the "Junior Achievement of the Bay Area, Inc.: Equipment Narrative" example is Junior Achievement of the Bay Area, Inc.

The source of the "Clara Mateo Alliance, Inc.: Equipment Narrative" example is the Clara Mateo Alliance, Inc.

In Chapter Fourteen the source of the "Consider Software Upgrades Carefully" Planning in Practice case is Scott Render, chief executive officer, American Red Cross, Santa Clara Chapter.

The source of the "Youth Science Institute: Software Table" example is the staff of the Youth Science Institute.

The source of the "Cupertino Community Services: Software Table" example is Cupertino Community Services.

The source of the first "Cupertino Community Services: Software Narrative" example is Cupertino Community Services.

The source of the "Junior Achievement of the Bay Area, Inc.: Software Narrative" example is Junior Achievement of the Bay Area, Inc.

The source of the second "Cupertino Community Services: Software Narrative" example is Cupertino Community Services.

In Chapter Fifteen the source of the "Presentation Center: LAN/WAN Narrative and Inventory" example is the Presentation Center.

The source of the "Hope Rehabilitation Services: LAN/WAN Narrative and Diagram" example is Hope Rehabilitation Services.

The source of the "Hope Rehabilitation Services: LAN/WAN Diagram" example is Hope Rehabilitation Services.

The source of the "Child Care Coordinating Council of San Mateo County, Inc.: LAN/WAN Diagram" example is the Child Care Coordinating Council of San Mateo County, Inc.

The source of the "EMQ Children and Family Services: LAN/WAN Diagram" example is EMQ Children and Family Services.

In Chapter Sixteen the source of the "Parents Helping Parents, Inc.: Other Technologies" example is Parents Helping Parents, Inc., of Santa Clara County.

The source of the "American Red Cross, Santa Clara Valley Chapter: Other Technologies" example is Santa Clara Valley Chapter, American Red Cross.

The source of the "Cupertino Community Services: Other Technologies" example is Cupertino Community Services.

In Chapter Seventeen the source of the "Hope Rehabilitation Services: Facilities Plan" example is Hope Rehabilitation Services.

The source of the "Clara Mateo Alliance, Inc.: Facilities Plan" example is the Clara Mateo Alliance, Inc.

In Chapter Eighteen the source of the "Junior Achievement of the Bay Area, Inc.: Security Plan" example is Junior Achievement of the Bay Area, Inc.

The source of the "Parents Helping Parents, Inc.: Security Plan" example is Parents Helping Parents, Inc.

In Chapter Nineteen the source of the first "San Jose Repertory Theatre: Technology Support Plan" example is the San Jose Repertory Theatre technology plan.

The source of the "Cupertino Community Services: Technology Support Plan" example is Cupertino Community Services.

The source of the second "San Jose Repertory Theatre: Technology Support Plan" example is the San Jose Repertory Theatre technology plan.

In Chapter Twenty the source of the "Presentation Center: Training Plan" example is the Presentation Center.

In Chapter Twenty-One the source of the "Mission Hospice, Inc.: Evaluation and Continuous Improvement Strategy" example is Mission Hospice, Inc., of San Mateo County.

The source of the "Services for Brain Injury: Evaluation and Continuous Improvement Strategy" example is Greg Marlan of Services for Brain Injury, who made SBI's tech plan a reality.

In Chapter Twenty-Two the source of the "Junior Achievement of the Bay Area, Inc.: Acceptable Use Policy" example is Junior Achievement of the Bay Area, Inc.

The source of the "San Jose Repertory Theatre: Acceptable Use Policy" example is the San Jose Repertory Theatre technology plan.

In Chapter Twenty-Three the source of the "Getting the Best Value for the Nonprofit Money" Planning in Practice case is James Madden, systems manager, Andover Newton Theological School.

The source of the "San Jose Repertory Theatre: Budget" example is the San Jose Repertory Theatre.

The source of the "Presentation Center: Budget" example is the Presentation Center.

In Chapter Twenty-Four the source of the "Services for Brain Injury: Implementation Timeline" example is Greg Marlan of Services for Brain Injury.

The source of the "Child Care Coordinating Council of San Mateo County, Inc.: Implementation Timeline" example is the Child Care Coordinating Council of San Mateo County, Inc.

The source of the "Hope Rehabilitation Services: Implementation Timeline" example is Hope Rehabilitation Services.

In Chapter Twenty-Five the source of the "Girl Scouts of Santa Clara County: Appendix" example is the Girl Scouts of Santa Clara County.

The source of the "Parents Helping Parents, Inc.: Appendix" example is Parents Helping Parents, Inc., of Santa Clara County.

In Chapter Twenty-Eight the sources of the "Using Technology Plans to Leverage Donations" Planning in Practice case are Pam Brandin, executive director, Peninsula Center for the Blind and Visually Impaired; Patricia Marie Mulpeters, executive director, Presentation Center; Michael Edell, former executive director, AIDS Community Research Consortium; and Felicia Sullivan, director of interactive media and community outreach, Lowell Telecommunications Corporation.

Made in the USA
San Bernardino, CA
07 March 2014